U.S.-Japan
Science and Technology Exchange

Published in cooperation with
The Japan-America Society of Washington, Inc.

U.S.-Japan Science and Technology Exchange

Patterns of Interdependence

EDITED BY

Cecil H. Uyehara

Westview Press
BOULDER & LONDON

Westview Special Studies in International Economics and Business

Published in 1988 in the United States of America by Westview Press, Inc.; Frederick A. Praeger, Publisher; 5500 Central Avenue, Boulder, Colorado 80301

Library of Congress Cataloging-in-Publication Data
U.S.-Japan science and technology exchange.
    (Westview special studies in international
economics and business)
    1. Science — International cooperation. 2. Technology
— International cooperation. 3. Science and state —
United States. 4. Technology and state — United States.
5. Science and state — Japan. 6. Technology and
state — Japan. I. Uyehara, Cecil H. II. Title:
US-Japan science and technology exchange.
III. Title: United States-Japan science and technology
exchange. IV. Series.
Q172.5.I5U15   1988   338.97306   87-10572
ISBN 0-8133-7415-4

Printed and bound in the United States of America

The paper used in this publication meets the requirements of the American National Standard for Permanence of Paper for Printed Library Materials Z39.48-1984.

6   5   4   3   2   1

Contents

Foreword

"Patterns of Interdependence," the subtitle of the Second symposium on U.S.-Japan Science and Technology Exchange, well expresses the fundamental spirit of the symposium and the objective of those who sponsored the two-day seminar, November 17-18, 1986, at the Sheraton Tysons Corner Hotel near Washington, D.C.

Unlike the first symposium in 1981, when it seemed to be more a matter of transfer of science and technology from the United States to Japan, the situation in 1986 had shifted significantly toward a true two-way exchange. For example, the 1981 symposium began with a report that was basically on the one-way transfer of science and technology, not an exchange on the management and legal aspects of such transfers. In stark contrast, in 1986 we began with an assessment and comparison of U.S. and Japanese science and technology more or less on an equal standing. The assumption underlying the second symposium was that there is something that can be learned from both sides as to how Americans and Japanese manage innovation. This approach was not even considered in 1981! It is also noteworthy that the symposium workshop subjects had advanced from steel, semiconductors, and robotics in 1981 to biotechnology, computers and communications, new materials, and mechatronics in the 1986 symposium. Our 1986 symposium also devoted a second day (unlike the 1981 symposium) to considering how the United States and Japan could improve and foster cooperation between themselves in science and technology. This is a dimension in our overall relationship that is bound to be of critical importance in the future.

This symposium was made possible not only by the registration fees of the more than 110 participants but also by the generous contributions of the symposium's co-sponsors, which included the Japan-America Society of Washington, the George Washington University Sino-Soviet Institute, the *Japan Economic Journal* in Tokyo, the National Bureau of Standards of the U.S. Department of Commerce, the Westinghouse Corporation, and the Associated Japan-America Societies of the United States, Inc. Publication of the symposium proceedings was partially funded by a grant from the Japan-U.S. Friendship Commission.

Once again, we are most indebted to Mr. Cecil H. Uyehara, president, Uyehara International Associates, for organizing the symposium, a challenging and time-consuming assignment. The logistical and administrative support for the smooth operation of the symposium was ably provided by Ms. Patricia Kearns, the society's executive director. Ms. Jeanne Moore, Lana Bian, Erica Baumer, and Mr. Jon Choy provided the first drafts of the discussion summaries after each chapter.

Comments we have received from many symposium participants confirm my strong impression that the quality of speakers, discussants, and moderators was exceptionally high, leading some of us to hope that perhaps a third symposium can be held in 1991, thus maintaining a five-year periodic reexamination of this vital issue.

I am deeply grateful to all the participants for their useful contributions to the success of the symposium, and I hope this record will be of value both to participants and those who were unable to attend.

Marshall Green
President, the Japan-America Society of Washington

1

U.S.-Japanese Science and Technology: A Comparative Assessment

Gerald P. Dinneen

This chapter was written in conjunction with the opening session of the Second Symposium on U.S.-Japan Science and Technology Exchange: Patterns of Interdependence, sponsored in part by the Japan-America Society of Washington, D.C.

As a participant in the symposium, I was asked to provide a comparative assessment of science and technology development in the United States and Japan. My initial reaction was that another chapter on the subject would be redundant because an abundance of books and papers and conferences have already addressed it. After studying much of this material, however, I found that most discussions have focused on specific Japanese industries, programs, and technologies rather than on the generic issue of science and technology. Therefore, I would like to step back from the issue of U.S.-Japanese competition in automobiles, steel, semiconductors, and computers and, instead, examine the underlying base of science and technology that contributes to that competition.

As I assess the two countries' comparative position in science and technology, I will also discuss how leadership in science and technology influences a nation's goals and international competitiveness. If the only issue were who has the most patents, Nobel prizes, and papers in prestigious journals, that can be easily determined. The more difficult question is, what difference does that make to a nation's national security — a major concern of both the United States and the Soviet Union — or to a nation's productive capacity — a major concern of Japan, the United States, Western Europe, and the Soviet Union? I raise the question because government officials tend to focus on the application of science and technology to achieve increased national security and international competitiveness.

A university president, however, working to get his or her university recognized as a leader in science and technology, will measure the number of technical publications, patents, Nobel prizes, and other technical awards. Although the application of science and technology is of interest to him or her, it is not a primary objective. A director of research in a Japanese or U.S. company, on the other hand, seeks leadership in the application of science and technology as a means to increase competitiveness. Although I have had experience as both a government official and a professor, I write today as the director of research for a U.S. corporation. Therefore, I will draw my comparison from the viewpoint of industry. This should not limit the scope of my discussion because most of the activity in science and technology in both countries is conducted in industry. In Japan, for instance, very little research and development (R&D) capital is spent on national security; most is applied to commerce, and most of the scientists and engineers work in industry. In the United States, most R&D, including defense, is carried out in industry. Of the approximately $120 billion budgeted for research and development, more than $60 billion comes out of the earnings of U.S. industry and is spent in industry. A large portion of the remaining $60 billion, most of which comes from the Department of Defense, is also spent in industry. As a result, most of the scientists and engineers in the United States are employed by industry, just as in Japan. An industrial perspective, however, requires that I go beyond a purely numerical comparison of the two countries to ask, so what? What impact does the difference in science and technology have on each nation's competitiveness?

This chapter, then, will examine the science and technology base in the United States and Japan, including the institutions and the people who work in them, and this chapter will do so in light of the impact this base has on the industrial competitiveness of the two nations. The following general observations will introduce the main themes of the chapter.

1. Japan has achieved outstanding success in competing with the United States in a number of targeted industries. This has occurred despite the fact that the United States continues to lead overall in basic science and technology.[1]

2. The governments of Japan and the United States have influenced the course of science and technology. However, significant differences exist in how that influence has been exerted and on what sectors — university, industry, etc.

3. Most of Japan's past economic success is not linked to scientific and technological development. A significant change, however, is underway in Japan regarding science and technology policy. It appears that the Japanese are placing more emphasis on knowledge-based information-processing industries. Moreover, the Japanese are devoting more resources to the *inter-*

nal development of basic technology and, therefore, are becoming less dependent on imported technology.

Japan's shift from a strong dependence on manufacturing and trade—based on imported science and technology—toward a reliance on nationally derived science and technology, which is then applied to the new knowledge-based information-processing industries, will be discussed in section IV.

4. If the aforementioned shift is in fact occurring and if it continues, there will be a significant change in the type of competition we currently see between the United States and Japan. This change in competition could create some interesting opportunities for cooperation between the two countries in basic technology.

QUANTITATIVE ASSESSMENT OF U.S.-JAPANESE TECHNOLOGY DEVELOPMENT

The relationship between science and technology and the achievement of a country's national goals, especially economic goals, is complex. Japan does a far better job of directing the development of science and technology toward achieving economic goals than does the United States. However, neither nation can aim basic research at a desired target; basic research is too full of surprises. The United States can provide nurturing environments for basic research, promote advanced education for scientists and engineers, and supply adequate funds to conduct research, but the United States cannot "command" creative and innovative basic research to bring about a particular result. Not so long ago, for example, no one could conceive of a transistor, and, certainly, no one could have commanded its invention.

Although the utility of basic research can never be predicted, the United States has long considered basic research the cornerstone of its economic and social development. In constant 1972 dollars, for example, spending on basic research in the United States has increased from $3.7 million in 1975 to $5.7 million in 1985. Table 1 shows U.S. spending during the last decade on basic research, applied research, and development as a percentage of total R&D expenditures. Although spending for basic research has increased in actual dollars, the spending mix among basic research, applied research, and development has remained relatively constant. This is probably not the case in Japan, although recent quantitative data are not available. Nevertheless, it seems likely that Japan has increased both the percentage of total R&D expenditures spent on basic research and absolute funding levels.[2]

Although the United States has increased its funding levels for R&D, Japan is increasing its support at a faster rate than the United States is.

Table 1
U.S. R&D expenditures, by character
of work, as a percent of total R&D expenditures

	1976	1980	1985
	Percent		
Basic research	12.8	12.9	12.5
Applied research	23.2	22.4	21.5
Development	64.1	64.6	66.0

Adapted from Science Indicators - 1985

According to *Japan and the World in Statistics, 1986,* issued by the Tokyo
Chamber of Commerce and Industry, U.S. expenditures for research in 1973
were $30.7 billion, while Japanese expenditures were $7.3 billion. In 1983,
U.S. expenditures increased by 185 percent to $87.7 billion, while Japanese
expenditures increased 275 percent to $27.4 billion. Perhaps more mean-
ingfully, Figures 1 and 2 relate R&D spending to each country's gross national product, showing that Japan's expenditures are rising while the United
States' are remaining constant. Figure 1 includes R&D expenditures for
defense.

Figure 2 illustrates that Japan invests more heavily as a percentage of
GNP than the United States does in nondefense R&D. Certainly, some of
the defense-related R&D in the United States is transferred to industry,
especially for fundamental research programs, but to what extent such a
transfer occurs is difficult to estimate. Most defense funding is allocated for
weapon system development, which does not have many commercial applications. Another way to quantify U.S.-Japanese R&D expenditures is to
compare spending as a percent of sales among large Japanese and U.S. companies. Table 2 shows dramatic differences in most of the sectors targeted
by the Japanese. The apparent exception is the General Motors-Toyota
comparison, in which one might expect a higher percentage of spending by
Toyota. The likely explanation for the similarity between the two is that by
1983, the Japanese had already achieved many of their objectives in this targeted industry.To illustrate the effectiveness of Japan's R&D spending in
targeted industries and advanced technologies, a researcher from AT&T's
Bell Labs assembled the data shown in Table 3. The data show that Japan's
advances in technology will ensure its continued competitiveness in, if not
domination of, world high-technology markets.

Figure 1
**National expenditures for performance of research
and development, including defense-related R&D,
as a percent of gross national product by country**

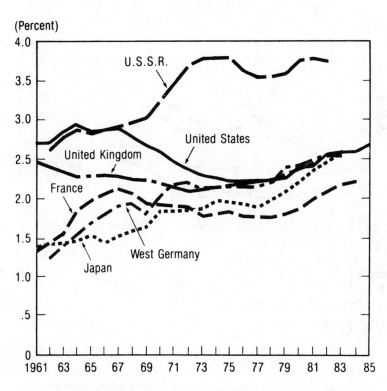

Adapted from Science Indicators-1985

6

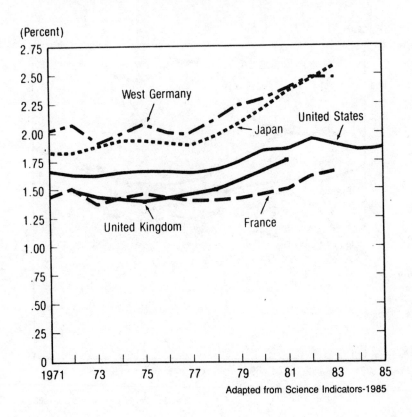

Figure 2
**Estimated ratios of non-defense R&D expenditures
to gross national product for selected countries**

(Percent)

West Germany

Japan

United States

United Kingdom

France

1971   73   75   77   79   81   83   85

Adapted from Science Indicators-1985

Table 2
Research and Development as Percent of Sales (1983)
for U.S. and Japanese Companies

U.S. Company	R&D (%)	Japanese Company	R&D (%)	Difference
General Electric	3.4	Hitachi	7.9	+4.5
General Motors	3.5	Toyota	3.9	+0.4
Eastman Kodak	7.3	Fuji Photo Film	6.6	-0.7
DuPont	2.7	Toray Industries	3.1	+0.4
U.S. Steel	o.5	Nippon Steel	1.9	+1.4
Xerox	6.6	Canon	14.6	+8.0
Texas Instruments	6.6	NEC	13.0	+6.4
RCA	2.4	Matsushita Electric Industries	7.2	+4.5
Goddyear	2.6	Bridgestone	4.5	+1.9
Eli Lilly	9.7	Shionogi	9.6	-o.1

Source:
Abegglen, James C., and Stalk, George, Jr. Kaisha: The Japanese Corporation.
Basic Books, Inc., New York: 1985.

Table 3
U.S.-Japanese Status in Key Technologies
for Advanced Processing

The United States holds the technological edge in three established areas:

- Ion implantation
- Thin film epitaxy (CVD, MBE and MOCVD)
- Film deposition and etching

Within the past year, the U.S. has lost control of:

- Optical lithography

The Japanese lead in the following emerging technologies:

- Microwave plasma etching
- Lithographic sources
- Electron and ion microbeams
- Laser-assisted processing
- Compound semiconductor processing
- Optoelectronic integrated circuits
- Three-dimensional device structures

Clearly, Japan's commercial R&D investments have paid off. Figure 3 shows the sharp increase in a Japanese worker's productivity compared to the relatively flat curve for a U.S. worker. In industrial sectors targeted by the Japanese, productivity is greater than that in the United States. For example, a U.S. employee in the motorcycle industry made 15 units per year, while his Japanese counterpart made 200 units in the same period.[3] In untargeted industries, however, such as textiles, lumber, and glass, U.S. productivity is substantially ahead of that in Japan.

Much has been published about innovation in Japan and the United States. Innovation and creativity, however, are notoriously difficult to measure directly, and indirect measures leave much to be desired. For example, Japan has won 4 Nobel prizes in science, while U.S. researchers have won 158. During this same period, however, most scientific publications by Japanese workers were printed in the Japanese language and thus were largely unavailable to Western readers, including the Nobel Committee.

Figure 3
Real gross domestic product per employed person in selected countries, in constant 1972 dollars*

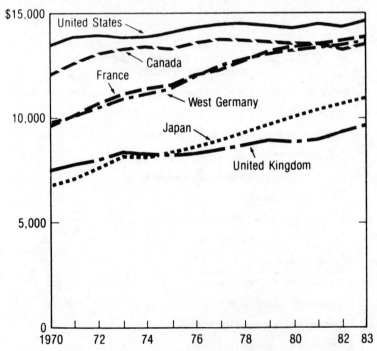

* GNP implicit price deflators used to convert current dollars to constant 1972 dollars.
Adapted from Science Indicators-1985

Patent activity is one of the indirect measures of technical innovation. Figure 4 shows that from 1969 to 1982, the number of U.S. patent applications fell about 50 percent, while Japanese patent applications increased about 50 percent. This suggests that inventiveness in Japan is increasing relative to the United States, although in general, patents are considered a less-important gauge today than they were in previous years.

Quantifying the number of scientists and engineers is another indirect way of measuring technical innovation. Figure 5 shows that from 1968 to 1983 Japan doubled the number of scientists and engineers engaged in R&D per 10,000 workers in the labor force, while the United States maintained a constant number of R&D workers. Given that half the R&D in the United States is defense related, Japan employs more R&D workers per capita in civilian areas than the United States does.

Figure 4
External patent applications by residents of selected countries

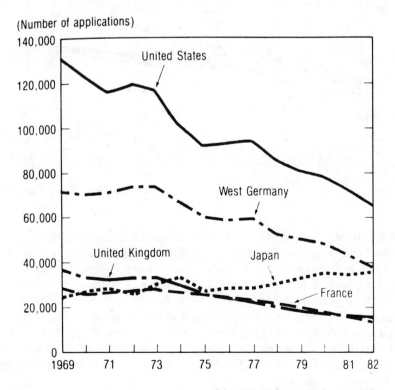

Adapted from Science Indicators-1985

Figure 5
Scientists and engineers engaged in research and development per 10,000 labor force population by country

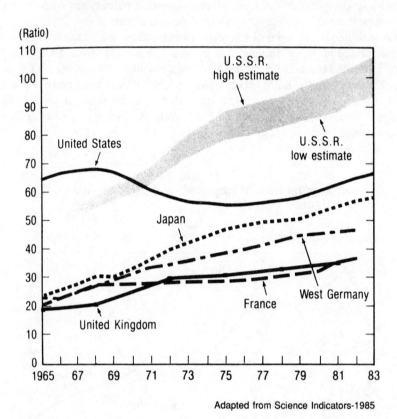

Adapted from Science Indicators-1985

R&D, by nature, looks ahead to the development of new technologies that will lead to new applications for new products. How different are these forward-looking views in the United States and Japan? One way to answer the question is to look at Japan's highly organized and publicized plans for new research programs and then determine whether the United States has similar programs. Japanese organizations such as the Ministry of International Trade and Industry (MITI) and the Science and Technology Agency plan and sponsor local new-research thrusts. One example is the Fifth Generation Computer Project (ICOT) to promote and advance information-processing technology.

Two new research programs in Japan are the Human Frontiers Plan (HFP) and the New Functional Element (NFE) Program, both sponsored by MITI and other organizations. The HFP has three main objectives: (1) innovation of production processed based on an understanding of analogous biological/biochemical processes; (2) development of new information-processing and control systems that functionally resemble animal nervous systems; and (3) development of power systems modeled after the locomotor systems of biological organisms.

The NFE Program is composed of three main elements: (1) new materials, such as membranes, plastics, synthetic metals, composites, alloys, and ceramics; (2) biotechnology, such as bioreactors, cell cultivation, and recombinant DNA; and (3) new functional elements, such as superlattice devices, three-dimensional integrated circuits, and bioelectronic integrated circuits.

Work in these research areas is already underway in U.S. universities and in government and industrial laboratories, which suggests that Japan and the United States exhibit striking similarities in their research efforts. Apparently, both countries see the same need for particular technologies on which to base future products and services.

Both Japan and the United States are leaders among nations in investment in research and development, including basic research. Overall, the United States continues to spend more in absolute terms than does Japan, but the Japanese have achieved remarkable success in targeted research areas and industries. Therefore, explanation for Japan's relative advantage over the United States must be sought in areas other than overall investment in science and technology.

THE ROLE OF GOVERNMENT IN SCIENCE AND TECHNOLOGY POLICY

The governments of Japan and the United States play an important role in setting policy for science and technology and in supporting its implementation and application. The support manifests itself in a number of ways— for example, direct funding, government direction, government analysis of the priorities of different titles, tax policies, regulatory policies, trade policies, international agreements, direct help to troubled industries, and government support of technical education.

Some general observations can be made about the role each government plays:

> 1. The Japanese government has been especially active in establishing an industrial policy, while the U.S. government

has largely avoided anything that could be considered an industrial policy.

2. The U.S. government has been very active in directing and funding science and technology in support of national security, while the Japanese government has withheld such support because of national policy and Japan's constitution.

3. The U.S. government also has been very active in supporting basic research, both for commercial and military applications, while the Japanese government generally has been less active in basic research, although, as I indicated earlier, this appears to be changing.

In the early 1980s, the term *Japan, Inc.* was widely used to describe the nature of Japan's success in international, particularly U.S., markets. As is so often the case with shorthand expressions and generalizations, the term was misleading. It implied that the Japanese government—specifically, MITI—played a major role in promoting commercial applications of technology developments.

Recent works have offered a more balanced view of technology policy in Japan, thus lessening somewhat the dominant role previously attributed to MITI. In *Kaisha: The Japanese Corporation*, Abegglen and Stalk propose that Japan's success is the result of, first, effective management in large Japanese companies and, second, the competitive fundamentals these companies have chosen, such as a bias for growth, a preoccupation with the actions of competitors, the creation and ruthless exploitation of competitive advantage, and the use of corporate financial and personnel policies that support the first three fundamentals.

Abegglen and Stalk's arguments are persuasive and seem consistent with the success Japanese companies have shown. Moreover, these arguments still allow for my belief that the advisory role of the Japanese government in establishing research and development priorities has been critical to Japan's success. Although Japan does not have a centrally *controlled* economy, the case can still be made that the Japanese have a *planned* economy, with the government doing the planning.

Abegglen and Stalk, for example, describe how the Japanese government assesses Japan's capability in various technologies in relation to other countries and then takes action to improve the situation in those areas in which the Japanese are behind. For instance, the Japanese have assessed that they are ahead in semiconductors, office automation, computer hardware, robotics, unmanned protection systems, optics, and new materials such as ceramics and composites. However, the Japanese believe that they lag behind the United States in aerospace, computer software, data communications, and space hardware and are only now just catching up in biotechnology.

The United States presents a dramatically different situation. Whenever the U.S. government makes a comparative assessment with respect to other countries, it is usually with the Soviet Union and concerns, of course, national security. After the assessments are made, the government — specifically, the Department of Defense — takes action to narrow the gaps, if they exist. Recently, however, several presidential commissions have examined such factors as U.S. productivity and have made recommendations for government action. In all the studies that I am aware of, however, the commissions fall far short of recommending the kind of market-related or product-related influence that MITI exerts.

In the United States, the system for setting science and technology policies involves a wide range of organizations from the executive and legislative branches of government and from the private sector. The central component of U.S. policy concerns the support of basic research and the importance of research in the universities. This theme goes back as far as the end of World War II, when Vannevar Bush published *Science: The Endless Frontier*, which established the federal government's responsibility for the support of basic research and, to a great extent, the health of the research universities.

To place emphasis on the policy of supporting basic research and to be sure that it can be implemented, the U.S. government created the National Science Foundation, which is the principal federal government arm for support of fundamental research. The foundation receives advice from a distinguished board called the National Science Board, which represents the industry and the universities. Other federal agencies, such as the Department of Defense, the Department of Energy, and the National Institute of Health also support basic research and development, although most of their support is for mission-oriented development programs.

Organizations in the private sector take up this clarion call for basic research, including the National Academy of Sciences, the National Academy of Engineering, the Institute of Medicine, and the National Research Council, as well as numerous professional societies. Another influential organization is the American Association for the Advancement of Science (AAAS), which has 136,000 scientists and engineers as members and affiliations with 285 other scientific, engineering, and technical societies and organizations, bringing the total membership to approximately 5 million members. The AAAS publication, *Science*, is a strong voice for basic research and is, of course, a vehicle for communication of the results of that basic research.

In this discussion, I have tried to show that both the Japanese and U.S. governments exert a strong influence on science and technology policy. However, they do so in very different ways. The U.S. government's policy is to support and shape basic research but to leave industrial policy to industry, whereas the Japanese government emphasizes industrial policy and the development of products and new markets.

A very clear statement of U.S. policy under President Ronald Reagan was given by George A. Keyworth, formerly the president's science adviser, at a November 21, 1985 workshop on the federal role in research and development, arranged by the National Academy of Science's Committee on Science, Engineering, and Public Policy. Dr. Kenworth states, "From the start and continuing through each budget cycle, we have trimmed federal support for commercially intended development projects that were sheltered from market forces." His statement reflects his belief, and the administration's belief, that the "government is ill-equipped to take the steps, or even to encourage others to take the steps, to move technology into usefulness." Keyworth points out, of course, that defense-related technology is the one exception because defense is a unique responsibility of government. Therefore, the federal government provides support for defense-related research from idea to product and significant funding for development. Keyworth goes on to explain his view of basic research:

"Basic research is a major source of growth in our society because it provides the talent and the technology we must have if we expect to compete with countries like Japan or Korea or China."

The United States has long considered it necessary to develop its own technology. In some sense, this is an acceptance of the need to repay other nations from which the United States gained technology in earlier years. Prior to World War II, for example, much U.S. work in physics, mathematics, and chemistry was based on technology imported from England, France, Germany, and other European countries.

Because the United States traditionally has developed its technology, the nation has turned away in recent years from the notion of accepting and adapting technology from other countries. Japan, it seems, does just the opposite.

According to Abegglen and Stalk, the government of Japan effectively recognizes and accelerates the forces at work in the marketplace. Because MITI plays a significant role in developing heavy industry in Japan, it is not unusual, at least not surprising, that Japanese industry accepts the advice and guidance from MITI. There seems to be a friendly relationship between government and business in Japan, whereas the relationship is usually adversarial in the United States. The U.S. government's reluctance to guide or direct commercially oriented research must be seen as a reflection of industry's reluctance to accept government guidance.

QUALITATIVE ASSESSMENT OF U.S.-JAPANESE
SCIENCE AND TECHNOLOGY

In the introductory paragraphs of this chapter I indicated that my perspective on scientific and technological developments was that of an industrialist. This perspective requires that, having offered some statistics and having described the role of government in the two countries, I ask the question, what is the impact on industrial competitiveness? The answer *should be* that U.S. technological superiority produces a competitive advantage that, in turn, leads to economic success. Unfortunately, some discrepancies emerge from the statistics. For example, if one looks at the percentage of U.S. GNP devoted to research and development, it seems logical to conclude that the United States should enjoy a significant economic lead over Japan. This is simply not the case. What, then, are the factors that account for this difference? At least five factors are at work:

- Different educational systems
- Greater commitment to industrial competitiveness in Japan
- Different business environments
- Lower input costs for products in Japan
- A buy-versus-make approach to technology in Japan

First, the United States looks with some envy at the Japanese educational system, particularly at the K-12 level. The Japanese stress the quality and intensity of education, and Figure 6 shows that this emphasis produces results as early as the eighth grade. The higher test scores may result from the fact that Japanese children spend more time in school each year, with more hours of classroom instruction devoted each day to science and mathematics. It may also be due to the so-called examination hell, which is an exhaustive test that Japanese children must pass in order to enter college.

Whatever the cause, Figure 7 shows that even the best U.S. college-preparatory high school mathematics ("calculus") students do not perform as well as average Japanese students. Moreover, Figure 8 shows that the United States confers about twice as many first degrees in science and engineering as Japan. Japan, however, trains slightly more engineers than does the United States. The Japanese system has been extremely successful, achieving a 99 percent literacy rate; 94 percent of Japanese children go to high school, and 37 percent go to college.

Although Japan's educational system has served it well as a supplier of highly skilled labor for rapid industrialization, the Japanese are examining their system with some concern. As Japan looks to create its own technology, it may need highly developed special skills rather than the more average skills that are appropriate for rapid industrialization. In simple terms, the

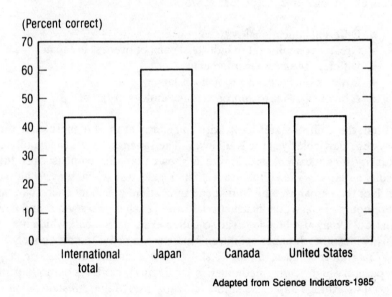

Figure 6
Algebra test scores at end of eighth grade,
for selected coutries: 1982

(Percent correct)

International total — Japan — Canada — United States

Adapted from Science Indicators-1985

Figure 7
Mathematics test scores at the end of secondary
school, for selected countries: 1982

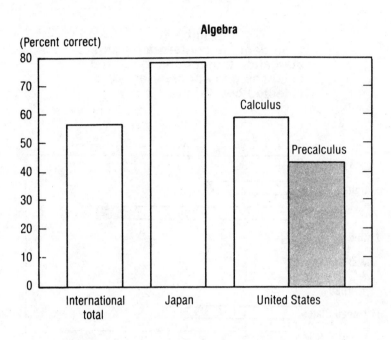

Algebra

(Percent correct)

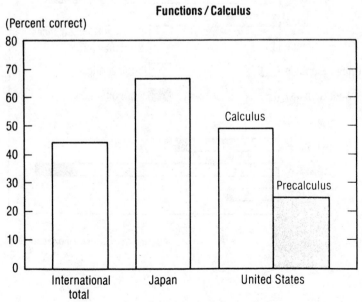

Functions / Calculus

(Percent correct)

Adapted from Science Indicators-1985

18

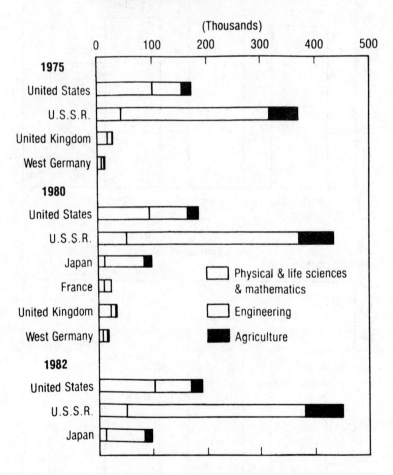

Figure 8
First degrees conferred by higher education institutions in natural sciences and engineering for selected countries

(Thousands)

Physical & life sciences & mathematics

Engineering

Agriculture

Adapted from Science Indicators-1985

system might require a change from rote learning to the command and control of robots and other aspects of industrial Japan. Naohiro Amaya, a senior adviser to MITI and a member of the Prime Minister's Ad Hoc Commission on Education Reform, is particularly critical of the current norm of rote learning and methodical teaching styles.

Another point of concern is that the strength of Japan's K-12 system is counterbalanced by an apparent weakness in Japanese universities, particularly in the graduate schools. Students often feel a need to recover from the intense competition in the secondary schools and, therefore, are not prepared to work hard at the beginning of their university careers. Consequently, many Japanese who desire more intense university education from to the United States. The number of Japanese receiving postsecondary education in the United States grew by about 527 percent between 1960 and 1983 from 2,168 to 13,610. About a third of these were graduate students.

In contrast to Japan, the United States has a strong university system, which should have a significant impact on U.S. industrial competitiveness because the university-industry relationship is stronger in the United States than in Japan. The relationship was nurtured during World War II with large government-sponsored activities, such as the Radiation Laboratory at MIT. During that period, senior professors from the universities worked on important national programs and became closely involved with industry as well as with government. The relationship, however, has deteriorated somewhat since then for reasons too many to cite here.

In Japan, the government works closely with industry in the application of science and technology. Therefore, one would expect the universities to play similar role. In addition, there are cultural differences between Japanese in industry, government, and the universities. As a result, although there is some movement from government to industry, there does not appear to be significant movement from academia into either government or industry. This, of course, is quite different than the situation in the United States. Frank Gibney sums up the situation: "The lack of effective communication between government, business and the academic is not merely a social failing, it is one of Japan's most serious potential limitations as a modern industrial great power."[4]

Finally, state university professors in Japan are civil servants and, as such, are not allowed to receive industry consulting fees. This further strengthens the view that the worlds of Japanese universities and government and industry are kept separate. Japan has been promoting a new research policy that relaxes some of the rules that interfere with free communication among the universities, government laboratories, and private industry, so some of the differences discussed earlier may be diminished. It remains clear, however, that the strength of Japan's educational system at the K-12 level is a major factor behind Japan's ability to convert foreign development in basic science and technology into world-leading commercial applications.

The second factor explaining Japan's disproportionate economic success is that Japan emphasizes the operational aspects of doing business, while the United States emphasizes financial analysis as the "glamor" function in U.S. corporations. Honeywell's chairman and chief executive officer, Edson W. Spencer, puts it this way in a speech before The Executives' Club of Chicago: "In American business schools, the study of marketing and production has been replaced by mathematical models and the analysis of the earnings stream. The financial side of the learning experience has overshadowed the more prosaic course favoring manufacturing productivity."[5]

While this country's best business minds are going into investment banking, Japan's best minds are running its factories. The United States emphasizes the movement and manipulation of products. The impact of this difference on production processes is no more evident than in the semiconductor industry. Data from Robert F. Graham and Hambrecht & Quist, Inc.[6] compare the typical yields of saleable chips from silicon wafers. While 17 percent of the wafer-derived integrated circuits are saleable in the United States, fully 54 percent are saleable in Japan. This, of course, gives Japan a tremendous advantage in reduced processing costs.

Similarly, U.S. technological endeavors emphasize basic science, while Japanese endeavors emphasize applied technology. A recent survey in *The Economist* notes, "American technology reaches out for the unknown."[7] This orientation toward production and application gives Japan a lead in *applying* science and technology in selected areas despite a less-favorable position in *creating* new science and technology. The third factor is the Japanese business environment. Japan's unique capital markets allow corporate senior management to make longer-term investment decisions. Japanese corporations are highly leveraged. Hostile takeovers are almost unheard of in Japan; and Japanese investors take the long view and, in many cases, favor the reinvestment of capital over increased dividends. U.S. managers, on the other hand, have a capital structure dependent on equity investors rather than on borrowed capital. These investors, many of whom are institutions, as a group have a shorter perspective than do sources of borrowed capital. The banker is worried about the servicing of a loan during the long term. The institutional investor, usually evaluated on the basis of his or her quarterly performance, is looking for short-term return on investment. In addition, the U.S. manager is always looking over his or her shoulder for a corporate raider. To avoid a hostile takeover, stock prices must be kept high, which again puts undue emphasis on short-term performance.

The fourth factor is the lower input costs the Japanese have for their intellectual and physical products. Capital investors are not only more patient but also provide capital at a lower cost. Recent data[8] indicate that gross fixed capital formation as a percentage of gross domestic product is 17.9 percent for the United States and 27.8 percent for Japan. This is a result of the strong propensity of the Japanese people to save. The average Japanese saved 15.7 percent of disposable income in 1985. The comparable American saved only 4.7 percent.

Cash wage rates, although rapidly catching up with the West, are still lower in Japan than in the United States. If fringe benefits are included, however, wages for U.S. manufacturers have actually increased. The Bureau of Labor Statistics reports that U.S. hourly labor costs have risen from $3 more than Japanese hourly costs in 1975 to nearly $6 more in 1983.[9] This means that the cost of manufacturing final products and the cost of conducting research are less in Japan.

Finally, in the past, technology itself was cheap for Japan to acquire from the West. The Japanese were more open to buying technology or to licensing technology rather than making it themselves. The United States realized, rightly so, that it needed to bolster Japan's technological and economic base after World War II to support U.S. national-security objectives. This is now changing. Japan's Economic Planning Agency sponsored a 1982 study of developments in Japan's economy and society through the year 2000. The study, according to Abegglen, notes that Japan has completed a full turn of the economic sequence. The Japanese have shifted from labor-intensive activities to activities emphasizing raw materials and energy and then to the present concentration on competitiveness and the manufacture of mass-produced goods such as autos, cameras, office equipment, and machine tools. It is worth noting that past progress did not require development of any new technology. The next stage, however, will involve a move from mass-produced goods into leading technology sectors. Special emphasis will be placed on electronics-driven and biology-related products as well as on knowledge-intensive service sectors such as software and communications.

As one moves through each sequence in development, the importance of science and technology increases. Up to now, Japan has been able to rapidly increase its share of export markets, penetrate U.S. markets, and increase Japanese productivity with little or no new developments in science and technology. This will certainly change in the future. "Henceforth, industrial competition between America and Japan is going to range fiercely along the high-tech frontier — where both countries take a special pride in their industrial skills and cherish sacred beliefs about their innate abilities."[10]

One way of measuring this shift is to talk about Japan's invisible balance of technological trade — that is, Japan's receipts compared with payments for patent royalties, licenses, etc. This balance of technological trade had a ratio of 1:47 two decades ago and came very close to being in balance last year. Japan probably still buys its high-tech goods and knowhow predominantly from the West and sells them mainly to the developing world, although that is rapidly changing. For example, it is generally believed that Japan is ahead now in fiber optics for telecommunications, gallium arsenide for integrated circuits, numerically controlled machine tools and robots, computer disk drives, computers, and magnetic storage media. If this is the case, then Japan must turn to its own resources for new technology that will enable Japan to retain leadership in those areas.

In this discussion, I have tried to show that developments in science and technology have not been deciding factors in industrial competitiveness between the United States and Japan. Education, operations, savvy, patient capital markets, lower input costs, and cheap Western technology have been the source of Japan's advantages in the past. In the future, however, scientific and technological superiority will probably become major competitive factors.

U.S.-JAPANESE COOPERATION
IN BASIC RESEARCH

Although *applied* technology may become a competitive factor, *basic* research is a very different proposition. As I indicated at the beginning of this chapter, basic research cannot be easily guided, it is costly, and it does not have immediate returns. Both countries have something to offer in this area. The Japanese offer the long-term perspective necessary to push basic research to its fruition. U.S. individualism, however, is most likely to provide the "spark of genius" that makes basic research successful. Both countries, therefore, should work together to gain the rewards that appropriate cooperative endeavors in basic science and technology can bring.

We should all feel comfortable with this proposition. As the September 1984 report of the United States-Japan Advisory Commission notes:

> The scope and depth of (current) scientific and technological cooperation between the United States and Japan is unique. Hundreds of cooperative arrangements exist among private corporations; some thirteen government-to-government agreements are designed to meet public needs; and countless additional interchanges occur among individual scientists in private and international forums.[11]

Specifically, several basic technologies that are very expensive or are of high mutual interest to the United States and Japan warrant cooperation. The previously cited Report of the United States-Japan Advisory Commission lists as possible cooperative efforts the Fifth Generation Computer Project, machine translation between English and Japanese, high-energy physics research, life sciences and cancer research, and development of scientific and engineering standards.[12]

In an area particularly important to Honeywell, cross-investment in R&D in each country's markets is a way to prevent protectionism. If a company is willing to make foreign R&D investments as well as investments in foreign manufacturing facilities, that company is generally viewed favorably by foreign governments.

Japan and the United States could also take additional steps to promote technological cooperation. First, Japan has no equivalent to the U.S. Academies of Science and Engineering. This makes it more difficult for Japan to conduct bilateral discussions from a nongovernmental perspective. Japan should consider the creation of private-sector organizations that match the academies in function, if not in structure. This is important because most technology issues will continue to be in the private sector. Issues such as university or private-sector technology exchanges would be handled more efficiently by a national organization than by individual scientists or companies.

Second, both countries should retain adequate safeguards on intellectual property. In 1984, MITI proposed a substitution of patent-like concepts for copyright protection on software. The Advisory Council on Japan-U.S. Economic Relations, expressing the views of U.S. industry on MITI's proposition, says simply: "None of [the] elements [of this proposal] are acceptable in whole or in part to the U.S. computer, software, or related industries. They cannot be prioritized and the degree to which they are unacceptable cannot be rank ordered."[13]

MITI recognized that this proposal would substantially hamper the transfer of technology to Japan in precisely the area such technology is most needed — software development — and wisely withdrew its proposed statute. The lesson we should all learn is that propositions that prevent the developers of technology from realizing the fruits of their labors are ill-advised in the long run. Such propositions should be avoided in the future if we wish to promote technological cooperation and exchange.

Third, U.S. businesses must take action to position themselves for commercial and technical exchange with the Japanese. Current preparation is woefully inadequate. A survey of 108 U.S. companies indicated that 81 percent of U.S. companies recognize that U.S. "corporations should attempt to get more Americans with a working knowledge of the Japanese language and culture into business positions where they are working with Japanese business issues."[14]

Unfortunately, few companies have policies or programs to reach that objective. If the United States is to gain from cooperative arrangements with Japan, Americans must be willing to take the same steps that the Japanese have taken to understand this country's language and culture. This is particularly true because future activities will be characterized by valuable information flow in both directions. In the past, when the Japanese had less to offer from a scientific and technological perspective, Americans had less need to understand Japanese intellectual products. In the present and future, both U.S. and Japanese scientific research is valuable, and the United States will be at a disadvantage if only Japanese scientists can avail themselves of this entire body of thought.

CONCLUSION

Japan has been extremely successful in the industries it has targeted — automobiles, consumer electronics, office automation — while the United States has been more successful overall. Japan owes much of its success to superior application of high technology and innovative manufacturing. Moreover, the Japanese government is more involved in industry and in science and technology than is the U.S. government, but the United States enjoys stronger cooperation between industry and the universities.

There are two movements underway, however, one in Japan and one in the United States, that are changing the competition between the two countries. Japan is moving away from the exploitation of foreign technology, particularly from the United States, toward the development of its own technology in order to establish a strong presence in information-processing, knowledge-based industries. Japan is at the point where it feels it has hit a technology ceiling and must create its own technology in order to take the next step in the evolution of its economy. Consequently, Japan is putting greater emphasis on basic research through increased collaboration between universities and industry and between the private sector and the government.

The movement in the United States is less certain. The United States is still reacting to Japan's success, creating organizations like the Microelectronics and Computer Technology Corporation to determine whether this country can do a better job of exploiting technology, but also investing in basic research in the universities in hopes that the United States will become competitive again. This will succeed, however, only if more emphasis in the universities is placed on manufacturing. As long as the U.S. government and U.S. industry do not want an industrial policy, the private sector must balance its basic research and industrial development investments.

The implication of these two movements is that Japan, by emphasizing the funding of basic research, may find itself in the same dilemma the United States now faces — that is, the United States has an abundance of basic research that has not translated into increased global competitiveness. Japan's success has been built on the exploitation and application of technology through superior manufacturing and marketing. Shifting the emphasis from manufacturing toward basic research could make Japan less competitive in the years to come.

NOTES

Acknowledgment is given for numerous discussions held with Steve Heer, Paul McAdam, K. C. Nomura, Stirling Stackhouse, and Hiroshi Yamashita. For an understanding of the Japanese management of research and development, I have relied heavily on my colleagues in Japan in the company Yamatake-Honeywell. Particular appreciation is expressed to Ichiro Ido and Kozo Tanaka, of Yamatake-Honeywell.

1. For an excellent review of this subject and of Japanese industry overall, see Abegglen, James C., and Stalk, George, Jr. *Kaisha: The Japanese Corporation* (New York: Basic Books, 1985).

2. Data obtained informally from Mark Eaton, Microelectronics and Computer Technology Corp., Austin, Texas.

3. Davidson, W. H. *The Amazing Race* (New York: John Wiley & Sons, 1984).

4. Gibney, Frank. *Japan: The Fragile Superpower* (New York: W. W. Norton Company, 1975).

5. Spencer, Edson W. "Playing Poker with American Industry" (Address to the Executives' Club of Chicago, April 18, 1986).

6. "Is It Too Late to Save the U.S. Semiconductor Industry?" *Business Week*, August 18, 1986, p. 66.

7. "High Technology Survey," *The Economist*, August 23, 1986, p. 16.

8. *OECD Economic Outlook* (May, 1986): 85, 91, 176.

9. "High Technology Survey," p. 6.

10. Ibid., p. 4.

11. United States-Japan Advisory Commission, *Challenges and Opportunities in United States-Japan Relations: A Report Submitted to the President of the United States and the Prime Minister of Japan* (Washington, D. C.: United States-Japan Advisory Commission, September 1984, p. 97.

12. Ibid., pp. 101-102.

13. Advisory Council on Japan-U.S. Economic Relations, *High Technology Position Paper* (Washington, D. C.: U.S. Department of Commerce, November 1984), p. 13.

14. Strategic Information Research Corporation for the Advisory Council on Japan-U.S. Economic Relations, Japanese Expertise in U.S. Corporations (Washington, D. C.: U.S. Department of Commerce, July 1985), p. 12.

BIBLIOGRAPHY

Bush, Vannevar. *Science: The Endless Frontier*, Washington, D. C.: U.S. Office of Scientific Research and Development, 1945.

Hirota, Toshiro. "Technology Development of American and Japanese Companies." *Kansai University Review of Economics and Business* 14, nos. 1-2 (March 1986).

Japan-U.S. Businessmen's Conference Joint Study. "Understanding the Industrial Policies and Practices of Japan and the United States: A Business Perspective." Washington, D. C.: Advisory Council on Japan-U.S. Economic Relations, July 1984.

Keizai Koho Center. "Japan 1985: An International Comparison." Tokyo: Keizai Koho Center, 1985.

Landau, Ralph, and Rosenberg, Nathan. *The Positive Sum Total: Harnessing Technology for Economic Growth*. Washington, D. C.: National Academy Press, 1986.

National Science Board. *Science Indicators/The 1985 Report*. Washington, D. C.: National Science Board, 1985.

Passin, Herbert. *Society and Education in Japan*. New York: Teacher's College Press, 1965.

Spencer, Edson W. "A Survey of U.S./Japan Economic Relations." Address to the Economic Council of Keidanren (Japan Federation of Economic Organizations), May 11, 1984.

DISCUSSION SUMMARY

The discussion began with two thought-provoking questions: Why, if the United States is the great innovator and Japan the great imitator, is the United States behind in science and technology? More importantly, why is the United States seemingly losing its number one position to Japan — a country that has been described as everything but innovative? It was suggested that the United States might study the educational system in Japan, particularly kindergarten through the twelfth grade. During those formative years, Japanese children are exposed to a rigorous program that instills a sense of discipline. A substantial portion of the curriculum focuses on English language training, and an equally important part emphasizes mathematics and science. By the time Japanese children are in junior high school, they are already ahead of their U.S. counterparts in these subjects. After graduating from college, they enter companies that train them for specific tasks.

Although inadequate language training may be hindering U.S. performance, not only in science and technology but in manufacturing as well, the lagging U.S. economy was attributed to a reluctance on the part of U.S. management to invest in R&D. Smaller companies do tend to concentrate relatively more resources on R&D, but the size of these companies limits the absolute amount of money budgeted for these purposes. Therefore, the United States has to devise a way to fund and encourage the smaller companies where innovation exists but where funds are not plentiful.

Recently, Secretary of Commerce Malcolm Baldridge has said that the United States has not been as successful as it could be because management tends to look at short-term profit rather than long-term commitment. This was described as a "bum rap," for U.S. senior management clearly understands the need for R&D investment and does its best with what it has to work with.

When the question was raised as to whether Japan was willing to invest in science and technology projects, particularly the basic sciences, it was explained that investments in the two countries are "different" and perhaps conflicting. While the United States has a high-tech image in terms of space technology and defense, Japan thinks on a more basic level (such as basic electronics). The Japanese are skilled at learning technology and applying it to their everyday needs.

It was emphasized that while Congress wants quick, simple solutions— temporary solutions that will carry senators and representatives through the next election—the real need is to shift U.S. thinking into the "long-term mode" and to realize that changes do not take place overnight. The United States has to begin by revamping the educational system, so that it can produce more innovative and creative people. Congress needs to provide information to the public that shows the benefits of long-term investment. The financial industry and government should prepare to share a larger part of the burden for long-term investment, as is the case in Japan. Congress also needs to think carefully about the consequences of eliminating the R&D and capital investment tax credits.

Overcoming the oft-mentioned not-invented-here syndrome must begin at basic levels within institutions. For example, it was maintained that chemical and electronic divisions of the same company in the United States are often unaware of what their neighboring divisions are doing. This split between divisions proves inefficient because both sections should draw on each other's knowledge. In addition, there is often very little incentive or encouragement from top management to collaborate. Research is usually done at one's own risk, with little or no backing from colleagues. It was suggested that "prestige compensation" in addition to monetary rewards should be awarded to creative people because people are by nature interested in personal success and like to see their ideas carried through to the end. Career advancement should result from these successes. The United States needs to encourage these creative thinkers to work on the shop floor, where they can contribute to grass-roots manufacturing, instead of joining prestige academic positions.

2

Technological Progress and R&D Systems in Japan and the United States

Gary Saxonhouse

It is easy to be dazzled by the fascinating and far-reaching advances in microelectronics, materials engineering, and biotechnology and to forget that the past one and one-half decades have seen a relatively modest rate of economic improvement in the world's advanced industrialized societies (see Table 1). Indeed, it is possible for serious observers to wonder whether the scientific opportunities for improving economic well-being on the scale of the early postwar decades may be diminishing (see Table 2).[1]

Support for such an outlook can be culled from several indicators. In almost all the fifty countries for which data are available, for example, patents per scientist and engineer as well as per unit of research and development (R&D) expenditure have declined. This is true in spite of the large absolute increases in R&D resources committed by most industrialized countries since the mid-1960s. The rate of return from R&D investments measured by the number of patents obtained per scientist and engineer has fallen sharply.

The sole exception to this worldwide pattern of seemingly diminished returns is Japan (see Table 3). This is in striking contrast to most other economies where patent rate of return has fallen as the number of scientists and engineers has expanded sharply. Although nationals of major industrial powers such as France and West Germany are only receiving 55 percent of previous peak levels, the number of patents received by Japanese has almost quadrupled during the years between 1967 and 1984 (see Table 4). The Japanese have been so active in overseas patenting that their contributions have offset what otherwise would have been a much sharper decline in the patents granted in the other major industrialized economies. If, for instance, patent approvals for Japanese nationals had been excluded from U.S. patent

Table 1. Average Annual Growth Rates of Productivity in the Advanced
Industrial Economies, 1960s to 1980s

Country	Growth in GNP		Growth in Productivity	
	Period	Percent	Period	Percent
United States	1965-1973	3.8	1960-1973	2.9
	1974-1979	2.8	1974-1984	2.3
	1980-1985	2.2		
West Germany	1965-1973	3.6	1960-1973	5.9
	1974-1979	2.4	1974-1984	3.7
	1980-1985	1.2		
France	1965-1973	4.8	1960-1973	6.4
	1974-1979	3.1	1974-1983	4.8
	1980-1985	1.2		
Japan	1965-1973	8.7	1960-1973	11.0
	1974-1979	3.7	1974-1984	6.9
	1980-1985	4.4		

Source: Bank of Japan, *Kokusai hikaku tokei, 1984* (Tokyo: Bank of Japan, 1985).

Table 2. Average Annual Rate of Growth of Total Factor Productivity
in the United States and Japan, 1959-1979

Period	United States	Japan
1959-1963 and 1964-1968	2.25	1.66
1964-1968 and 1969-1973	0.92	2.59
1969-1973 and 1974-1976	0.39	-0.03
1974-1976 and 1977-1979	0.63	1.06
1977-1979 and 1983-1984	0.58	0.97

Source: Daniel Okimoto and Gary Saxonhouse, "Technology and the
Future of the Economy," in Kozo Yamamura and Yasukichi Yasuba (eds.),
The Political Economy of Japan: Domestic Transformation (Stanford, Calif.:
Stanford University Press, 1987).

Table 3. Patents Granted to National Scientists and Engineers (1966, 1981) and Average Annual Change in R&D Expenditure per National Scientist/Engineer (1966-1981)

Country and Year	Patents Granted to National Scientists/ Engineers	No. of National Scientists/ Engineers (000)	Patents Granted to National Scientists/ Engineers (000)	Average Annual Change in R&D Expenditures per National Scientist/Engineer
United States				
1966	54,634	521.1	104.8	
1981	39,224	691.4	56.7	-1.35%
United Kingdom				
1966	9,807	52.8	185.7	
1981	6,076	87.7	69.3	-1.41%
West Germany				
1966	13,095	61.0	214.7	
1981	6,537	122.0	53.6	+1.09%
France				
1966	14,881	47.9	310.7	
1981	6,855	72.9	94.0	+0.39%
Japan				
1966	17,373	128.9	134.8	
1981	42,080	302.6	139.1	+1.3%

Source: Daniel Okimoto and Gary Saxonhouse, "Technology and the Future of the Economy," in Kozo Yamamura and Yasukichi Yasuba (eds.), *The Political Economy of Japan: Domestic Transformation* (Stanford, Calif.: Stanford University Press, 1987).

Table 4. Patents Granted in Selected Countries

Country	Patents Granted to Nationals		Patents Granted to Foreigners		Patents Granted to Nationals in Foreign Countries	
	1967	1984	1967	1984	1967	1984
United States	51,274	38,364	14,378	28,837	73,960	55,201
West Germany	5,126	11,402	8,300	10,356	41,775	35,050
United Kingdom	9,807	4,442	28,983	14,425	17,579	11,868
France	15,246	7,651	31,749	16,015	14,393	15,135
Switzerland	5,388	2,351	16,462	11,626	12,452	9,221
Canada	1,263	1,427	24,573	19,118	2,789	2,358
Japan	13,877	51,690	6,896	10,110	6,843	29,328

Source: World Intellectual Property Organization, *Industrial Property Statistics* (Geneva: World Intellectual Property Organization 1968, 1985).

totals, the recorded 0.5 percent increase in total patents granted between 1967 and 1984 instead would have turned into a 15 percent decline.

Japan's R&D performance raises a number of important questions. How should such technological progress as the data indicate? What characteristics distinguish the Japanese R&D system from that of the United States? What are the advantages and disadvantages of Japan's R&D system?

TECHNOLOGICAL PROGRESS

Patents

International comparisons of patent data may overstate Japan's technological accomplishments. Quantitative indicators reveal little about the quality of patents. Many Japanese companies, including many of the technological giants, give their employees special bonuses when employee inventions result in the filing of a patent application and when and if the patent application is granted.[2] This may mean the Japanese have applied for and registered more patents than others have because the knowledge the Japanese seek to protect tends to be less significant technologically. Larger quantity may reflect lower quality or at least a greater propensity to seek patents for knowhow that others would consider too mundane or short-lived to bother about.

Note that Japan's rate of increase in patents received is exceeded considerably by Japan's rate of increase in unsuccessful patent applications. Nearly half the applications made by Japanese to their own Patent Office are turned down[3] compared with less than 20 percent of foreign applications.[4] In the United States, the ratio of approvals to applications for Japanese nationals is about 75 percent that of U.S. citizens and only 60 percent that of other foreigners.[5]

Although an unusual zeal to protect run-of-the-mill products and processes may explain the sharp rise in Japanese patent applications, it does not account for the simultaneous decline elsewhere. One explanation may be that patent protection has never been an important feature of the incentive structure underlying R&D investment in the United States and Western Europe. In certain industries, the pace of technological change may be so rapid as to make the lengthy patent approval process an inferior device for protecting property rights.[6] Moreover, with greater public access to the proprietary information contained in patent applications, U.S. and European companies may feel that patents simply cannot be obtained without disclosing vital information that will help competitors. Also, patenting processes entail increasingly costly legal fees, and the protection provided by patents (assuming applications gain approval) may not be so foolproof as to be worth incurring the up-front costs of the application process.

The risk of leaking information to competitors is not new. The term *trade secret* long antedates the industrial revolution. What is new is the mounting concern in the United States and Western Europe that the advanced state and current orientation of Japanese R&D place Japan in an advantageous position to derive special benefits from the disclosure of proprietary information.[7]

If the rise in the production of patents per unit of R&D effort in Japan and its fall elsewhere truly reflect contrasting changes in the quality of innovative effort, a change in the structural relationship linking R&D effort and the productivity of economic activity more generally might also be expected. Evidence on this critical relationship is not easy to find. What evidence exists is remarkable. It suggests that at least until the late 1970s the relationship between productivity and R&D expenditure was stable.

If research and development expenditures played an increasingly important role in explaining Japanese economic growth, it is probably not because Japan was more efficient in making use of its expenditures but rather because Japan was just increasing such expenditures dramatically. Between the mid-1960s and the late 1970s, the estimated rate of return on R&D expenditures rose modestly not only in Japan but also in the United States and West Germany. There was no monotonic rise in research productivity. Despite a sharp decline in the number of patents per scientist and engineer in recent years, West Germany and the United States continued to record rates of return for R&D expenditures roughly comparable with Japan (see Table 5).

Other Indicators

Crude confirmation of Japan's technological progress might also be gleaned from data on Japan's technological balance of trade. Throughout the entire postwar period, Japan has run a sizable deficit in its technological balance of trade. Japan has relied heavily on imports of foreign knowhow to upgrade its manufacturing capabilities and step up the tempo of industrial output. Although Japan, like West Germany, still runs a large deficit today, the imbalance is shrinking steadily as the value of exported technology rises. Using balance-of-payments data, in 1971, the ratio of exports to imports stood at 0.12; but by 1983, it had risen to 0.29.[8]

Given that trade statistics include royalty payments for foreign licenses purchased in the past, such data may understate the pace at which Japanese technology has advanced since the 1970s. To measure the flow of technological trade at any particular amount, royalty payments for past purchases must be sorted out from technological transactions newly entered. Unfortunately, such transactions data are not available. What is available are data on the overall size of newly contracted Japanese programs of technology sales and purchases. According to this data, Japan's ratio of newly contracted technology exports to imports exceeded 1 as long ago as 1972 and by 1984 had risen to 1.76.

Table 5. Rates of Internal Return on Net Investments of Capital and R&D for Manufacturing in Japan, the United States, and West Germany, 1965-1977

	United States	Japan	West Germany
Capital	10	13	9
R&D	11	15	13

Source: Pierre Mohnen, M. Ishaq Nadiri, and Ingmar R. Prucha, "R&D, Production Structure and Rates of Return in the U.S., Japanese and German Manufacturing Sectors," *European Economic Review* 30 (1986):749-771.

Disaggregating Japanese technology trade data according to source and destination can be illuminating. For example, consider the destination of Japanese exports of technology. As of 1984, only about 40 percent of Japan's new technology was sold to advanced industrial states; 60 percent was sold to developing countries.[9] By contrast, more than 85 percent of U.S. technology exports went to advanced industrial states, with less than 15 percent being transferred to developing countries. This implies that the bulk of Japanese technology exports may not be state of the art or concentrated in the most sophisticated sectors of high technology. Much of the exports appear to fall into the category of incremental improvements in production technology for the heavy manufacturing sectors, especially chemicals, iron and steel, and transportation machinery (Japan's biggest export earners).

Trade data on technology contracts may also be misleading in that a significant portion of technology exports represent intracompany transactions, with overseas subsidiaries purchasing patents and other knowhow from parent companies based in Japan (presumably for tax or accounting purposes). By contrast, virtually all technologies imported into Japan are arms-length transactions between foreign and Japanese firms. Moreover, the data on technology contracts include both current and future receipts and expenditures. In a period of Japanese technological progress, such calculations into the future bias Japan's reported balance of trade on new technology upward. This bias is probably exaggerated because the responses by Japanese firms to the questionnaires that constitute the sole basis for this data tend to magnify the value of technology sold and underplay the cost of technology purchased. This is easily seen. Despite Japan's apparent surplus in the balance of trade in new technology since 1972, the Bank of Japan's data on actual receipts expenditures on technology transactions continue to show Japan in heavy deficit.[10]

Progress in Basic Research

Data on patents and technology sales cast light on applied research and commercial development, the two areas where Japanese government policy has placed overriding emphasis. But what progress is Japan making in basic research? Has improvement here been retarded by the seemingly low priority assigned to basic research? Because advances in basic research are closely related to at least some of the breakthroughs in applied technology, Japan's capabilities in basic research have a bearing on the nature and scope of the nation's applied R&D, especially in high technology industries such as biotechnology and fine ceramics.

According to Japan's surprising official data, Japan has long allocated a disproportionate share of its R&D resources to basic research.[11] As long ago as 1967, Japan was seemingly devoting 28.2 percent of all its expenditures to basic research. Moreover, since that time the real rate of growth of Japan's R&D expenditure for basic research has almost always exceeded the real growth rate in the United States.[12] Is Japan a basic research paradise? Japan's apparent preoccupation with basic research is an artifact of Japanese definitions of R&D expenditures. In contrast to U.S. and European practice, Japan treats the salaries of all university and college science teaching personnel as if they were full-time researchers. This leads to a substantial overstatement of Japan's overall R&D expenditures, a substantial overstatement of the academic sector's role in Japanese R&D and, given that university research is treated largely as basic research, a substantial overstatement of the role of basic research.

An illustration of how important this statistical convention has been in shaping Japanese R&D data is given in Table 6. By one new estimate of Japanese R&D personnel, the official statistics for 1965 overstate by some nineteen times the number of scientists and engineers in Japanese universities and colleges engaged in R&D activities. Over time, it appears that this overstatement has diminished by a factor of nine. This means that starting from an extremely small base in 1965 there was an extraordinarily rapid increase in the research role of Japanese universities and colleges and an increased role for basic research within Japan's R&D effort. Even today, however, the aggregate Japanese effort in basic research remains modest by U.S. standards.

It is well known that Japan is not among leaders in the number of Nobel prizes won in the natural sciences and engineering. Between 1901 and 1985 Japan won only 4 of the 370 science and medicine Nobel prizes awarded, compared with 137 by the United States, 63 by England, and 51 by East and West Germany. Countries with populations a fraction of the size of Japan's such as Sweden, the Netherlands, Switzerland, Austria, Denmark, and Belgium, have had more Nobel recipients than Japan has. This rank ordering accords with the widespread perception of Japan as a country that has contributed few revolutionary breakthroughs to the world's storehouse of fundamental knowledge.

As a measure of overall progress in basic research, however, the number of Nobel prizes is at best incomplete because the prizes are skewed so heavily toward seminal breakthroughs at the frontiers of theoretical knowledge. Such a measure reveals little about the degree to which aggregate advances have been made by a growing legion of basic researchers working both inside and outside Japanese universities. Other indicators are needed to round out this incomplete picture.

The number of published research papers, which must pass peer review before being issued, probably provides a fuller, more representative indicator of a country's overall state of basic knowledge. In 1982, Japan ranked third in research papers published in the world's leading scholarly

Table 6. Scientists and Engineers at Japanese Universities and
Colleges Engaged in R&D, (in thousands)

Year	Official Series	Series Corrected by Sample Survey
1965	39.1	2.1
1966	43.6	3.3
1967	48.5	4.1
1968	54.3	7.2
1969	52.4	7.6
1970	55.2	19.0
1971	59.7	18.0
1972	60.5	18.7
1973	75.2	33.1
1974	79.2	35.2
1975	81.9	36.4
1976	88.0	41.4
1977	92.8	45.9
1978	91.5	45.7
1979	96.7	50.2
1980	100.7	46.7
1981	102.6	44.0

Source: Daniel Okimoto and Gary Saxonhouse, "Technology and the
Future of the Economy," in Kozo Yamamura and Yasukichi Yasuba
(eds.), *The Political Economy of Japan: Domestic Transformation*
(Stanford, Calif.: Stanford University Press, 1987).

journals, accounting for 7.3 percent of the world's total, behind the United
States (33.2 percent) and England (7.9 percent), but ahead of the Soviet
Union (6.4 percent) and West Germany (5.7 percent). This research output
and ranking are broadly consistent with revised data on what Japan has actually been spending on basic research relative to other advanced industrialized countries.[13]

Since the mid-1960s, moreover, Japan has increased basic research not
only absolutely but also, as the new Japanese R&D expenditure series in
Table 6 suggests, relative to what other countries are doing. In 1982, for example, Japan accounted for nearly 12 percent of all scholarly papers on
chemistry published in the world, placing it third behind the United States

(21.9 percent) and the Soviet Union (15.3 percent) but well ahead of West Germany (6.4 percent) and England (5.7 percent). In the telecommunications field, between 1981 and 1984 Japan accounted for nearly 10 percent of the research papers accepted by the Comite Consultatif International Telegraphique et Telephonique, thereby ranking second behind the United States. In fields such as chemistry, telecommunications, and semiconductors, the Japanese have become major participants in both leading-edge research and in the communication of this research in scientific publications.[14]

JAPANESE AND U.S. R&D SYSTEMS

There is no doubt that summary statements about Japan's technological position are liable to be misleading. Japan's technological position cannot be summarized simply because there is enormous variance across sectors. According to a particularly authoritative survey of Japanese businessmen done in 1982 and doubtless now outdated as to the details, Japan had reached state-of-the-art technology in a variety of areas: iron and steel production, agricultural chemicals, new materials, nuclear energy processing (for example, fast breeder reactors), semiconductors (metal oxide semiconductors and gallium arsenide mass memory chips), computer peripherals, office automation, robotics, flexible manufacturing systems, certain areas of telecommunications (power transmission cables and digital switching equipment), pharmaceuticals (artifical blood), biotechnology (fermentation and gamma interferon from synthetic genes), and industrial lasers.[15]

These survey results are interesting because there is a pattern to these areas of excellence. There is a common core of technological and industrial characteristics that appears to fit the particular strengths of Japan's R&D system. Typically, it seems the theoretical parameters surrounding these technologies are well known (for example, solid state physics). The technological trajectories are predictable, and product advances are made in continuous or incremental steps (for example, random access memory chips). Small adaptations in proprietary designs, such as miniaturization, based on foreign knowhow often create vast new commercial opportunities.[16] Similarly, incremental improvements in production technology (such as automated bonding equipment), lower costs, and upgrade reliability are making Japanese products more competitive in world markets. Although such technological changes cannot be considered "pathbreaking," their cumulative impact on the commercial competitiveness of Japanese industry has been substantial. From an economic standpoint, therefore, their significance should not be underestimated.

Progress has been slower in technologies where the theoretical parameters for problem solving are highly complex (jet aircraft design) and technological trajectories are not readily predictable (advanced software). Japanese firms have not been as apt to make seminal inventions that lead to the creation of whole new industries, owing in part to the relatively low level of government R&D sponsorship and to the (until recently) narrowly applied nature of much of commercial R&D. Whereas Japanese companies excel at electronic components, they have not been as competitive when it comes to complicated systems integration (for example, aerospace), an area U.S. firms have tended to dominate.

Not surprisingly, therefore, in this 1982 survey Japan was found to lag far behind the United States in various military technologies: aerospace, jet aircraft, avionics, computer-aided design and computer-aided manufacturing, security-related information processing, and so forth. Japan fares better in certain dual-purpose technologies (that is, technologies with both military and civilian applications) where commercial markets are large and the barriers to new entry are not prohibitively high, such as superconductivity components (gallium arsenide), nuclear energy, and supercomputers. Although still behind in lasers and artifical intelligence, Japan was thought to be catching up rapidly, owing to the motivation imparted by the enormous commercial potential of those technologies.[17]

The Locus of Innovative Activity

Japanese innovative successes are often attributed to the dominant domestic market positions held by a small number of giant corporations. Joseph Schumpeter noted decades ago that market concentration can enhance innovation because concentration makes the fruits of R&D more appropriate.[18] Because Japanese industrial organization is said to be dominated by corporate giants, R&D is thought to be heavily concentrated in the big business strata. Indeed, this is assumed to be one of the defining characteristics of Japanese R&D and a central reason for both its achievements and its limitations.[19]

However, the actual situation is more complicated. Japan is no more dominated by large firms than are other countries. If anything, the opposite may be closer to the truth. In 1981, for example, Japanese firms with less than one thousand employees accounted for 18.5 percent of all R&D expenditure by private business in Japan.[20] It may surprise market-oriented venture capital to learn that as late as the early 1980s no more than 4.1 percent of the R&D conducted in the United States by private business was undertaken by firms with less than one thousand employees.[21]

Over time, the role of small firms in R&D seems to have become less important in both Japan and the United States. Interestingly, this appears to be occurring more rapidly in the United States than in Japan. Data are not available in the United States for more recent years, but between 1975 and

1980, the share of smaller firms in total private business R&D expenditures declined by almost 20 percent. In Japan during roughly the same time period and starting from a share of total private R&D expenditures almost four times as large, the R&D expenditures of small firms fell by only 10 percent in relative share.[22]

The relatively large amount invested in R&D by small firms in Japan and the comparatively modest proportion spent by small firms in the United States may seem surprising in view of current policies in both countries. The U.S. government, unlike its Japanese counterpart, has devised policies consciously aimed at allowing small, research-oriented firms to play a critical role in the development of new technology. Accordingly, in the United States the R&D tax credit can be used to offset 100 percent of corporate income. The R&D tax credit in Japan, which once served as the model for the U.S. credit, allows only 10 percent of corporate income to be offset. Consequently, small firms in Japan, for whom research is a primary activity, do not benefit greatly from the R&D tax credit. Neither do they enjoy the tax encouragement that their U.S. counterparts have received until recently from limited R&D partnerships, sub-Chapter S corporations, small business investment corporations, pension fund investments in venture capital partnerships, and simplified registration requirements for initial small public offerings of equity. All these U.S. incentives emerged out of legislative and administrative changes since the mid-1970s, and some have even survived the Tax Reform Act of 1986, thereby causing concern in Japan that the United States may have acquired new, special advantages in the promotion of high technology.[23]

Although small-scale Japanese firms account for a much higher proportion of R&D expenditure than do their U.S. counterparts, the level of research intensity is lower. In 1981, R&D expenditures of small firms with less than one thousand employees in the United States were 1.6 percent of their total sales. For Japanese firms of this size, R&D expenditures can be explained by the larger overall presence of these firms in the Japanese economy. Indeed, the long-term decline of R&D expenditures by small firms in the United States (from 11 percent of R&D in 1957 to 4.1 percent in 1980) is only marginally affected by changes in the research intensities for large versus small firms; the main explanation is the smaller number of firms that employ less than one thousand workers in the U.S. economy. Because the aggregate number of small and medium-size firms in Japan has not shrunk as much as it has in the United States, the R&D expenditures of small Japanese firms have declined only modestly since the mid-1960s.

Such data do not need to be understood within the context of different corporate environments and organizational structures. Differences in Japanese and U.S. legal, accounting, and tax practices, for example, have made it advantageous for many Japanese firms to eschew the formal vertically integrated structure characteristic of large firms in the United States. Only since 1977 have large Japanese corporations been required to maintain common settlement dates and to consolidate balance sheets and income and earnings statements of their less than wholly owned subsidiaries. This makes it entirely possible that some significant portion of the R&D carried out by small Japanese firms is actually initiated and administered by much larger companies.

It should also be understood that the relative shares of R&D expenditures borne by small versus large firms are not closely correlated with most of the prominent measures of research productivity for both groups. In 1980, small firms accounted for only 4.1 percent of business R&D expenditures in the United States, but these firms produced 19 percent of all patents.[24] By contrast, in Japan small firms, which accounted for 18.5 percent of all business R&D expenditures, produced only 13 percent of all patents. Given the much lower R&D intensity of small firms in general, the U.S. figures imply a high patent productivity per unit of R&D intensity. Despite the major differences that were noted earlier in Japanese and U.S. behavior with respect to the filing of patent applications, small U.S. firms produce patents at a higher rate (per unit of input) than do either larger U.S. firms or small Japanese firms. Moreover, at least one comprehensive study suggests that small U.S. firms of one thousand employees or less produced more so-called major innovations that did larger firms (more than five thousand employees) between 1953 and 1966 and an equal number between 1967 and 1973 (see Table 7).

Table 7. Distribution of Major U.S. Innovations by Size of Company, 1953-1973

No. of Employees in Company	Percentage (and Number of Innovations)			
	1953-1959	1960-1966	1967-1973	1953-1973
Less than 100	23 (23)	27 (29)	20 (20)	23 (72)
100-1,000	26 (27)	23 (25)	23 (23)	24 (75)
1,000-5,000	14 (14)	14 (15)	12 (12)	13 (41)
More than 5,000	37 (38)	36 (38)	46 (46)	39 (122)
Total	100 (102)	100 (107)	100 (101)	100 (310)

Source: Gellman Research Associates, *Indicators of International Trends in Technological Innovation* (Washington, D.C.: Gellman Research Associates, 1976).

The record of Japanese companies with respect to major innovations poses a striking contrast to that of U.S. firms. Although U.S. firms were responsible for 310 major technological innovations, Japanese firms accounted for no more than 34.[25] Of these 34 innovations, 33 were accomplished during the last decade of the twenty-year survey period. All but 2 of the 34 innovations were the result of R&D activities by large firms.

Therefore, small U.S. firms, despite the fact that they spend much less money as a proportion of total R&D expenditures, play a more crucial role in stimulating major technological innovations than their Japanese counterparts do. That small Japanese firms have not played so prominent a role in the past or present, however, does not foreclose the possibility of greater future contributions. Nor does it mean that there are no institutions in Japan capable of serving as effective substitutes for the role that small, technologically innovative firms play in the United States.[26]

Recently, there has been considerable interest in Japan about the role that small firms might play in the development of high-technology industries. The Ministry of International Trade and Industry's (MITI) Office of Venture Business Promotion and Small and Medium Size Enterprise Agency have devoted much attention to the identification and analysis of small, innovative Japanese firms. Quite apart from their fewer numbers, such Japanese businesses currently differ markedly from U.S. venture businesses. In particular, few Japanese venture businesses are new firms. In MITI's sample of 850 venture businesses, less than 4 percent had existed for less than three years![27]

Government Sponsorship of R&D

Japan's R&D system also differs markedly from the U.S. system in the role played by the government. The Japanese government spends much less to underwrite industrial R&D than the U.S. or European governments do. The U.S. government funded 29.3 percent of all business R&D expenditures in 1983; the Japanese government supplied no more than 1.8 percent.

Aggregate expenditures are reflected at the sectoral level (see Table 8). Although virtually all U.S. manufacturing sectors receive substantial government funding for R&D, few Japanese industries depend on government financing for a significant share of their R&D funding. Over time, U.S. government funding has become less concentrated in aircraft, missiles, and telecommunications equipment but has risen to 25 percent in the iron and steel industry and almost 40 percent in nonferrous metals. By contrast, the Japanese government has reduced its share of R&D funding for the machinery industry from 15.5 percent in 1971 to 0.81 percent in 1981. This is significant because the Japanese machinery industry was the last industry in the early 1970s to receive a substantial share of its R&D funding from the government.

Some Japanese think that they are at a disadvantage in competing with the United States in high-technology industries because their government underwrites so little of the business sector's R&D in comparison to the U.S. government.[28] (See Table 9.) If what motivates the U.S. government to underwrite a substantial proportion of R&D is a sense that it must compensate for market failures, such as externalities, increasing returns to scale, incomplete information, or even unemployment, then if Japanese firms faced the same market failures but were forced to meet them without government intervention, they would certainly be disadvantaged.

It is even possible that Japan's knowledge-intensive industries may be handicapped in competition with their U.S. counterparts, even in those industries where the provision of public goods, such as national defense, dominates U.S. allocation of government R&D funding and compensation for spillovers and incomplete information dominates Japanese funding. The scale and scope of U.S. government and private R&D spending may be so large that civilian spillovers from defense R&D may well tilt the board to the advantage of the United States. It is no coincidence that U.S. competitive strengths have long resided in such industries as aircraft, electrical machinery, telecommunications, and health products, all of which enjoy enormous government support. On balance, however, Japan's knowledge-intensive industries have probably not been placed at a disadvantage by U.S. government R&D funding during the past fifteen years. Already in 1971, if government funding is subtracted from total R&D expenditures, at least four of the U.S. industries listed in Table 8 had become less research intensive than their Japanese counterparts. Subtracting the full amount of government-funded R&D may distort the comparison, but there is evidence that the private rate of return for U.S. government R&D spending may be very low.[29] The low return may be due to externalities and restrictions on the appropriability of government-funded innovation. It is particularly important to understand that these externalities are no more internal to the U.S. economy than they are to the U.S. firm.

Consideration must also be given to evidence suggesting that rather than being a substitute for private R&D, government funding actually stimulates additional private R&D spending.[30] Not only is R&D allocation heavily shaped by government funding and directed toward supporting the procurement of public goods in the United States, but publicly funded R&D may also generate additional, privately financed R&D. To the extent that private sector R&D is directed toward the commercialization of spinoffs from government-financed R&D, the competitiveness of U.S. industry may well be enhanced. On the other hand, to the extent that private R&D is undertaken in the hopes of improving a firm's ability to successfully compete with

Table 8. Government Funding and Research Intensity in Japanese and U.S. Manufacturing Industries, 1971 and 1981, (percentage of total R&D; R&D as percentage of total sales)

Industry	Japan				United States			
	1971		1981		1971		1981	
	Govt. Funding	Research Intensity	Govt. Funding	Research Intensity	Govt. Funding	Research Intensity	Govt. Funding	Research Intensity
Chemicals	0.29%	2.56%	0.82%	3.05%	10.0%	3.91%	7.19%	3.83%
Petroleum, Refining, & Extraction	1.11	0.30	4.48	0.18	3.36	1.04	7.29	0.72
Rubber Products	0.48	1.41		2.32	23.9	2.31	23.8	2.56
Ferrous Materials	0.46	0.77	4.49	1.44	1.39	0.75	25.9	0.81

Nonferrous Metals	0.66	1.04	2.82	1.37	3.12	1.06	37.6	1.21
Fabricated Metal Products	1.51	0.64	0.14	1.34	4.54	1.28	12.5	1.40
Machinery	15.5	1.64	1.63	2.18	16.9		10.9	2.57
Electrical Machinery	1.65	3.21	1.69	4.52	51.4	7.38	37.9	6.82
Telecommunications Equipment	1.15	3.64	1.63	4.72	54.1	8.21	33.9	8.90
Transportation Equipment	0.78	1.67	3.88	2.69	62.8	8.26	59.8	8.37
Precision Instruments	0.92	2.35	0.46	3.73	22.0	5.71	17.3	8.38

Source: Daniel Okimoto and Gary Saxonhouse, "Technology and the Future of the Economy," in Kozo Yamamura and Yasukichi Yasuka (eds.), *The Political Economy of Japan: Domestic Transformation* (Stanford, Calif.: Stanford University Press, 1987).

Table 9. Distribution of Government Support of R&D by National Objective and Country
(percentage)

	United States		Japan		West Germany		France	
Objective	1975	1980	1975	1980	1975	1980	1975	1980
Social development & social services	2.1	2.3	2.5	1.7	8.5	6.0	1.2	1.4
Advancement of knowledge	4.3	3.0	3.0	3.5	15.7	14.2	17.1	15.0
Government R&D as percentage of GNP		1.11		0.56		1.14		1.07

Source: Adapted from OECD, *OECD Science and Technology Indicators* (Paris: OECD, 1982).

other firms for government procurement contracts, the opposite may be true.

Japan's low level of defense-related procurement has had important implications for Japan's R&D system: (1) macroeconomic policies aimed at expanding aggregate demand have played a greater role than targeted industrial policy has in promoting the growth of high-technology products; (2) MITI has had to rely predominantly on supply-related incentives, not demand-pull measures; (3) inefficient resource allocation, waste, and politicization have been kept under relative control; (4) this has prompted Japanese management to stress applied research and development instead of basic or prototype-development research; (5) with no assurance of government demand for new products, Japanese companies have followed a fairly conservative approach to R&D, emphasizing reasonably high prospects of commercial feasibility; (6) this may be one reason why the Japanese have not been noted for creating whole new industries or major new product designs; and (7) Japanese engineers and scientists have not been diverted from commercially oriented R&D to carry on highly specialized research for military and space applications.

Training and Innovation Management
in Japan and the United States

From the 1960s through the early 1980s, the total number of scientists and engineers in Japan's labor force, especially scientists and engineers engaged in R&D, increased at a rate that surpassed that of every other major industrialized economy, including the Soviet Union. Indeed, this rate of increase has been so large that the Japanese economy added more scientists and engineers in absolute terms to its R&D labor force between 1969 and the early 1980s than did any other advanced industrialized economy, including the United States.[31]

Japan's rapidly growing scientific and technological labor force is stirring anxieties in the United States somewhat reminiscent of old fears concerning the Soviet Union's capacity to turn out large numbers of scientists and engineers. In recent years, careful study of the Soviet Union's higher educational programs in science and technology has added a qualitative dimension to what had been crude, quantitative comparisons. According to the National Science Board:

> Soviet graduate training programs are considered to be more narrowly specialized, oriented toward the specific needs of research institutes and geared towards applied science, while U.S. graduates receive a broader based and more flexible theoretical education. Moreover, a third of all nondoctorate U.S. scientists and engineers have increased their skills through further formal training in master's degree programs while the Soviet Union does not have such programs. Therefore, it may be that U.S. specialists, although fewer in number, are better prepared to deal with future problems and goals.[32]

Significantly, this assessment could be applied to the situation in Japan! Modern industrialized economies face the difficult problem of encouraging a socially optimal accumulation of skills. Until the postwar period, there were few alternatives to self- or family-financing for the acquisition of new skills. With worker mobility, firms providing general training implicitly charged their workers for this service by providing less than market wages. At the same time, because skills are embodied in individuals and therefore no tangible collateral is created that could be confiscated for nonpayment of loans, it is difficult to seek financing for skill accumulation from financial intermediaries. In consequence, in both prewar Japan and the United States, there was probably a persistent underaccumulation of socially beneficial skills, with skill accumulation heavily dependent on personal or family resources.[33]

The growing complexities of industrial life have come to require a more rapid accumulation of industrial skills. Immediately after World War II, a number of extremely significant programs were organized in the United States to subsidize skill accumulation directly or to facilitate the use of financial intermediaries to underwrite advanced training. These programs, including Veterans Educational Benefits, which began with the G.I. Bill of Rights, and Guaranteed Student Loans, required that training be conducted in accredited educational institutions. Thanks to these programs, the demand for, and supply of, vocational undergraduate and graduate education in the United States has expanded enormously.

In Japan, skill accumulation has assumed a very different institutional form. There have been no major government programs directly subsidizing individual education. The number of public institutions providing education at a heavily subsidized, low rate of tuition has increased to some extent, but the steep rise in the number of Japanese receiving higher education has come about largely through an increase in enrollment at private universities that finance themselves to a considerable degree out of tuition fees.[34]

Financial stringency has strapped university-based research. Lacking large government grants, most Japanese universities until recently have been unable to develop and sustain extensive research programs, particularly in the sciences and engineering. There has been only a relatively modest effort to provide specialized graduate programs. The $4.8 billion that the U.S. government provides in support of R&D universities and colleges is roughly five times what Japanese universities receive in R&D support from their government. Not surprisingly, U.S. academic institutions in 1981 awarded six times as many doctoral degrees in the sciences and engineering as did Japanese institutions.[35] In biology, the United States graduates thirty-six times the number of Ph.D.s and ten times the number in chemistry. Although a third of all U.S. scientists and engineers without doctorates have enhanced their skills through further training in master's degree programs, less than 5 percent of the same group in Japan have received further academic training.[36]

Although a Ph.D. can be a prerequisite for participation in the U.S. corporate R&D laboratory, it is not required in otherwise comparable Japanese facilities. More than twelve hundred Ph.D.s work in U.S. biogenetic engineering, according to a 1982 survey by the Office of Technology Assessment and the National Academy of Sciences.[37] In contrast, a Keidanren (Federation of Economic Associations) survey found only 161 scientists and engineers with doctorates doing firm-based R&D work in biotechnology in 1982, including Japanese with Ph.D.s from U.S. universities. A number of subsidized public universities including Tokyo, Kyoto, Osaka, and Kyushu have significant programs in biotechnology, but these programs train only a limited pool of advanced research personnel for Japanese industry. A MITI survey of 104 firms found that about 80 percent of the research personnel have been trained exclusively in their own firms, a rather surprising figure for a dynamic, technologically sophisticated industry like biotechnology.[38] However, more than 40 percent of the biotechnology firms surveyed in 1981 and 1982 indicated some engineering and scientific personnel would be sent abroad for either primary or supplementary training.[39]

Japanese companies have apparently discovered cheaper ways of training than sending large numbers of employees through doctoral programs. Sometimes the right mix of skills and knowledge can be obtained by using foreign consultants on a temporary basis. The in-house training Japanese R&D personnel receive is less general and less theoretical than what might be received through U.S. graduate schools, but it is more closely coordinated with the Japanese firm's operational needs. Less emphasis is placed on training well-rounded members of a profession, occupation, or craft.[40] Where advanced academic knowledge is needed, the facilities of Japan's relatively few graduate research institutions can be used or scientists and engineers can be sent abroad for additional training.

The differing locus and auspices of training in Japan have led, in part, to much lower interfirm mobility of scientific and engineering personnel than in the United States or Western Europe. The absence of pervasive extrafirm training programs and the absence of a real market for allocating experienced scientific and engineering personnel make for relatively insulated R&D staffs. The informal exchange of useful information, often working as a lever to job mobility that is characteristic among U.S. technologists, is far less prevalent in Japan. To facilitate such informal cooperation, which in the United States encourages technological progress and diffusion, Japan has created formal programs. The well-known Japanese government cooperative R&D programs in very large-scale integration in electronic chips, in flexible manufacturing systems, and in fine ceramics are also attempts to extract information from the technological leaders in Japan for the rest of the industry; these programs also are efforts to overcome technological bottlenecks. In this way, the Japanese government seeks to break down information flow barriers even as it pursues procompetitive policies by building up rivals to leading Japanese firms. With cooperative R&D projects of this character, it is not surprising that Japanese companies are sometimes reluctant to join efforts in areas of Japanese expertise.

Japanese labor market practices have built walls preventing certain kinds of information flows among Japanese firms—walls that government policy has broken down only with difficulty. Nevertheless, Japanese firms have not necessarily faced many more difficulties than have U.S. firms in benefiting from the market and nonmarket diffusion of proprietary and nonproprietary information available within and outside the Japanese economy. In this connection, many of the so-called reciprocity issues that are raised about Japanese trade in goods recur in a potentially even more dramatic way for technology flows.

Is Japan a technology sponge? Specialized university graduate training and research programs are by their very nature largely committed to the production and diffusion of nonproprietary information. Such programs have developed far more in the United States than in Japan. When Japanese firms have needed the information produced in graduate research programs, these firms have been able to send their employees to study in the United States. For the most part, until recently a reciprocal of Americans going to Japan would not have made sense. Similarly, the much greater professional orientation of U.S. personnel and the selective disclosure of highly useful generic and even proprietary information by individuals and by business leaders, both in print and informally, long ago persuaded Japanese firms and the Japanese government to maintain technological and economic listening posts in the United States. Quite apart from quality, U.S. scientists and engineers publish five times as many technical papers as do their Japanese counterparts. The relative lack of such formal and informal disclosures of information in Japan may well mean that many of the new U.S. listening posts being established there by private and public bodies could yield far lower rates of return for their efforts than are now being confidently anticipated.

In analyzing strategic sector policy, the differing U.S. and Japanese experiences with training and with information generation and diffusion should be kept in mind. One U.S. response to the specter of foreign competition has been a renewed emphasis on university-based science and technology training and research. Unhappily, strategic sector analysis suggests that unless the creators of new science and technology are also best at applying them, much of the benefit will be as helpful to Japanese firms as it is to U.S. firms. Indeed, if the contemporary Japanese experience suggests anything, it is that there is no particular connection between the creation and application of technology. It remains to be seen whether this will be as true in the future as it has been in the past.

SUMMARY AND CONCLUSION

Japan's technological progress has been remarkable — not so remarkable as either comparative patent data or new agreements on international trade in technology might suggest, but, nonetheless, Japan's progress has outstripped the performance of all the other advanced industrialized economies. Japan's technological success was built on a rapid increase in its commitment of resources to research and development and not on the resources being particularly productive once committed.

Public policy has played a critical role in shaping the differing R&D systems in Japan and the United States. The relatively unimportant role of small firms in Japan as a source of critical innovation, the strength in Japan of process and production technology, and the strength of the United States in basic research reflect differing fiscal choices made in Japan and the United States.

The differing means for financing training for scientists and engineers in Japan has lead to a different mix of institutions imparting such training, to different kinds of training being important, and ultimately to the kinds of scientists and engineers being trained. The Japanese approach to training puts more burden on Japanese firms for financing, but leads to a labor force more directly in touch with its needs. The U.S. economy's pervasive extrafirm training programs and the market allocation of experienced scientists and engineers mean that by contrast with Japan large amounts of potentially proprietary scientific and technological information readily become global public goods.

If too much potentially proprietary information diffuses among firms and across borders in the U.S. system, it is possible that because of permanent employment, too little information diffuses in the Japanese system. In the same way that industrial policy in Japan has operated to ensure that the concentration of capital in Japan did not lead to a misallocation of resources, so also does complementing Japanese government science and technology policy work to ensure that the barriers to interfirm transfer of information created by Japanese employment practices does not slow the pace of technology diffusion within Japan.

NOTES

1. William D. Nordhaus, "Policy Responses to the Productivity Slowdown" in *The Limits of Productivity Growth* (Boston: Federal Reserve Bank of Boston, 1980); and Martin N. Bailey, "The Productivity Growth Slowdown by Industry," *Brookings Papers in Economic Activity*, No. 2 (1982).

2. Teruo Doi, "The Role of Intellectual Property Law in Bilateral Licensing Transactions Between Japan and the United States" in Gary Saxonhouse and Kozo Yamamura (eds.), *Law and Trade Issues of the Japanese Economy: American and Japanese Perspectives* (Seattle: University of Washington Press, 1986), pp. 157-194.

3. Tokkyocho, *Tokkyocho nenpo* (Tokyo, 1982).

4. Sampson Helfgott, "Statistical Study of the Japanese Patent Office's Handling of Foreign Patent Applications" *Patents and Licensing* 3 (Spring 1983).

5. U.S. Patent and Trademark Office, *Indicators of Patent Output of U.S. Industry* (Washington, D. C.: U.S. Patent and Trademark Office, 1982).

6. Christopher T. Taylor and Z. Aubrey Silberston, *The Economic Impact of the Patent System* (Cambridge: Cambridge University Press, 1973); Edwin Mansfield, Mark Schwartz, and Samuel Wagner, "Imitation Costs and Patents: An Empirical Study," *Economic Journal* 91:34 (December 1981);

and Frederic M. Scherer, *The Economic Effects of Compulsory Patent Licensing* (New York: New York University Graduate School of Business Administration, 1977).

7. See the discussion in Gary Saxonhouse, "Tampering with Comparative Advantage," *Testimony Presented Before the United States International Trade Commission Hearings on Industrial Targeting* (June 15, 1983).

8. Nihon Ginko, *Kokusai shushi tokei geppo*, various issues. This series on Japan's technological balance of trade is the only one based on actual transactions. Japan's Statistics Bureau has an alternative series based on sample survey data. Unfortunately, that series does not present technology trade data on a receipts and expenditure basis, but on the entire value of new and continuing programs, including both current and future contractual receipts and expenditures. In a period of Japanese technological progress, this biases Japan's balance of technology trade upward. For example, not only are the Statistics Bureau estimates of total technology sales 63 percent larger than the comparable Bank of Japan figures for 1983, but the Statistics Bureau estimates of technology purchases are also 41 percent smaller than the Bank of Japan figures!

9. Somucho, *Kagaku gijutsu kenkyu chosa hokoku* (Tokyo, 1984), Tables 12 and 13.

10. Differences in the pattern of payments between technology sales and purchases may also account for the balance of trade in new technology being in Japan's favor for the past twelve years without Japan's overall balance of technology moving into surplus. If Japanese sales of technology typically involve lump-sum payments at the time of contract but Japanese purchases rely more heavily on future royalty payments, it is possible that the two series could be reconciled.

11. Hajime Eto, "Behavior of Japanese R&D Organizations" in Hajime Eto and Konomu Matsui (eds.), *R&D Management Systems in Japanese Industry* (Amsterdam: North Holland Company, 1984), p. 214.

12. Kagaku Gijutsu Cho, *Hakusho* (Tokyo, 1984), p. 21.

13. Daniel Okimoto and Gary Saxonhouse, "Technology and the Future of the Economy," in Kozo Yamamura and Yasukichi Yasuba (eds.), *The Political Economy of Japan: Domestic Transformation* (Stanford, Calif.: Stanford University Press, 1987).

14. Ibid. These data have been supplied by the Institute for Scientific Information. Alternative estimates that have put Japanese scientific publications at as much as one-third the U.S. level have been made by Mitsubishi Sogo Kenkyusho in *Kagaku gijutsu jiho no kokusaiteki ryutsu no arikata ni kansuru chosa hokoku* (Tokyo, 1982). Note, however, that the Japanese journals group used by Mitsubishi Sogo Kenkyusho does not appear to be comparable in quality to their U.S. data set.

15. Kagaku Gijutsu Cho, *Minkan kigyo no kenkyu katsudo ni kansuru chosa hokoku* (Tokyo, 1982).

16. For a discussion of technological trajectories and their influence on economic development, see Okimoto and Saxonhouse, "Technology and the Future of the Economy"; and Richard C. Levin, Alvin K. Klevorick, Richard R. Nelson, and Sidney G. Winter, "Survey Research on R&D Appropriability and Technological Opportunity: Part 1," Working Paper (New Haven, Conn.: Yale University, July 1984).

17. Okimoto and Saxonhouse, ibid.

18. Joseph Schumpeter, *The Theory of Economic Development* (New York: Oxford University Press, 1961), Chaps. 2 and 6.

19. Semiconductor Industry Association, *The Effect of Government Targeting on World Semiconductor Competition* (Cupertino, Calif.: SIA, 1983).

20. Sorifu, *Kagaku gijutsu kenkyu chosa hokoku, 1982* (Tokyo, 1983).

21. Okimoto and Saxonhouse, "Technology and the Future of the Economy."

22. Between 1976 and 1981, the share in total private business R&D fell from 20.5 percent to 18.5 percent. Between 1981 and 1984, however, the share fell to 17.4 percent. Sorifu, *Kagaku gijutsu kenkyu chosa hokoku, 1984* (Tokyo, 1985).

23. The operation of these incentives for U.S. firms are described in more detail in Gary R. Saxonhouse, "Industrial Policy and Factor Markets: Biotechnology in Japan and the United States" *Prometheus* (December 1985). For new Japanese policies toward smaller high technology firms in Japan, see Chusho Kigyo Cho, *Hakusho* (Tokyo, 1986). These policies are a modest response to U.S. practices.

24. U.S. Patent and Trademark Office, *Small Business Patenting* (Washington, D. C.: U.S. Patent and Trademark Office, 1982).

25. Gellman Research Associates, *Indicators of International Trends in Technological Innovation* (Washington, D. C.: Gellman Research Associates, 1976).

26. Saxonhouse, "Industrial Policy and Factor Markets."

27. Bencha Bisenesu Kenkyu-kai, *Chukan hokoku* (Tokyo, 1984).

28. Such arguments figured in the discussions surrounding Japan's celebrated Very Large Scale Integration Project. See Daniel Okimoto, Takuo Sugano, and Franklin B. Weinstein (eds.), *Competitive Edge: The Semiconductor Industry in the U.S. and Japan* (Stanford, Calif.: Stanford University Press, 1984).

29. Zvi Griliches, "Returns to Research and Development Expenditures in the Private Sector" in John W. Kendrick and Beatrice N. Vaccara (eds.) *New Developments in Productivity Measurement and Analysis* (Chicago: University of Chicago Press, 1980); and Nestor Terleckyj, "Direct and Indirect Effects of Industrial Research and Development on the Growth of In-

dustries," in David M. Levy and Nestor Terleckyj, *Government-Financed R&D and Productivity Growth: Macroeconomic Evidence* (Washington, D. C.: National Planning Association, 1981).

30. Edwin Mansfield, "R&D and Innovation: Some Empirical Findings," National Bureau of Economic Research Working Paper no. 1132 (April 1983); and John T. Scott, "Firm Versus Industry Variability in R&D Intensity," National Bureau of Economic Research Working Paper no. 1126 (Cambridge, Mass.: National Bureau of Economic Research, April 1983).

31. National Science Board, *Science Indicators, 1982* (Washington, D. C.: National Science Board, 1983). Note that for more recent, shorter time periods, this is not necessarily the case. In particular, although the number of Japanese scientists and engineers engaged in R&D increased 24.4 percent between 1975 and 1981, the number of U.S. scientists and engineers increased during the same period by 29.8 percent. The rate of increase is diminished further if the unofficial statistics from Table 6 are used.

32. National Science Board, *Science Indicators, 1980* (Washington, D. C.: National Science Board, 1981).

33. To the extent that public subsidy was important in keeping down tuition costs for higher education in Japan and the United States, students were not totally on their own. In prewar Japan, as in postwar Japan, such benefits were limited to relatively small groups of individuals. In the prewar United States, publicly subsidized education was much more broadly available, but if the cost of training includes foregone wages plus living expenses and tuition, even this subsidy was relatively small.

34. Horiuchi Akiyoshi, "Daigaku kyoiku rieki, hiyo oyobi hojokin — Nihon ni tsuite no jisshoteki kento" (The benefits, costs and subsidization of higher education: An empirical study on Japan), *Nippon rodo kyokai zasshi* (April 1973).

35. National Science Board, *Science Indicators, 1982*; Sorifu, *Kagaku gijutsu kenkyu chosa hokokusho (Tokyo); and Kagaku Gijutsu Cho, aku gijutsu yoran* (Tokyo).

36. Mombusho, *Gakko kihon chosa hokokusho*; and National Center for Educational Statistics, *Digest of Education Statistics 1982* (Washington, D. C.: National Center for Educational Statistics, 1982).

37. U.S. Congress, Office of Technology Assessment, *Commercial Biotechnology: An International Comparison* (Washington, D. C.: Office of Technology Assessment, 1984).

38. Baiotekunoroji Shinko Iinkai, *Hokokusho* (Tokyo, 1983).

39. Ibid.

40. Ronald Dore, *British Factory—Japanese Factory (Berkeley: University of California Press, 1973).*

DISCUSSION SUMMARY

It was pointed out that the number of patents issued is not the best indicator of "who is ahead" in science and technology. Innovations in several areas, such as microelectronics and systems software, may not be patentable. The Japanese practice of aggressively building portfolios of patents for use as leverage in cross-licensing agreements was also noted. While many companies actively encourage their employees to patent discoveries, many others are more selective in submitting patents.

On the issue of basic research, in terms of aggregate effort, basic research in Japan is modest, especially in the life sciences and military areas. In optoelectronics and other communications technology fields, however, Japanese companies are involved in research and are competitive with or exceed their U.S. counterparts. In the U.S. construction industry, it is rare to have scientists involved in research. In the Japanese construction industry there are 200-300 scientists, 20-30 with Ph.D.s, conducting research.

The number of Nobel prize winners was also seen as an inaccurate indicator of "who is ahead," with the intrinsic delay in recognition and a Western bias in the selection process cited. In addition, Nobel prizes are not given in many areas of scientific research. It was predicted that Japanese scientists eventually will receive recognition from the Nobel committee. In the meantime, Japanese scientists continue to receive a proportionately large share of engineering society prizes.

In Japan, doctorate degrees are generally obtained after joining an institution or company. There are two ways of getting doctorate degrees: through graduate study at a university or by submitting to one's alma mater a thesis based on ten to fifteen years of work. In an effort to improve graduate studies, more companies in Japan are hiring students with doctorates. In the past many of these students aspired to work in academe; now they hope to work in industrial laboratories. It was suggested that the Japanese need to acknowledge the benefits they have gained from the West. The Japanese have benefited from Western technical literature, study in Western universities, and a free-trade system. By depending on the United States for its defense needs, Japan has been able to redirect its resources toward development of commercial goods and technologies.

The Japanese culture and mind are not unique or extraordinary; both the United States and Japan need to admit that they are similar in many ways and have much to learn from each other. The diligent and highly skilled Japanese work force could serve as a model for the United States, as could the role of cooperation and competition in the work place. The Japanese need to contribute more to the international community in science and cul-

-ture, remove some of their rigidity and hierarchy, and increase the flow of skills across academic and research and development organizations. The Japanese could also learn from the U.S. tradition of corporate philanthropy and pay more attention to exchange grants and fellowships.

With regard to the number of engineers that the United States is producing, the situation is worse than many people understand. Part of the problem is the "sticking ratio" — the number of engineers who continue to follow a career in engineering. Society does not recognize their worth and pays them accordingly. Of all the students in MBA programs, the largest percent are former engineering students. The United States simply is not producing practicing engineers. Of the scientists that it does produce, 50 percent are foreigners, and 80 percent of all new young faculty members are foreigners.

Western scientists advance their careers in part by publishing scientific papers. The difficulty is that such papers soon become "global public goods." Companies involved in research and development are reluctant to share information because a return on investments cannot be gained once the information becomes common knowledge. The patent application system has not kept up with technology; thus, a patent is no guarantee of protection.

The Japanese are not making a mistake by patenting new discoveries because the Japanese carefully chose specific areas of innovation. There is a need, however, for patents in cross-licensing negotiations.

3

The Japanese Technical Literature
Act of 1986

Mark R. Policinski

It is encouraging to note that despite the competition between Japan and the United States, both countries have been cooperating in recent years. Although trade surpluses and deficits have dominated our attention, we continue to work closely in many areas. In fact, we would like to improve our relationships to recognize mutual interests and goals.

In science and technology, the United States and Japan have initiated thirteen bilateral agreements since 1957. One was negotiated and implemented at the presidential level—the U.S.-Japan Agreement for Cooperation in Research and Development in Science and Technology. Signed in 1980, it covers all nonenergy fields and will expire in 1987. Preparations among U.S. agencies started in July 1986 to develop positions for joint talks in December. The United States certainly wants to capture and upgrade its science and technology relationship with Japan in the service of the following long-term goals:

- Increasing the world's knowledge base through joint research in areas where pooling of resources and talent can accelerate the rate of discovery
- Expanding the global economy so as to enhance the well-being of the people of both countries
- Enhancing the domestic R&D capabilities of both countries
- Improving reciprocity in exchange of personnel and use of research facilities and enhancing mutual access to emerging trends and research results in both countries

Let us briefly consider technology and its role in international competitiveness. Both the United States and Japan have used advanced technology extensively to drive economic growth. Since World War II, both countries have made great strides. Japan has been particularly adept at commercial applications of scientific discoveries, many of which originated in the United States. Japan has also been very successful in its strategy of basing its economic growth on exports and on importing most of the required natural resources and technology. Prime Minister Yasuhiro Nakasone has called for efforts to stimulate the domestic economy in order to encourage more imports, particularly of manufactured goods.

Japan has done a thorough job during the last three decades of monitoring the world's scientific laboratories and industrial technological developments. Many times, Japanese firms have marketed commercial products faster than have the U.S. firms who developed the scientific knowledge. Japan has developed outstanding skills in product design and manufacturing productivity.

Following a national tradition, U.S. research laboratories have been open to Japanese visitors, and U.S. universities have been open to Japanese students. On both governmental and institutional levels, the United States has cooperated with Japan in many ways. Japanese came here because the United States had the best scientific base and laboratories in the world — and still does.

However, there is a competitiveness problem for U.S. industry that has resulted in excessive trade deficits for the last few years. The total U.S. trade deficit for 1986 is expected to be around $170 billion, while Japan will have a trade surplus of $86 billion. Just last week the U.S. Department of Commerce announced that the U.S. trade deficit with Japan was running at an annual rate of $72 billion.

The Reagan administration continues to support open markets and fair trade. Secretary Malcolm Baldridge has taken a leading role in initiating agreements that would open markets to U.S. exports, negotiate scientific exchange agreements, and avoid protectionism. For example, the International Trade Administration has sponsored evaluations of Japanese technology to help U.S. business-people, and the National Bureau of Standards is participating in a bilateral exchange program with the Nippon Telephone and Telegraph Laboratories.

In response to competitive pressures, U.S. firms must do all they can to improve their performance, both in securing domestic markets and in penetrating foreign markets. During the 1960s and early 1970s, one of the strongest U.S. trading strengths was products incorporating high technology, with continual improvement as new technology allowed. Recently, U.S. firms have been under siege. Even so, U.S. technology is still a key weapon, an area where the United States can maintain, and improve, its comparative advantage. In this process the United States needs to tap all the sources it can for ideas and scientific knowledge. The United States does not have a monopoly on new scientific knowledge and successful technological applications. Therefore the United States must monitor foreign scientific and technological developments more effectively than we have in the past.

As an example of the need for closer monitoring, I offer the recently publicized process of diamond coating. A low-cost process has been demonstrated that deposits a thin carbon coating having the hardness, high heat conductivity, and transparency of natural diamonds. This has great commercial potential for wear-resistant coatings for cutting tools, scratch-proof optical coatings, improved solid-state microelectronic circuits, military technology, and even long-wearing razor blades. The Soviets accomplished the initial scientific work about ten years ago. Japanese firms have been conducting the applied research during the intervening years, and in 1986, Sony offered commercial products using this technology. The scientific literature covered these advances, but little or no attention was given to this area in the United States. A crash catch-up effort was started about three months ago when the Strategic Defense Initiative and the Office of Naval Research announced a $2.7 million program called the Diamond Technology Initiative involving Penn State, Research Triangle Institute, and the Lincoln Laboratory. One materials expert says the United States is ten years behind the Soviets and Japanese in this field. Who knows when better monitoring might have allowed U.S. researchers to join the game. This example certainly provides food for thought.

There should be no question that Japan is a prime source of relevant scientific and technical information. This is particularly true as Japanese institutions continue to shift their resources to support fundamental research rather than technologies having direct commercial applications. I refer to recent efforts such as the Exploratory Research for Advanced Technology program sponsored by the Science and Technology Agency, the Ministry of International Trade and Industry (MITI) program to conduct research on fundamental- level basic technologies needed for next-generation industrial applications, and the Fifth Generation Computer Project.

During the last three years, there has been considerable discussion on the value of actively monitoring Japanese scientific developments and on the need for more federal action in this regard. Several conferences on this topic have been held, beginning with the 1981 symposium on U.S.-Japan science and technology sponsored by the Japan-America Society of Washington and organized by Cecil H. Uyehara. Professor Richard Samuels of MIT's Japan Science Program organized conferences in 1983 and 1985, the Woodrow Wilson Center in spring 1985, the National Bureau of Standards in June 1985, and the National Science Foundation sponsored a workshop. The House Subcommittee on Science, Research, and Technology held hearings in March 1984 and June 1985 on the general availability of current and important Japanese scientific and technical literature.

The U.S. Congress has recently given the federal government a new impetus to help industry in this area by passing the Japanese Technical Literature Act of 1986, which the president signed into law on August 13, 1986. Its objective was to improve the availability of Japanese scientific and engineering literature in the United States. The Department of Commerce was assigned the responsibility of implementing the act. We have started developing some implementation plans, which I want to share with you.

The act authorized $1 million for fiscal year 1987 to carry out its purposes. The normal process of requesting appropriations would be the next step, a process that is uncertain and time consuming. However, the problems of wrestling with excessive budget deficits led the administration to carry out the purposes without requesting new funds, that is, by reprogramming from existing funded programs.

The other necessary action was to assign specific responsibilities to specific organizations and people. The deputy secretary asked the National Bureau of Standards (NBS) to manage the new program as a departmental effort. The director of the new program, Dr. Kenneth Gordon, and the deputy director of NBS will report to the deputy secretary regularly on progress and will receive policy guidance from him. This approach should ensure a department-wide viewpoint and maximum coordination of the many federal activities involved with Japanese technical literature.

The following four factors have guided our thinking thus far in formulating implementation plans:

1. Many federal agencies operate programs that monitor or disseminate information on Japanese technical development — these include the National Science Foundation, the National Technical Information Service, and the Office of Naval Research. The new Commerce function will not take over any of these activities in any sense. Its assignment is coordination — with the goal of increasing effectiveness and ultimate availability to U.S. users.

2. Many private services exist, or are being started, as sources for the translation or distribution of Japanese technical literature to U.S. users. However, the sales thus far have been very limited. This new federal program is intended to encourage — not to interfere — with these private services and help increase the demand for these services as well as the supply of materials.

3. Priorities must be established. For example, we cannot underwrite large-scale translation or publication of Japanese literature; however, we might provide seed money for development of new approaches or services on an experimental basis. If information services do not become self-supporting at some reasonable point, the conclusion must be that they are not meeting an important user need.

4. The federal role in persuading researchers and industrial managers to find and use technical information from Japan is limited. The government

can only encourage, facilitate, coordinate, study problems/opportunities, and perhaps start test programs. The most critical actions are up to the users.

In conclusion, let me list some specific tasks that our initial planning has identified as worthwhile to achieve the objectives of the act:

1. Define and evaluate the various federal activities that already contribute to such information dissemination.

2. Convene a conference of these federal groups to improve coordination and gain further participation.

3. Survey nonfederal producers of such information that offer services to users.

4. Publish a directory of federal sources of Japanese technical literature and related activities.

5. Help government and private users learn of the value of foreign technical developments and make use of available and expanded sources.

6. Identify significant gaps in U.S. coverage of Japanese technical literature and work to fill those gaps through U.S. or Japan-based activities.

7. Study the current status of computer-assisted translation of Japanese literature and its applicability to this problem in order to promote appropriate use.

8. Sponsor assessments or state-of-the-art reviews of Japanese literature or developments in selected technical areas.

9. Increase information availability by providing seed money or other assistance in the start-up of new translation or dissemination services.

The priorities for carrying out these tasks are directly affected by costs and available resources and are still being studied. We welcome your suggestions for actions needed to best achieve the objectives of the Japanese Technical Literature Act of 1986.

4

New Materials

George B. Kenney and H. Kent Bowen

In order to address the issue of patterns of interdependence with respect to U.S.-Japanese science and technology exchange in new materials, it is helpful first to establish the role and importance of materials within various industries and society as a whole. At the societal level, materials have established the very level of human development and standard of living since the Stone Age and on through the Bronze and Iron Ages. One of the first human domestic appliances was crude pottery fashioned from raw clay and fired, probably first, in an open fire. For thousands of years, long before there even was a dream of a discipline called materials science, materials processing was an essential part of society, practiced best by skilled artisans who worked with materials to enhance their utility and aesthetic appeal. For illustrations of materials meeting societal needs, we can turn to such well-known examples as the beautiful and functional pottery, textiles, and cast arts of Asia Minor of five thousand years ago, the beautiful and formidable Japanese swords of nine hundred years ago, medieval ironmaking, and the ubiquitous U.S. blacksmith. In all cases, the level of materials development established the standard of living and sometimes the military status of each society.(22)

The knowledge base of these past materials artisans was empirical, and the processing they did can best be described as "materials craftsmanship." The properties and performance of various materials were achieved and enhanced through various processing methods but without the benefit of basic material science as in modern materials processing and without the essential modern concept that properties and performance are controlled through control of the structure of materials. During the last century, the crucial role of control of structure at both the micro- and macroscopic levels was vigorously explored and studied, as was the essential linkages of materials processing to the science base and societal need. Largely as a result of the continue to be a field critical to current national needs.

The status of the major developed nations can be measured in terms of materials development and application. Beginning with the steel industry nearly a century ago, the United States plowed its farmland and built an infrastructure of railroads, bridges, cities, industries, and ships. Unscathed by World War II, U.S. industry led the world in materials processing and manufacturing on practically all fronts. This was clearly reflected in the U.S. standard of living, while much of the rest of the industrialized nations prepared to rebuild both their industrial base and infrastructure.

With its infrastructure in place, the United States stood ready to provide the steel export requirements of war-ravished Europe and Japan as well as of developing Third World nations. The United States also rapidly expanded its aluminum industry during the 1950s to support its new aerospace, construction, and consumer products industries. Polymers, which were developed during World War II, became the boon of the 1960s and now permeate society from the clothes we wear to the planes we fly.

Undoubtedly, the 1970s represented the growth of the silicon age, which gave birth to the information/computation age. The 1980s, besides being the information age, appear to be the period when new and advanced materials create myriad industrial, consumer, and military applications.

According to a recent issue of *Scientific American* (October 1986), which dealt exclusively with materials for economic growth, per capita U.S. consumption of nonrenewable, nonfuel mineral resources exceeds 20,000 pounds per year(1). Advanced materials shipments represent 14 percent of this total, or roughly $70 billion.

However, advanced materials do not usually represent the end products of commerce. Instead, advanced materials represent the foundation and critical components upon which depends the performance and operation of larger, more complex transportation, aerospace, communication, computation, and energy conversion systems(2). Materials science and subsequent processing technology also represent a critical element in the determination of such fundamental economic issues as resource supply, availability of strategic materials, maintenance of economic growth and productivity, creation of capital, and industrial/national competitive position.

Semiconductor devices are an excellent example of an area in which advanced materials are of critical economic importance. It is generally held that leadership in semiconductor materials and in semiconductor processing equipment are necessary for a competitive strategy. However, although the dollar value of semiconductor processing equipment sales is relatively small (roughly equivalent to the wine cooler market), the U.S. electronics industry, which depends on such equipment, had an aggregate sales value of $172 billion in 1984.

MATERIALS USAGE AND DEVELOPMENT
IN JAPAN

Basic materials provide the foundation necessary to establish the infrastructure of developing and developed nations, while advanced materials and processes provide the basis for industrial renewal, new technologies, and new industries. Nowhere is this recognition more apparent than in Japan. During the last forty years, Japan has accomplished the incredible feat of totally rebuilding its industrial and economic infrastructure and has established itself as a productivity and technology leader. What makes this truly remarkable is not that this feat was accomplished in only forty (really thirty) years, but that it has been accomplished by a small island nation which possesses no substantial raw materials or energy base! Besides hard work and dedication, the formula for Japanese success consists of technology acquisition, rapid exploitation, and continued development.

Japan began with the acquisition of state-of-the-art steelmaking technology during the 1950s to complement existing steelmaking capability. Steel was first required to rebuild Japan's cities, bridges, railroads, and factories. It is not surprising that shipbuilding was an industry upon which Japan focused immense early attention. Ships were required to haul raw materials and fuel to factories located around major port facilities. These same ships were also needed to export Japanese products to foreign markets. With no substantial indigenous export products of its own, Japan was totally dependent upon the exportation of processed imports to provide foreign currency and profits necessary to sustain its own consumption and economic growth.

After shipbuilding came automobiles, which consumed steel and other basic materials, and engine technology acquisitions. Japan also built, through technology acquisition, plastics and aluminum production which was expanded during the 1950s and 1960s. Basic electronics technology, most notably the transistor, was also acquired as Japan progressed from cars to television, radios, and the full spectrum of consumer electronics.

One of the reasons for Japan's past successes and economic growth was the importation, rapid implementation, and vigorous enhancement of foreign technology without shouldering much of the initial research investment risk. Automobiles, an excellent illustration of a materials-intensive product, are an example of where Japanese industry was almost entirely dependent upon Western technology.

Specifically, automobile engine technology was acquired during the 1950s and 1960s through four U.S., one Canadian, two German, and one French patent. As Japanese engine technology evolved from this base to world leadership status, foreigners grew reluctant to license new technology to Japanese manufacturers. In partial response to the general loss of offshore sources of new science and technology, the Japanese government established a ten-year initiative — the Research and Development Project of Basic Technology for Future Industries. The aim of the initiative was to establish a scientific and technology base in Japan that would sustain future industry.

One of the most remarkable features of Japanese industry is its ability and willingness to respond rapidly to changes in economic climate. The energy crises of 1973 and 1979 are excellent cases in point. Japanese industry responded immediately in 1973 to the order-of-magnitude increase in oil prices by acquiring, developing, and installing energy efficient or conservation technology within the basic materials industry. These early capital investments further enhanced production efficiency and further widened the existing competitive advantage. The second "oil shock" in 1979 led to even more dramatic industrial shifts. For example, Japan's relatively new aluminum industry simply moved offshore. With 1.5 million tons per year of production in 1979, the Japanese aluminum industry was rapidly rationalized to a current level of less than 0.2 million tons. This represented a rapid and significant industrial adjustment to compensate for externally driven changes of competitive position, especially for companies with a general philosophy of lifetime employment. Many of these companies simply adjusted their emphasis to other materials and processing technologies.

The willingness of Japanese firms to rapidly initiate new businesses to compensate for restructuring is part of a general philosophy to continually seek new markets for existing product lines while also looking for new opportunities based on extensions of resources, people, plants, and technology. This approach provides the growth flexibility and the mechanisms to absorb labor rendered redundant by fading lines of business.

Advanced materials, with the leverage they provide into a full spectrum of basic and high-tech applications, represent an extremely attractive field for both Japanese and U.S. industries. One particularly exciting example is advanced ceramics. This generic class of material provides leverage into a broad spectrum of useful products and devices, such as

- fibre optics in communications
- heat-wear resistant components in fuel-efficient adiabatic engines
- enhanced and innovative electronics devices and sensors
- improved biological implants
- superior cutting tools and industrial equipment

This leverage effect of advanced ceramics into a full spectrum of business opportunities is illustrated in Figure 1. The most current example is the potential revolution in all industrial sectors that high T_c, superconducting ceramics may offer.

George B. Kenney and H. Kent Bowen

Figure 1. Functions, properties, and applications of advanced ceramics

From an alternative perspective, various industrial sectors can be profoundly influenced by the full complement of advanced materials. This is particularly true in the energy sector where advanced materials can have both direct impact on the cost of energy production and the efficiency with which energy is consumed(2). Table 1 illustrates this situation for segments as diverse as coal mining, power generation, and energy conservation. Differing advanced materials are required in various energy systems to meet a multitude of mechanical, thermal, pressure, and chemical environmental requirements. Given that the overall thermodynamic efficiency of energy consumption throughout the U.S. economy is on the order of only 10 percent, room for improvement exists, and much of this is dependent upon the development and proper use of advanced materials.

Table 1. Advanced Materials Requirements in Energy Systems

	Electrical Materials	Ceramics	Advanced Polymers	Composite Materials	Advanced Metals
Mining	High-Temperature Electronics	Hard Drill Bits	Packers and Seals		Corrosion-Resistant Metals
Refining		Catalysts			Corrosion-Resistant Metals
Coal Refining and Combustion		Catalysts; Erosion-Resistant Ceramics		Erosion-Resistant Composites	
Nuclear Energy	Radiation-Resistant Electronics	Radioactive-waste Immobilizers; Plasma Insulators			Radioactive-waste Cannisters; High-temperature Radiation-Resistant Alloys

Table 1. (continued)

Electricity Generation and Transmission	Superconductors	Turbine Components	Insulators		Turbine Blades; Steam-handling Components
Solar Energy	Low-cost Solar Photovoltaic Cells	Selective Light-Absorbers	Solar-cell Encapsulation		
Waste Combustion					Corrosion-Resistant Metals
Geothermal Energy	High-temperature Electronics				Corrosion-Resistant Metals
Energy Conservation	Efficient Magnets Energy Control Systems	Heat-Transfer Components	Low-weight Vehicle Components	Low-weight Vehicle Components	High-temperature Alloys Recycling

Source: R. S. Claussen and L. A. Girifalco, "Materials for Energy Utilization," *Scientific American* 255, no. 4 (October 1986): 109.

Materials will continue to play a critical role in determining standards of living, technological leadership, and international competitiveness. The fortunes of companies, industries, and nations have risen and, just as quickly, disappeared based on the application of, and advantages provided by, advanced materials. Consequently, an examination of the interdependency of U.S. and Japanese materials should provide some valuable insight. What follows is discussion of steelmaking technology as an example of a basic material and industry that has matured in both the United States and Japan; polymers as a growing industry; and electronic materials as a modern, high-tech industry still undergoing great changes.

STEELMAKING TECHNOLOGY AND INDUSTRY EVOLUTION

The issue of technology exchange in the steel industry was addressed by Dr. H. W. Paxton of U.S. Steel Corporation at the First Symposium on U.S.-Japan Technology Exchange in 1981. No attempt will be made here to fully update Dr. Paxton's report. With respect to technology exchange, it is interesting to note that U.S. Steel Corporation established USS Engineers and Consultants' Corporation in 1969 for the express purpose of licensing its steelmaking technology and engineering resources. Other U.S. steel companies quickly followed in establishing similar organizations. It is also interesting to note that both U.S. and Japanese steel production peaked in 1973 with the U.S. steelmakers 23 percent ahead of their Japanese counterparts (see Table 2).

Table 2. Steel Production by the United States and Japan (million tons)

Year	United States	Japan
1973	135	110
1981	110	102
1985	79	105

The United States and Japan were at roughly equivalent steel production levels going into the 1982 economic recession. U.S. steelmakers, with 160 million tons of capacity, had resisted modernization and energy efficiency improvements similar to those installed by Japan in response to the 1973 and 1979 energy crises. By 1981, for example, Japan was continuously casting more than 70 percent of its hot metal while U.S. continuous casting capacity was at the 20 percent level. This energy-efficient and cost-effective technology eliminates several process steps between ingot casting and cold rolling operations. Japanese steelmakers were also very busy installing ladle refining technology in response to consumer demand for higher product quality and improved performance. By 1981, Japan was the undisputed technology leader and lowest cost integrated producer of steel worldwide. Continuous casting capacity had increased to 91 percent in Japan by 1985, with U.S. producers climbing to 44 percent.

Between 1982 and 1985, individual U.S. steelmakers lost $7 billion; invested $7 billion in capital expenditures; generated $2.6 billion from operations; and watched imports soar to 25 percent, which resulted in production decreases of nearly 20 percent. If anything, the situation in the United States has further deteriorated over the past year.

Although major Japanese steelmakers remained profitable through 1985, the situation has changed over the last year due essentially to the 50 percent increase in the value of the yen against the U.S. dollar. Foreign market share is being lost by the Japanese to Korean and other foreign steelmakers whose currencies have moved in tandem with the U.S. dollar. The strong yen has also caused a broad economic slump in Japan, which has further reduced domestic sales. All five major Japanese steelmakers announced substantial losses ($1.2 billion) for the first half of 1986(5).

For the first time ever, Japan's two largest steelmakers, Nippon Steel Corporation and Kawasaki Steel Corporation, are publicly discussing the possibility of layoffs(6). The Japanese unions are expected to accept the layoffs, which are expected to be short term, with laid-off workers receiving up to 90 percent of their average wages. In the meantime, steelmakers are attempting to reduce their labor forces through attrition, assignments to affiliated companies, and the creation of subsidiaries to absorb redundant workers.

Japanese steelmakers are diversifying into related areas of advanced materials, which are a logical extension of the industry's knowledge and production base. For example, coal, tar, pitch-based, and carbon fibers for metallic and ceramic matrix composites applications are a natural extension of coke-making operations, and advanced ceramics are a logical extension of refractory operations.

Kawasaki Steel and Nippon Kokan plan to have 40 and 50 percent of their respective businesses in nonsteel areas by the end of the century(7). Nippon Steel has the largest research and development effort in advanced materials, with three hundred staffers spread between the new materials project bureau and central laboratory for research and development. These special project teams are focused on advanced composites, fine ceramics, specialty metal alloys, shape memory alloys, semiconductors, high performance magnets, etc. Clearly, the emphasis is on diversification and expansion through knowledge-intensive research and development efforts which build on existing technological strengths and facilitate entry into closely allied advanced materials fields with future growth potential.

The strategy of U.S. steelmakers stands in stark contrast. U.S. Steel has become USX to reflect its new status as an oil company. The U.S. Steel component has recently experienced a protracted strike. This component's once world-class research and development facilities and staff of fifteen hundred have shrunk to less than fifty people and are a lost resource. Ironically, USX is currently trying to defend itself from corporate raider Carl Icahn. Other U.S. steelmakers have severely cut their research and development efforts as typified by Bethlehem Steel's sale of a major portion of its Homer Research Labs to Lehigh University. On the even darker side, LTV has followed Wheeling-Pittsburgh into Chapter 11 bankruptcy in July 1986, becoming the largest U.S. company ever to make such a filing. This puts additional pressure on Bethlehem Steel and Armco, the latter having recently barely survived its ill-timed diversification into insurance. Armco has since rationalized its position and refocused on its own internal strengths in materials. By way of comparison, the total cumulative research and development effort of U.S. steelmakers has shrunk to less than that of Nippon Steel alone in terms of number of researchers.

Another event to note is the 50 percent equity interest in National Steel taken by Nippon Kokan. It is reported that Nippon Kokan has steadily boosted its role in managing the company. A total of four of the seven largest U.S. steelmakers have sold equity positions to Japanese companies or formed joint ventures with them. The results of a policy twenty years ago to license technology appears to be returning foreign equity buyers with their own advanced technology. However, these equity moves into the United States on the part of Japanese steelmakers appear to be motivated by a fear of protectionism and a desire to maintain access to the U.S. marketplace from within.

With mature, modern steelmaking technology readily available worldwide, the production cost advantage has shifted to those countries with the lowest cost factor inputs of raw material, energy, and, above all, labor. This leaves U.S. and Japanese steelmakers at a disadvantage. Their continued survival will depend upon their ability to cope with and compete in a changing economic climate and to access technology that might change the nature of competition. Nippon Steel has responded by establishing an office in Cambridge, Massachusetts, not to sell steel but to access the nearby sources of new and emerging technology. In contrast to this Japanese approach, the technology licensing subsidiary of Bethlehem Steel—Bethlehem Steel Corporation—was recently sold to Australia's Broken Hill Proprietary, Ltd. This move appears to complete U.S. Steel's 1969 technology licensing initiative and represents the sale by Bethlehem Steel of its remaining technology in an attempt simply to survive!

POLYMER TECHNOLOGY FLOW, DEVELOPMENT, AND LEADERSHIP

In May 1986, the Japanese Technology Evaluation Program (JTECH) completed its report, "Advanced Materials in Japan"(8). The purpose of JTECH is to provide definitive technical assessments of emerging Japanese thrusts in selected high-technology areas. These assessments are performed by panels of U.S. technical experts and focus on the current status and long-term direction and emphasis of Japanese research and development efforts. (What follows is taken largely from the chapter on polymers of this JTECH report.)

Three major Japanese chemical companies were examined in some depth to illustrate four key trends that differentiate Japanese and U.S. chemical companies:

1. A well-defined reversal in flow of technology from the United States to Japan
2. An increased emphasis on industrial research and development (R&D) in Japan along with increased productivity per employee
3. A tendency toward decentralization, which fosters an improved environment for new ventures
4. A pattern of vertical integration toward higher value-added product lines.

Licensing Patterns

Toray Industries provides an excellent example of how the flow of technology from the United States to Japan changed directions in the 1970s. Toray (originally known as Toyo Rayon) was established in 1926 by Mitsui to manufacture rayon. In 1980, Toray had $2.5 billion sales of which 70 percent was fiber and 13 percent plastics. At that time, Toray also had eighty affiliates and subsidiaries. The licensing patterns for Toray are shown in Table 3, starting in the 1950s when Toray began by licensing technologies for nylon and polyester. This pattern shifted in the 1960s toward setting up joint ventures in specialty polymers. During this period, Toray also acquired the technology for polypropylene, acrylonitrile-butadiene-styrene (ABS), and acrylics. By the 1970s, there were practically no commercial polymers remaining to be licensed. In the meantime, Toray had underway R&D programs designed to upgrade the processes and products it had licensed earlier. Because of its close attention to technical and marketing details, Toray was able to make significant improvements in many of these polymers to the extent that the upgraded polymer technology was licensed back to the United States during the 1970s. It is noteworthy that UCC and Borg Warner, pioneers in the development of carbon fibers and ABS, respectively, appear now to have become dependent on Toray for advanced technology for these products.

Development of Escaine (Ultrasuede) is also indicated because it is considered by several Japanese scientists as the only new innovation to emerge from the Japanese chemical industry. This development can be readily traced to the confluence of two programs—namely, the efforts in Japan in the late 1960s to develop a synthetic silk and also the emergence at that time of techniques for spinning very fine fibers.

Table 3. Licensing of Technology by Toray, 1951-1979

Licensed technology from		
DuPont	nylon	1951
ICI	polyester	1957
Joint ventures in Japan with		
DuPont	elastomeric fiber	1964
Dow Corning	silicones	1966
Thiokol	polysulfides	1969
Licensed upgraded technology to		
Dow	polyethylene foam	1972
Borg Warner	ABS	1978
UCC	carbon fibers	1978
Milliken	heat resistant fabric	1979
New technology: Escaine (Ultrasuede)		
Developed by	Toray	1970
Technology licensing	Anic SpA Italy	1972
Joint venture	Anic SpA Italy	1975

Increased Productivity per Employee
and Increased Emphasis on R&D

This pattern of attention to the upgrading of processes and products also is dramatically illustrated by examining the changes in Sumitomo Chemical during the early 1970s(4). Sumitomo Chemical traces its roots back to the seventeenth century when it began as a copper smelting business. By 1925, however, it had become known as Sumitomo Fertilizer and in 1934 took the name it now bears. In 1984, Sumitomo Chemical had nearly $3.5 billion sales with seven thousand employees (50 percent of the sales were in plastics and petrochemicals). Two important points that should be stressed are that more than 25 percent of these seven thousand employees are in R&D and that the productivity per employee is $500,000.

Typically, a U.S. chemical company with $3 billion sales employs twenty-five to thirty thousand people and maintains a significantly smaller R&D effort. Productivity per employee is closer to $125,000. Since 1970, Sumitomo Chemical has effected dramatic reductions in numbers of employees (in 1970 the figure was approximately seventeen thousand), presumably through automation and robotization of processes. It is noteworthy that from 1979 to 1983, Sumitomo Chemical's R&D budget doubled even though sales were flat and the company suffered through a severe recession in petrochemicals. Sumitomo Chemical also split off eight affiliates from 1980 to 1984. These figures on ratio of labor to revenue appear to be typical of most of the Japanese chemical companies. Hence, in spite of the lack of raw materials in Japan, these chemical companies are positioned to be extremely cost competitive and to dominate those fields of polymers where innovation is a primary driving force.

Decentralization

In examining the growth patterns of Japanese chemical companies, it is apparent that these patterns do not follow the patterns of many U.S. companies with acquisitions, mergers, or formation of conglomerates. To the contrary, major chemical companies in Japan tend to split off subsidiaries or affiliates when that action is deemed advisable for the ultimate success of a new venture. For example, Sumitomo Chemical has 64 affiliates and subsidiaries with total sales of nearly $4 billion in 1984(10). These combined affiliates and subsidiaries employ fifteen thousand people which is probably consistent with the increased personnel necessary to support a far greater diversity of activities.

Marketing and manufacturing are independent of the parent organization; however, some cooperation may occur at other levels. Typically, each of these companies maintains its own R&D. An important advantage to this strategy for decentralization of responsibility is that local management now has the necessary autonomy to make key decisions and commit resources in a timely manner. Furthermore, such management will tailor the organization to be more competitive in the specific business environment associated with that product line. In the United States, a very different philosophy prevails in which success is measured primarily by profitability and growth. Because acquisitions can provide an instant response to such goals, a pattern has emerged in the United States where the chief executive relies more on acquisitions and less on R&D to achieve growth.

There are a few exceptions in Japan to the pattern of decentralization; however, these are usually associated with industries which are in financial difficulty. For example, until recently Japan was a major exporter of petrochemicals, with approximately nine chemical companies involved. With the increased production of low-cost petrochemicals from Canada and Saudi Arabia, Japan has become a net importer(11), and the petrochemical industry operates at a relatively inefficient 40-70 percent capacity. Both the Ministry of International Trade and Industry (MITI) and the leaders of the chemical industry now propose to form a cartel to operate three to four large plants which would function at greater than 90 percent capacity. Polypropylene manufacturing and sales have already been consolidated from eighteen to four companies, thereby resulting in far greater price stability and profitability(12).

Trend Toward Vertical Integration

Potential advantages and forward integration have not been lost on the Japanese chemical companies, and much of their R&D effort is directed toward high value-added products derived from plastics. Mitsubishi Rayon, with sales of $1 billion in 1984, provides an excellent example of this trend. This company recently put all of its rayon activities into a wholly owned subsidiary and has proceeded to focus its attention on polymethyl methacrylate and several synthetic fibers as the raw materials base for high value-added derivatives. In effect, Mitsubishi Rayon has entered those high value-added businesses such as electronics, medical devices, and energy saving processes based on its ability to integrate from raw material to end use(13). This type of focused R&D takes advantage of the ability of Japanese scientists to effectively address problems with clear-cut goals. Furthermore, within R&D the time from discovery to implementation can be greatly reduced when goals are clearly stated.

ELECTRONIC MATERIALS AND PROCESSING:
GATEWAY TO THE FUTURE

The Federation of Materials Societies sponsored a workshop in February 1986 to consider "Electronic Materials: A Key to U.S. Competitiveness?" Part of their summary is reproduced here to provide a review of the status of electronic materials and materials processing, current international trends, and prospects for the future.

Why Are Electronic Materials and Materials Processing a Key to U.S. Industrial Competitiveness?

Electronic materials are the key elements in many important high tech applications. For instance, lasers and detectors are fabricated from arsenide phosphide single crystals. Similarly, very carefully prepared piezoelectric quartz is required for frequency standards and timing circuits. Lasers fabricated in single crystal oxides are used for radar ranging and retinal eye surgery; and single crystal nonlinear optical crystals are essential for modulation and harmonic generation of optical frequencies. Electronic ceramics are used in capacitors and packages. Special property polymers are required to pattern integrated circuits, as encapsulants, and for printed circuit boards. These similar materials are the sine qua non of electronic devices.

Electronic devices are the building blocks which are used to make electronic systems such as computers, telecommunications systems, and military command and control systems. Microprocessors and sensors make possible, for instance, industrial process control and automobile fuel, ignition and pollution management. Modern electronic devices are the essential elements in VCRs [video cassette recorders], digital discs and hospital patient intensive care monitoring. Indeed, a second industrialization revolution is going on in the world today, brought about by the availability of inexpensive information acquisition, manipulation and distribution systems. This revolution was started by our ability to control electronic materials and processing. It began with the processing of electronic materials to fabricate the transistor, and it is fueled today by modern electronic materials and devices. The electronics industry has been among the largest and fastest growing segments of our economy. This industry is an important source of jobs, and gives us our edge in defense. U.S. success as an industrial nation is strongly tied to success in electronics.

All new devices and most improvements in device and circuit performance result from understanding, controlling and optimizing electronic materials and materials processing. The most efficient, reliable and flexible systems are made from optimized devices. Whoever controls the material and materials processing controls the devices, the systems, and ultimately, modern electronics.

Device performance, yield, cost, and reliability are the principal factors which determine systems competitiveness. They are strongly influenced by our ability to understand and control the synthesis and processing of electronic materials. The dollar value of electronic materials themselves is high, but the downstream leverage as an enabling technology is many times greater than the value of materials. Worldwide electronic materials consumption in 1985 was $2.4 billion. This supported an equipment market estimated at $388 billion.

What Is The Present Position of U.S. Electronic Materials Technology?

U.S. electronic materials technology started from a position of world dominance with the invention of the transistor and the integrated circuit and the first commercial preparation of silicon for these devices. Although early work on III-V semiconductor materials (such as gallium arsenide) began in Germany, most of the critical materials compositions and processes were discovered, invented, or perfected in the United States. Similar generalizations could be made about ceramics and other electronic materials. However, in the past decade, the U.S. lead in electronic materials technology has been severely eroded, and in many areas the United States is now behind. In 1984, Japan surpassed the United States in silicon consumption and in 1985 consumed more silicon than the United States and the rest of the world combined. At the current rate of growth of Japanese production, this gap will widen. The rate of increase in Japan is approximately twice the rate of increase in the United States.

Japanese domination of the low end of the consumer electronics market is, to a considerable degree, due to Japan's ability to manufacture low-cost devices with an appropriate level of reliability. Japan exceeded the United States in market share of computer memory DRAMs beginning in 1983. The more recent Japanese inroads into the higher end of the market are due largely to more rapid transfer of advanced electronic materials processing technology from lab to factory. At the high end, device dominance probably will lead to system dominance.

In optoelectronic devices, such as LEDs and communication lasers, the United States is losing ground. The loss of U.S. dominance is due to relatively high-cost, low-yield factory processes. This situation has been brought about by the U.S. neglect of electronic materials process science and manufacturing technology. In III-V materials, the Japanese have been especially quick to transfer laboratory process science into factory technology. Similar statements can be made about other electronic materials and devices.

The U.S. research base devoted to understanding the relationship between materials characteristics and circuit performance is not large, and the U.S. industrial commitment to new materials is confined to a few organizations. At the same time, the Japanese have targeted these areas as critical to the next generation of advances in device and circuit structures. At the present time, the United States still has a reasonably strong base and ongoing effort in basic electronic materials science and device physics, but as more of the manufacturing capability moves offshore, the research and technology development are likely to follow. Even now the offshore producers are often quicker than we are to incorporate U.S.-developed technology into their production lines.

As materials and device dominance move offshore and systems begin to follow, the United States national defense position erodes. The government no longer requires across the board that all components for its systems be made onshore. As more and more electronic devices and systems are built offshore, more and more foreign components will appear in U.S. defense hardware. Benjamin Franklin said, "For want of a nail . . . the horse was lost." Today one might say, "For want of an IC . . . the missile was lost." It is already true that in the case of certain strategic materials, the number of U.S. suppliers is shrinking rapidly, and for materials such as single crystal sapphire there is only one domestic supplier. It is not too late, but there is not much time to reverse the trend. As offensive and defensive weaponry become more sophisticated (electronic subsystems, microprocessors, electro-optic sensors), the ability of the United States to maintain a strong national defense will hinge on the viability of the domestic electronic materials and materials processing industry.

Basic electronic materials research directed toward the understanding of the connection between chemical bonding-structure and useful properties historically has been the source of all the materials used in modern devices. The first opportunity to design and exploit future new devices and resultant systems will go to the organizations and nations which pursue a vigorous fundamental electronic materials program. Silicon and gallium arsenide were once exotic new materials. New research results already indicate great future potential for materials which can now be made by new techniques, such as molecular beam epitaxy in which the control is at the level of individual atomic layers. The possibilities for new semiconductors based on the quantum levels in strained layer super lattices and new magnetic and optical materials are inherent in current research. New layered compounds which have potential for solid-state batteries, new compounds which simultaneously exhibit semiconductor and magnetic properties, organic conductors, and new electro-optic materials are but a few current examples of recent research findings. Research continues to have the potential to produce a cornucopia of materials results which, if history is any indicator, will lead to new devices and presently unimagined systems. The U.S. track record and continuing vigor in the basic aspects of materials science are encouraging, but the gap is narrowing, and foreign competitors have made basic materials science—especially electronic materials—their national priority.

Some Conclusions

Electronic materials production and processing capabilities have a large impact on device and circuit performance. Production and processing are the key to yield, cost, and reliability. Performance, cost, and reliability determine the competitiveness of electronic systems. The necessity to improve yield and reliability makes it essential that the United States increase its emphasis on the development of electronic materials, materials process science, and manufacturing technology.

The cost of electronic materials production and processing is highly leveraged at early stages of the production of high-value-added systems. Therefore, the loss of a competitive electronic materials base inevitably leads to a loss in competitiveness in the manufacture of circuits and systems.

Independent materials suppliers are generally not in a position to benefit from the value-added associated with materials control.

In light of the impact of materials on circuit yield, performance, and reliability, there is a disproportionately low amount of government funding of electronic materials technologies.

A weak link in the United States is technology transfer and implementation of processes from research and development to manufacturing.

Inherent U.S. strengths in physical chemistry and chemical engineering could provide the United States with a critical edge in improving process science with commensurate economic impact on manufacturing technology.

A significant amount of U.S. industrial resources is being consumed by intercorporation redundancy in the development of materials synthesis and processing technology.

The electronic materials community has not had the opportunity to impact decisions on government funding and industrial policy. Therefore, there appears to be a lack of appreciation among much of the management of both government and industry of the impact of materials and materials processing on cost, performance, and reliability and on the interaction between materials synthesis and device processing.

U.S. foreign competitors have targeted electronic materials as a key to the future of their industrial competitiveness.

If the current trend continues, it can be anticipated that the United States will be a minor force in the world market in electronic materials and systems by the early 1990s. Therefore, corrective action must be taken soon to reverse the precipitous decline of U.S. competitiveness.(14)

THE ROLE OF THE JAPANESE GOVERNMENT IN ADVANCED MATERIALS

The JTECH report referred to earlier provides an excellent overview of the role played by the Japanese government in advanced materials acquisition, application, development, and licensing. The report indicates that the Japanese government has very well-defined goals with respect to materials science and technology—namely, to make Japan the world leader in high-technology business areas which depend on advanced materials. Achieving this goal is considered vital to Japan's future economy because Japan has very few raw material resources. The problems that confront government and industry are formidable. To establish and maintain a proprietary position on advanced materials requires a complete restructuring of the research methodology and includes building up a strong fundamental research effort in this area. If one accepts that much of the corporate-sponsored basic research on new materials is beginning to be curtailed in the United States, and hence is no longer available as a resource, it then becomes incumbent on Japan to establish its own infrastructure on basic materials science. Also, the need for more creative, entrepreneurial scientists is essential to translate this science into useful new materials. These thoughts are uppermost in the minds of the Japanese leaders as they attempt to formulate programs which will permit Japan to become the world leader in advanced materials.

Figure 2 outlines the organization of the Japanese government for research sponsorship and implementation. The Science Council, chaired by the prime minister, consists of the heads of the various ministries and selected representatives from the private sector(15). This group decides on broad issues concerning science and technology in Japan and also determines how much government money will be spent on R&D. The Science and Technology Agency is concerned with major projects such as Japan's space or breeder reactor programs. In 1961, this agency also established the Research Development Corporation of Japan (JRDC), which in recent years has provided support for start-up companies and now is attempting to improve the climate in industry for original research(16).

Figure 2. Japanese government organization chart

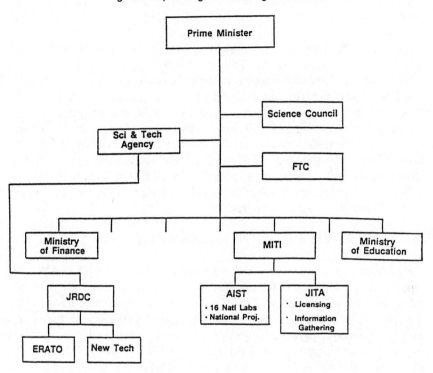

MITI provides a major thrust to development and technology implementation in industry, and this work is carried out through MITI's Agency of Industrial Science and Technology (AIST). The Japanese Industrial Technology Association (JITA), also under MITI, acts as the licensing agency for AIST-developed technology and plays an important role in tracking external R&D developments. The Ministry of Education which provides support for university research, is essentially autonomous in its selection of research agendas. The Ministry of Finance approves all R&D budgets, and its actions are not perfunctory. In the process of selecting government-sponsored research policies, government and industrial leaders arrive at a consensus on issues concerning the long-range interests of their nation. Arriving at this consensus is a difficult and arduous process, and arguments can be pursued in Parliament and are chronicled in the media. There are no paid lobbyists in Japan; hence, vested interests do not have much leverage in this process.

More than 75 percent of Japanese R&D occurs in industry. The government plan is that basic research will be done primarily in industry because university scientists are considered too independent and rigid in their approach. The Science Council has ordered that the annual R&D expenditures in Japan be increased from 2.5 percent to 3.5 percent of the gross national product, increasing total budgets from 7.2 trillion yen to approximately 10 trillion yen(15). This figure is half the value of total R&D in the United States; however, when one takes into account the lower costs for R&D in Japan and also the fraction of U.S. research sponsored by the Department of Defense, it would appear that in the near future Japan will be doing more nonmilitary R&D than will the United States. MITI's budget for R&D appears relatively small; however, because of its traditional relationship with industry, MITI has been unable to assume a major role in championing Japan's future as a technology leader. The income from technology exports appears substantial, but because of earlier licensing commitments, Japan still remains a net technology importer.

The Role of MITI in Advanced Materials

The primary effort on advanced materials is pursued in MITI's AIST, an organization that many years ago resembled the National Bureau of Standards in the United States. Today AIST consists of sixteen government laboratories with a total budget of 121.6 billion yen (fiscal year 1985)(17). The key programs on advanced materials are pursued under the general theme of Basic Technology for Future Industries (6.4 billion yen). There are a total of thirteen projects: seven on new materials, three on biotechnology, and three on new electronic devices. The seven material activities are indicated in Table 4. These seven projects run for eight to ten years, and the R&D is carried out completely in private companies. The companies are expected to share in some of the expenses and typically do not charge overhead. The intent of these programs is to generate knowledge and knowhow, and the participants meet regularly to review progress. Government laboratories maintain smaller efforts in these areas and interact closely with the industrial research groups.

MITI's licensing arm, the Japan Industrial Technology Association (JITA), formed in 1969 to license AIST-developed technology, claims to have licensed 10 percent of the thirteen thousand patents(18). JITA also carries out extensive surveys of recent scientific and technological advances in other countries.

Some three hundred university and government scientists who travel abroad are asked to participate in such assessments. An example is a detailed analysis of all the major chemical companies throughout the world, including strategy statements by the presidents of these companies.

MITI has established three new materials laboratories in polymers (Tokyo), ceramics (Nagoya), and metals (Tokyo) with the intent of providi

Table 4. AIST (MITI) Support of New Materials Research for Future Industries

Project Name	R&D Period (FY)	Total R&D Expenditure[a]	Budget[a] (FY 1985)
High performance ceramics	1981-90	13,000	961
Synthetic membranes for new separation technology	1981-90	10,000	556
Synthetic metals	1981-90	5,000	375
High performance plastics	1981-90	6,000	299
Advanced alloys with controlled crystalline structures	1981-88	8,000	610
Advanced composite materials	1981-88	11,000	721
Photoactive materials[b]	1985	--	70

[a] Unit = 1×10^6 yen.
[b] Basic plan in formation.

ing materials research support to start-up companies. These laboratories will be staffed with fifty to one hundred scientists and will not only evaluate new materials for the start-up companies but also provide them with seed money.

The cooperation between government, industry, and academia to create the necessary infrastructure for successful widespread use of advanced materials can be further demonstrated by the care of ceramics and metals.

The Japan Fine Ceramics Center (JFCC) was established in 1985 and will occupy a new $32 million, fully equipped research and development facility due to be completed early in 1987. The JFCC will promote more systematic R&D, providing technical knowhow and standardized methods of testing and evaluation. It will also promote the industrial use of advanced ceramics and integrate technical data base systems. The objectives of JFCC include

1. contributing to the advancement of fine ceramics
2. promoting university, government, and industry relationships in Japan throughout the world.

Although international cooperation is being sought, it is not clear that foreigners will be given equal access to all results and data base information.

The Japan Research and Development Center (JRDC) for Metals is attempting to develop and commercialize innovative new technologies in order to secure future industrial bases. This center serves to integrate the needs of producers and users; identify clear R&D targets; and implement efficient R&D programs based on industrial liaison and international exchange. The center's theme is materials and process development.

The Role of JRDC

JRDC was established about twenty-five years ago by the Science and Technology Agency to promote R&D for new technologies relevant to future national needs(19). JRDC tries to integrate efforts between the government, academia, and the private sector. Currently, JRDC is providing $25 million per year in support of work on new, high-risk technology. Such projects are usually contracted to industry and then go through a screening phase and a commercial development phase. In case the project is discontinued, JRDC absorbs all the costs.

In 1981, JRDC initiated a new program called Exploratory Research for Advanced Technology (ERATO), with the intent of stimulating a more creative and original style of research within the industrial environment.[20] Five projects were started in 1981 of which one was in specialty polymers (known as Ogata Fine Polymers). Each program was funded to the extent of $2 million per year for five years, with the majority of the effort conducted in industry. In the case of the Ogata Fine Polymer Program, the effort consisted of twenty-five to thirty people and was directed toward (1) high temperature monolayers, (2) separations of optical isomers, (3) conducting polymers, (4) molecular particles, and (5) adsorption systems. Although the five-year funding cycle was rather short, it appears that good progress was made in all five areas. With termination of the project, the hope is that industrial scientists who worked under the auspices of ERATO will continue to carry on a more independent and original style of research. Results of the first five years have been encouraging, and JRDC plans to continue and enlarge the program.

When viewed in its entirety, there is a well-defined strategy for advanced materials whose purpose is to place Japan at the forefront in high-technology industries by the late 1990s. This strategy speaks both to the welfare of the individual companies and of the nation. In arriving at this strategy, there are many competing forces that must be harmonized so that the desired consensus can be achieved.

MITI plays a very major role in defining, implementing, and homogenizing the long-range strategy for advanced technology. Typically, a president of a major company meets with MITI representatives two to three times a month to discuss his plans and strategies. MITI is thus able to monitor the activities of the entire industry and suggest directions consistent with the long-term national interest. In the late 1970s, MITI had its wings clipped by Parliament with respect to MITI's power to control the foreign exchange rate as well as license of foreign technology(15). Today, MITI appears in a position to coordinate industrial policy and through AIST to support financially areas of advanced materials technology. There are some checks and balances where, for example, the Ministry of Finance increasingly demands accountability with respect to MITI-supported R&D and the Japanese Federal Trade Commission questions the legality of questionable MITI strategies, such as forming cartels. In addition, the Science and Technology Agency through JRDC promotes programs on advanced R&D which are competitive with the MITI effort.

ADVANCED MATERIALS TO
HIGH-TECH LEADERSHIP

During the past forty years, Japan has accomplished the impossible in going from a position of minimum scientific infrastructure to international technological leadership. From a historical perspective, Japan began by importing existing technology. Early limited financial resources and long distances demanded that careful evaluation of available foreign technology be conducted to ensure the optimum return on investment. Clearly, the Japanese have never been encumbered by the crippling constraints of not-invented-here snobbery. The fact that in the past Japan was closed to direct foreign investment encouraged foreign sources of technology to provide their best assets to Japanese licensees as a means of secondary access to an otherwise closed marketplace.

With new technology in hand, the Japanese manufacturer had to rapidly become proficient in the use of such technology to first meet domestic demand. The manufacturer also had to produce products for the export market in order to generate the profits necessary to sustain raw materials imports and economic growth. The Japanese were quick to embrace Demming's teachings concerning statistical process controls and productivity. Cheap labor combined with increasingly efficient production and Demming-style quality control translated directly into international competitiveness, market penetration, profitability, and rapid growth.

Japan's success is due in large part to having avoided the economic trap of licensing dependency. As pointed out by Dr. Bela Gold at the first symposium five years ago:

> A strategy of relying heavily on licensing innovations by others is likely to be self-defeating, rather than economically wise: (1) because licensees rarely catch up with innovations within technologies involved—thus tending to ensure continuing lags; and (2) because failure to keep close to the current frontiers of technology undermines not only the prospects of catching up with competitors, but also undermines a firm's ability to make prompt and effective use of the licensed technologies.
>
> Licensing technological advances offers an effective means of reducing lag behind more successful innovators only if the licensee is already technologically advanced enough to grasp and utilize the incremental insights and techniques offered by the innovations; and only if other components of the production environment can be thoroughly adapted to the requirements of the innovation. To achieve and maintain international competitiveness, however, the licensing of innovation from others must be also combined with vigorous programs seeking to develop innovations which will offer competitive advantages over others from time to time(21).

Japanese licensees of materials technology in the 1950s followed up these licenses in the 1960s with joint ventures in Japan with foreign materials technology leaders, thereby rapidly gaining technological parity on an international scale (this model was illustrated earlier in the discussion of polymers). Materials processing parity combined with modern, efficient production and manufacturing systems operated by inexpensive, skilled labor established Japanese international price competitiveness even with near total dependence on imported raw materials and energy and geographic isolation from the world marketplace. At one time, Japanese cars enjoyed a $1,500 per vehicle labor cost advantage alone, before quality and reliability were factored in. In addition, while U.S. automakers considered *Consumer Reports* to be antibusiness, Japanese automakers scoured this magazine as a source of consumer preferences upon which to target and build a competitive advantage.

In building its industrial and technology base from the ground floor up with licensing and manufacturing followed by joint ventures and engineering, and now directed, long-term research and new concept design, Japan has built into its technology community a rapid development and applications capability. It is this short circuit between global science, directed research, targeted development, and rapid implementation of advanced materials, processing, and manufacturing technology which is the foundation of Japan's competitiveness in both basic and advanced technology systems. The interdependency of global materials and materials processing science and technological leadership is illustrated in Figure 3. In examining this relationship between access to the existing knowledge base of materials science and demonstrated technology, it is clear that international competitiveness and technological leadership are a strong function of the rate at which available science is converted to a commercial technology or research results become a developed product.

Figure 3 illustrates three distinct cases where the rapid application of existing scientific knowledge resulted in international technological and commercial leadership. In steelmaking, the Japanese rebuilt their steel facilities incorporating the latest Western technology and applied to this base the latest new "scientific" concepts involving both steel products and the steelmaking process. The rapid growth of Japanese steelmaking capacity was necessary to rebuild the nation and prepare it for trade with the rest of the world. By the mid-1970s, it was no secret that Japanese steelmaking had become second to none in quality, efficiency, and cost of production.

Figure 3. Technology role models and the application of science

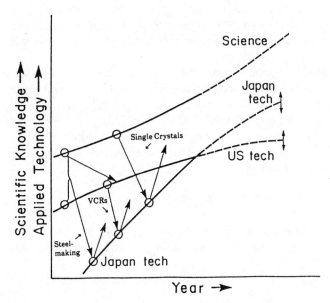

The second case illustrated by Figure 3 deals with VCRs. This technology was invented and first commercialized by two U.S. firms during the late 1970s. These bulky systems were considered too expensive to generate significant consumer demand. However, Japanese manufacturers picked up this existing technology, miniaturized it, and moved rapidly into mass production, thereby also solving the unit cost problem through mass production. Japan now supplies more than 90 percent of all VCRs worldwide.

The "single crystal" case in Figure 3 refers to the growth of single crystals in a strong magnetic field. In a magnetic field, it is possible to greatly reduce the thermal convection within the liquid melt from which crystal is pulled/grown. The reduced convection allows a much higher quality crystal with fewer and smaller defects. The science base for this materials processing technology was invented at MIT in 1969. However, the circuit architecture of that era was insensitive to existing defect levels, and so the new, patented, magnetic crystal growth process was placed "on the back shelf." By 1979, integrated circuit architecture had shrunk in size to the point where existing crystal defects were then the limiting step to further miniaturization. That same year, Sony announced its new, commercial, magnetic Czochralski single crystal growth technique, which delivered substantially higher integrated circuit yields through improved crystal quality. In one move, Sony had set the world standard in the quality and efficiency of single crystal production simply by retrieving existing technology from "the back shelf."

Unfortunately, science and technology and research and development are often considered single entities or activities. In reality, a distinct gap exists between both science and technology and research and development. The manner in which this gap is bridged directly determines the rate of technology development, which in turn establishes levels of international competitiveness.

The pattern of interdependency between advanced materials and high-tech systems is clearly recognized. However, the rate and efficiency with which new developments in materials and materials processing are applied determine technological leadership. The pursuit of new materials and processes through research is necessary but insufficient for commercial success. The key to success is an efficient mechanism which rapidly converts science into technology.

REFERENCES

1. *Scientific American* 255 no. 4 (October 1986):51.
2. J. P. Clark and M. C. Flemmings, "Advanced Materials and the Economy," ibid.
3. R. S. Claussen and L. A. Girifalco, "Materials for Energy Utilization," ibid.

4. *Iron and Steelmaker* (July 1986).

5. *Wall Street Journal*, November 12, 1986.

6. *Wall Street Journal*, October 16, 1986.

7. J. D. Kidd, "Advanced Materials Drive," *American Metals Market Magazine* (November 3, 1986).

8. JTECH Panel on Advanced Materials, *Advanced Materials in Japan*, (La Jolla, Calif.: Science Applications International, May 1986, JTECH-TAR.8502).

9. Toray Industries, *Annual Report 1979-80* (Tokyo, 1980).

10. Sumitomo Chemical, "Creating a New Age of Chemistry" (Tokyo, 1984).

11. *Chemical and Engineering News* (December 2, 1985):8.

12. Mitsubishi Rayon, *Annual Report* (Tokyo, 1984), p. 29. 13. Ibid, pp. 20-21.

14. "Electronic Materials: A Key to U.S. Competitiveness?" (Washington, D.C.: Federation of Materials Societies February 26-27, 1986).

15. "Science and Technology in Japan," *New Scientists* 21 (March 85):31-32.

16. Ibid, p. 33.

17. Science and Technology Agency Brochure (1985).

18. Brochure of Japanese Industrial Technology Association (1985).

19. Brochure of Research Development Corporation of Japan (1985).

20. Research Development Corporation of Japan, *ERATO* (1985).

21. Cecil H. Uyehara, ed., *U.S.-Japan Technological Exchange Symposium* (Washington, D.C.: University Press of America, 1982), p. 54.

22. C. S. Smith, *Metallurgy as a Human Experience* (New York: American Society for Metals and the Metallurgical Society of AIME, 1977).

DISCUSSION SUMMARY

It was emphasized that new materials research is the new wave of the future; the halcyon days of steel are gone. Japanese government, industry, and academia are focusing on new materials, particularly ceramics. There is a ceramic association in Japan that has more than two hundred corporate members. There is a kind of "new materials fever" in Japan that appears to be missing in the United States.

Although new materials research can be applied to all sectors of the Japanese economy, especially manufacturing, the United States lacks this diversification. New materials research in the United States is confined to specific, high-tech areas, such as space technology and defense, and its applications are more strategic. The Japanese are more concerned with basic research, and each company makes full use of its own resources, rather than going to another Japanese company for information. Japanese companies tend to start from scratch and employ a wide spectrum of their own scientists and engineers in research activities. This proves valuable because Japanese companies apply R&D efforts to specific goals rather than gather knowledge for its own sake.

In response to a query as to why Japan leans toward diversification while the United States leans toward specificity, it was explained that a Japanese company takes pride in R&D through its own channels, through employees that the company has trained. For example, Nippon Steel applied its own resources (scientists and engineers) in order to diversify into electronics. U.S. companies, on the other hand, would rather acquire another company or be acquired by another company rather than invest in new areas that are not guaranteed to deliver an immediate profit. In the United States, people are employed in a company and do one specific job for years. In Japan, employees are moved around to different sections of the company every few months. Through this system, employees become acquainted with all areas of the company and with their colleagues as well. This helps to create an incentive for the separate components to work together.

Japan's advancement in new materials can be attributed to Japan's scientists and engineers. The science and engineering fields have been integrated for many years, and the combined skills of scientists and engineers have led to new material development for new products.

Japanese companies also thoroughly investigate markets for their new materials and are interested in pleasing the consumer, and the Japanese consumer at all levels of society tends to be much more interested in sophisticated technology than is the U.S. consumer.

The problem is for the United States to find a way to interest its people in science and technology. There has to be a "new emphasis" on the basics and on training college students for careers that start out on the manufacturing level, rather than at the management level. Managers cannot direct a division if they do not know the basics.

It was emphasized that there was a need for cooperation in science and technology exchange between the United States, Europe and Japan. Countries should not hide their technology from one another because shared technology has the potential to result in further advances.

A number of participants commented that the Japanese are often evasive when asked about a particular technology or even long-range goals. Although it is not uncommon for a Japanese to present an American with a detailed questionnaire on a particular industry or sector, the American is often frustrated when the Japanese avoids questions about his or her business. One participant pointed out that some government agencies refuse to meet with the Japanese because previous meetings have not resulted in an equal exchange of information. Many meetings come to an immediate close when the Japanese visitors have completed their questions. Americans have decided that information exchange is a two-way street and are now reluctant to volunteer information when they get nothing in return.

It was suggested that it takes a lot of work for the United States and Japan to cooperate and compete at the same time. One suggestion was that the two governments should get together to support joint technical activities, bring in foreign scientists, or set up a "science exchange consortia" with foreign companies or joint ventures or joint research in precompetitive stages. However, none of these approaches is feasible unless both sides allow open access to their data bases. Another participant pointed out that although building a solid relationship with the Japanese is extremely beneficial, there is also a down side – the relationship is for life, and the relationship's implicit loyalty often forces a company to pass up business opportunities elsewhere.

The question was raised whether someone with a Ph.D. in a particular field could be a better leader than a multidisciplined chief executive officer (CEO) or manager. Some of the largest Japanese companies have presidents who hold Ph.D.s in physics, chemistry, etc. These company leaders, because of their focused backgrounds, have a long-term vision that multidisciplined CEOs in the United States often lack. It is not unusual for a scientist or engineer to head a company in Japan because promotion and key appointments are based on experience. In contrast, a CEO in the United States, it was maintained, is often promoted on the basis of his or her most recent achievements and his short-term record. Sometimes, his ability to make a quick profit for the company outweighs all other considerations. In the United States, people who hold Ph.D.s are often considered "academics" and really do not have a place in the business world. The truth is that U.S. industry needs their expertise and should use their knowledge, as the Japanese do in their companies.

5

Mechatronics

James L. Nevins

ABSTRACT

The term *mechatronics*, which was originated by the Japanese, is generally used to describe the union of mechanical and electronic engineering
needed to produce the next generation of machines, robots, and smart
mechanisms for applications such as manufacturing, large-scale construction, and work in hazardous environments. There appears to be no specific
definition for the term even among its originators. Its greatest significance
is not technology but the integrated approach to manufacturing problems
that has been used so successfully by the Japanese. This chapter, like the
report it is based on, divides mechatronics into nine areas for analysis:

- Flexible manufacturing systems (FMS)
- Vision systems
- Nonvision systems
- Assembly/inspection systems
- Intelligent mechanisms

The basis of this chapter is the Mechatronics Panel Final Report of the
Japanese Technology Evaluation Program (JTECH), sponsored by the U.S.
Department of Commerce and National Science Foundation, administered
by Science Applications International Corp., La Jolla, California, March
1985. Copyright by the Charles Stark Draper Laboratory, In., 1987.

The author wishes to express sincere thanks to the following people for
their support in editing this chapter: J. S. Albus, NBS; M. Kutcher, IBM;
and G. L. Miller, Bell Labs.

- Software
- Standards
- Manipulators
- Precision mechanisms

Comparisons between the United States and Japan were made in each area according to basic research, advanced development, and product implementation.

Technical Summary

Figure 1 shows the assessment summary for each technical area. The symbols indicate Japan's current status, and the arrows show the trend. The assessment summary shows Japanese basic research to be equal to U.S. research in all areas except vision and software. Furthermore, Japanese research is staying even with its U.S. counterpart in spite of the former's lack of large Department of Defense (DOD) and National Aeronautics and Space Administration programs. In vision the Japanese are not much behind, and they will probably catch up in the near future. In basic research, the Japanese are behind and falling further behind only in artificial intelligence (AI) software techniques. However, it should be noted that AI is not the only path to future intelligence systems, and Japan appears to be embarked on a broad approach. Thus, one can argue that an information-control versus AI approach to advanced robotics/process problems may be the method used by the Japanese to accelerate their basic research programs for intelligent machines. The Toshiba software factory has already demonstrated the Japanese ability to create high-quality software at productivity levels some seven times greater than those produced by Americans(1). In advanced development and product implementation, the Japanese are ahead or equal to their U.S. counterparts, and the rate of change is definitely in favor of Japan.

Conclusion

- In all categories of mechatronics except software, Japan is holding constant or gaining ground over the United States, and there is evidence that the lag in software is closing.
- The Japanese integrated approach to manufacturing systems coupled with government planning and support, which has been very successful in the past, is now being applied to the area of mechatronics.
- Japanese progress in mechatronics is of major importance because it addresses the very means of production. Mechatronics itself has a regenerative effect on manufacturing industries. Further, mechatronics identifies the

Figure 1. Mechatronics Assessment Summary

Category	Basic Research	Advanced Development	Product Implementation
FMS	0 →	0 ↗	+ ↗
Vision	− →	+ →	+ ↗
Non-Vision	0 →	0 →	0 ↗
Assembly	0 →	> ↗	> ↗
Intelligent Mechanisms	0 →	+ ↗ →	0 →
Software	< ↘	− →	− ↗
Standards	0 →	0 →	
Manipulators	0 →	+ →	+ ↗
Precision Mechanism	0 →	+ →	+ ↗

Coding System - Japan Compared to U.S.:

Present Status		Rate of Change	
<	Far Behind	↑	Pulling Away
−	Behind	↗	Gaining Ground
0	Even	→	Holding Constant
+	Ahead	↘	Falling Behind
>	Far Ahead	↓	Losing Quickly

Source: JTECH Mechatronics Panel, *Final Report* (La Jolla, Calif.: Science Applications International, March 1985).

need for, and offers a wide range of, new products that are key to the advanced/automated manufacturing systems of the 1990s.

Observations

- The Japanese have decided that software is indeed a key issue in the development of intelligent systems.
- Vertical integration significantly aids major Japanese companies in mechatronics development.
- Japan is able to focus national resources through the activities of the Ministry of International Trade and Industry (MITI).
- The major U.S. government funding of robotics and AI is currently through military agencies. This provides some commercial spinoff benefits to the U.S. economy, but is vastly less effective than the Japanese model of direct MITI-industry collaboration on mechatronics.

Recommendations of the JTECH Panel

- An appropriate national response to the Japanese challenge in the area of mechatronics needs to be formulated.
- A formal process of collecting and disseminating technical information on Japanese mechatronics activities is needed.

INTRODUCTION

Mechatronics is a term coined by the Japanese to describe the union of mechanical and electronic engineering. The term is used to emphasize a multidisciplinary, integrated approach to product and manufacturing system design. Mechatronics encompasses the next generation of machines, robots, and smart mechanisms necessary for carrying out work in a variety of environments. The environments are primarily manufacturing but extend to hazardous regions such as space, underwater, and nuclear as well as to disasters such as fire, chemical, explosion, and nuclear emergencies. Further, the Japanese are pursuing applications in the construction and service industries.

By both implication and application, mechatronics represents a new level of integration and approach to manufacturing systems and processes. The intent is to force a multidisciplinary approach to these systems as well as reemphasize the role of process understanding and control. Mechatronics can only speed up the already rapid Japanese process for transforming ideas into products.

Currently, mechatronics describes the Japanese practice of using integrated teams of product designers and manufacturing, purchasing, and marketing personnel acting in concert to design both the product and manufacturing system with minimal technical complexity. For the future, mechatronics offers a means for implementing advanced processes and production technology. The Japanese are already succeeding in specific areas. For example, the integration of VLSI technology and machine vision software algorithms is creating cheaper, more capable vision systems.

Mechatronics will have an impact on higher education. Engineers are needed who understand both processes and systems. There is a further need for business schools to be aware of new issues, options, and tradeoffs that mechatronics will create.

The principal goal of the JTECH study was to evaluate Japanese research and development (R&D) in mechatronics and to estimate the impact on U.S. industry. A second purpose was to comment on the availability of Japanese literature related to mechatronics.

BACKGROUND

The study group felt that the current Japanese mechatronics effort should rank high as an area of U.S. national concern for several reasons:

1. The pragmatic Japanese approach, coupled with Japan's particular infrastructure, allows the Japanese to create systems very rapidly with present technology. That is, using minimal on-line sensors the Japanese create systems by coupling product design to present technology and use people whenever the technology is missing or fails.

Because most large Japanese firms are supported by large production technology centers, these firms can produce the needed systems rapidly and independently of the supplier marketplace. In the United States, on the other hand, users depend on suppliers, and suppliers do not generate new systems unless they are assured of a marketplace with a good return on investment. In a sense this is an institutional problem. Mechatronics addresses the issues related to the way in which product design is carried out, the coupling of designers to manufacturing, and the coupling of users to suppliers.

In contrast, in the United States the factory-of-the-future (FOF) approach taken by a number of companies offers integration of product design and manufacturing systems, but does not address the user-supplier infrastructure issue. Several large U.S. companies, notably IBM and GE, are addressing the infrastructure issue by acting as their own supplier, but this does not help the midsize company. Until the user-supplier infrastructure question is addressed, the United States may continue to lag behind Japan in implementing these new systems.

2. Japan appears to be embarked on a broad spectrum approach to intelligent mechanisms. One can argue that an information-control versus an AI

approach to advanced robotics/process problems may be the method used by the Japanese to accelerate their basic research programs for intelligent machines. Currently, Japanese lag significantly behind their U.S. counterparts in intelligent systems and complex autonomous system research. (See the JTECH Computer Science Panel Report for more substantiation of these issues.) But, the Japanese have started such work, and the question is which strategy they will use.

3. Previous history of the Japanese for rapid implementation of products together with the potential of many new products and systems available from mechatronics is expected to provide strong advantage to Japan in worldwide economics.

In the next section a summary of each of the mechatronics subtopics identified by the study group for analysis is presented. The depth to which each subtopic was explored is not uniform due to several factors — such as Japanese activity in the area, a panelist's experience, and availability of relevant Japanese data. In most of the areas, the Japanese status and rate of change compared to those of the United States are summarized in Figure 1.

TECHNICAL ANALYSIS

FMS Development

In Japan, any multimachine system with some material handling ability and a degree of flexibility may be considered a flexible manufacturing system. The Japanese have been installing FMS of all types for more than a decade. A wide range of educational, cultural, and economic pressures have supported and pushed this movement to FMS, along with central planning and goal setting.

Installed FMS is growing rapidly. In 1981, Yamazaki opened a new plant with two fully automated FMS systems. Since then, two larger FMS systems have been installed. Toyoda, SNK, Niigatta, Makino, and other Japanese machine tool companies have also installed FMS and are competing strongly in the worldwide FMS marketplace. Table 1 lists systems which became operational in 1983-1984.

Japanese companies initially implemented FMSs with available technology. These companies did not delay implementation while more advanced systems were being developed. Consequently, the Japanese have become experienced users of FMS. The technology is not necessarily the most advanced, but the systems are being fully utilized. As Professor Sata points out in his paper (3) the real epoch-making step in the development of a flexible manufacturing system was the success of unmanned operations in the evening and night shifts that was achieved in 1975. This expanded the monthly

TABLE 1. EXAMPLES OF FLEXIBLE MACHINING SYSTEMS DEVELOPED RECENTLY.
(LISTED ARE MAINLY SYSTEMS WHICH STARTED OPERATIONS IN 1983 AND 1984)

COMPANY WHERE SYSTEM IS INSTALLED	KINDS OF PRODUCTS	OUTLINE OF SYSTEM		YEAR OF START OF OPERATION	Remarks
		MACHINE TOOL	EQUIPMENT AND TYPE OF TRANSPORTATION		
KOMATSU LTD.	CYLINDER BLOCKS OF MEDIUM ENGINE, 4 KINDS	MM 1, NC-H-BM 1, H-MC 1, DC 4, COMPLEX NC MACHINE 4 (COMBINATION OF H-MC AND MULTI-AXES ATTACHMENT)	GUILDED CART (LINEAR TYPE)	1983	AIMED AT COMPLETE UNATTENDED OPERATIONS DURING NIGHT SHIFTS. PLANNED TO INSTALL 18 FMS'S FROM 1983 TO 1985. NUMBER OF OPERATORS 1/3-1/4. LEAD TIME ABOUT 1/10.
	CYLINDER HEAD OF MEDIUM ENGINE, 3 KINDS	V-MM 2, H-MC 6, MM 1, DC 3, NC-DM 1 NC-H-BM-1	ROLLER CONVEYOR		
NIIGATA IRON WORKS CO.	PARTS OF MACHINE TOOL INTERNAL COMBUSTION ENGINE, RAILWAY VEHICLE, INDUSTRIAL MACHINE, ETC. ABOUT 70 KINDS	H-MC 5, NC-MM 1, NC LATHE 1	UNATTACHED CART (RANDOM TRANSPORTATION)	APRIL 1983	AUTOMATIC LOADING AND UNLOADING DEVICE OF WORK. UNATTENDED OPERATIONS DURING NIGHT SHIFTS.
YAMAZAKI MACHINERY WORKS LTD.	PARTS OF MACHINE TOOL, ETC. 534 KINDS	COMPLEX CNC LATHE 8 CNC LATHE 1, V-MC 4 H-MC 16, MC WITH CHANGABLE HEAD 7, NC BED GRINDER 2, GRINDING MACHINE 5	UNATTACHED CART AND GUIDED CART (LINEAR TYPE)	MAY 1983	AIMED AT FACTORY WITHOUT DRAWING. 5 LINES, WHICH ARE FLANGE LINE, SPINDLE LINE, BOX LINE, FRAME LINE AND LARGE FRAME LINE

Company	Parts/Products	Machines	Transport	Date	Notes
HITACHI SEIKI CO.	LARGE FLAT-BOX TYPE PARTS OF MACHINE TOOL, ETC. 79 KINDS	H-MC 4	UNATTACHED CART (LINEAR TYPE)	MARCH 1984	LINKED TO AUTOMATIC PROCESS PLANNING AND OPERATION PLANNING, IN-PROCESS TIME ABOUT 1/3.
	MEDIUM AND SMALL FLAT BOX-TYPE PARTS 131 KINDS	H-MC 2, V-MC 2	STACKER CRANE		
	MEDIUM AND SMALL CYLINDRICAL PARTS	H-MC 1, NC LATHE 3	CART		
MAKINO MILLING MACHINE CO.	PARTS OF MACHINING CENTER AND MILLING MACHINE ABOUT 300 KINDS	H-MC 10	UNATTACHED CART (RANDOM TRANSPORTATION)	APRIL 1984	DYNAMIC SCHEDULING IS ADOPTED.
YOSHIDA KOGYO CO.	LARGE CASTING	H-MC 8	UNATTACHED CART	MAY 1984	EMPHASIS IS GIVEN TO IMPROVEMENT OF SOFTWARE. PLANNED TO INTRODUCE 8 FMS'S BY 1987. ULTRA-HIGH SPEED MACHINING CENTERS (40000-50000 RPM) ARE ADOPTED.
	INJECTION MOLDING DIE AND ELECTRODE FOR EDM	H-MC 21	UNATTACHED CART		
MURATA MACHINERY LTD.	PARTS OF TEXTILE MACHINE AND MACHINE TOOL	H-MC 4	STACKER CRANE DIRECTLY LINKED TO CUBIC WAREHOUSE	JUNE 1984	SINGLE LOT. CONTINUOUS UNATTENDED OPERATIONS.
BROTHER INDUSTRIES CO.	FRAME OF SEWING MACHINE FOR INDUSTRIAL USE	H-MC 13	SELF TRAVELLING ROBOT	JUNE 1985	EACH MACHINING CENTER IS EQUIPPED WITH TABLE CARRYING FIXED JIGS.

MM:MILLING MACHINE, NC-MM:NC MILLING MACHINE, V-MM:VERTICAL TYPE MILLING MACHINE
MC:MACHINING CENTER, V-MC, VERTICAL TYPE MACHINING CENTER, H-MC:HORIZONTAL TYPE MACHINING CENTER,
NC-H-BM:NC HORIZONTAL TYPE BORING MACHINE, DC:DRILLING CENTER, NC-DM:NC DRILLING MACHINING
TC:TURING CENTER

Source: K. Iwata, "Recent Developments of Flexible Manufacturing Systems in Japan" (Proceedings of the ICMA Symposium on Flexible Automation in Production Technology, Hanover, East Germany, September 18-19, 1985), pp. 49-60.

operating time of systems to about five hundred hours. Initially this expansion was done with single machines; later companies did it with many machines, no central monitoring or diagnostics, and with minimum changes in manufacturing process. Reference 4 describes the work done at the Takatsuka plant of Daini Seikosha Company in 1980.

The newest systems (Table 1) employ extensive monitoring and diagnostics, AGVs, Stacker cranes, etc. According to Iwata(2), 279 systems for machining were introduced into 145 factories prior to 1982. One hundred seventeen systems at 57 factories were planned for 1983 and 139 systems at 61 factories in 1984. But as Iwata's questionnaire points out, the use of the term *FMS* is not specific. Thus, fully a third of the systems are for machining parts with similar shapes, and another 20 percent are for machining parts with the same method but with different shapes.

In the area of plastic forming the first FMS was not developed in Japan until 1975. Table 2 lists forming systems that came on line in 1983.

MITI has sponsored the Flexible Manufacturing System Complex at the Tsukuba test plant since 1977. This program is commonly known as the FMS With Laser. The Japanese have two goals:

> 1. To develop a manufacturing system with high flexibility and productivity for small lots of products
> 2. To base the system on the idea of "complex" — that is, total productivity is increased as the space occupied by the machines is reduced. Thus, it is necessary to carry out more than two kinds of operations at the same place, simultaneously or in sequence.

Due to such complex processing, the work material stays at the same place and therefore the transportation facility becomes needless or small scale depending on the degree of complexity. This approach and the marketing of the machines that result will probably be the only measurable output of this particular experiment.

Computer-aided design (CAD)/computer-aided manufacturing (CAM) integration in Japan is growing, but it is not as advanced as in the United States and Western Europe (see Figure 2). The Japanese have tended to buy U.S. CAD and production control systems. But as Professor Sata(3) indicates, this may not always be so. In addition, the Japanese tend to push toward standardized designs with firm production schedules and press distributors to absorb inventory when business is slow in order to keep plant productivity flowing.

TABLE 2. EXAMPLES OF FLEXIBLE PLASTIC FORMING SYSTEMS DEVELOPED RECENTLY.
(LISTED ARE MAINLY SYSTEMS WHICH STARTED OPERATIONS IN 1983)

COMPANY WHERE SYSTEM IS INSTALLED	KINDS OF PRODUCTS	OUTLINE OF SYSTEM		YEAR OF START OF OPERATION	REMARKS
		PLASTIC FORMING MACHINE	EQUIPMENT AND TYPE OF TRANSPORTATION		
TOSHIBA	PARTS OF POWER CONTROLLERS	PRESS 1	4 AXIS WORK FEEDING ROBOT, CONVEYOR	1983	INCREASE OF PRODUCTIVITY BY MORE THAN 3 TIMES. COMMUNICATION WITH CRT.
FUJI XEROX CO.	FRAME, COVER, DOOR (3500 PARTS/70 KINDS/MONTH)	NC TURRET PUNCH PRESS 3, NC SHEARING MACHINE 1, NC AUTOMATIC BENDING MACHINE 4, DEBURRING AND SELECTING MACHINE, NC WELDING MACHINE 1, NC WELDING ROBOT 1	AUTOMATIC CART	1983	SHORTENING OF PREPARATION TIME. REAL TIME CONNECTION TO HIGHER LEVEL COMPUTER.
NIPPON ELECTRIC CO.	MECHANICAL PARTS OF COMMUNICATION DEVICE AND DATA TERMINAL, ETC.	NC TURRET PUNCH PRESS 5, NC TAPPING MACHINE 1, NC SHEARING MACHINE 2	AUTOMATIC CART WITH AUTOMATIC LOADER	1983	TWO SEPARATE LINES FOR SMALL PARTS AND MIDDLE AND LARGE PARTS. AUTOMATIC GENERATION OF NC DATA FROM CAD INFORMATION. UTILIZATION OF OPTICAL DATA HIGH WAY.
FUJITSU CO.	PERIPHERAL DEVICE OF COMPUTER DEVICE (1500 PARTS/200 KINDS/MONTH)	NC TURRET PUNCH PRESS 2, NC SHEARING MACHINE 1, NC PRESS BREAK 3, NC HYDRAULIC PRESS 2, WELDING ROBOT 1, PAINTING ROBOT 2	CONVEYOR	1983	UNIFIED INFORMATION SYSTEM FOR CAD AND CAM. CAPABLE OF UNATTENDED OPERATION FOR 24 HOURS. EACY TO COPE WITH CHANGES OF DESIGN AND PRODUCTION ENVIRONMENTS. LEAD TIME REDUCTION TO HALF.

TABLE 2. (cont.)

Company	Products	Equipment	Material Handling	Year	Description
KUBOTA IRON WORK CO.	FRAME OF BENDING MACHINE (2500 PARTS/30 KINDS/MONTH)	NC TURRET PUNCH PRESS 5, PRESS BREAK 1, TANGENT BENDER 1, BLANKING SHEARING MACHINE 1, WELDING ROBOT 4, BEAD GRINDING ROBOT 1	CONVEYOR, UNATTACHED CART	1983	CONSISTENT SYSTEM FROM SHEET METAL FORMING TO ASSEMBLY. CONTROL WITH USE OF LAN (LOCAL AREA NETWORK). REDUCTION OF STOCK TO 1/3-1/4.
KAWASAKI HEAVY INDUSTRIES CO.	SMALL SHEET METAL PARTS FOR RAILWAY VEHICLE	NC TURRET PUNCH PRESS 1, (56 STATIONS) BLANK SHEARING MACHINE 1	NONE DIRECTLY LINKED TO WAREHOUSE	1983	SCHEDULE CONTROL WITH USE OF MINI COMPUTER SAVING OF MAN POWER.
MITSUBISHI ELECTRIC CO.	FRAMES OF VARIOUS CONTROL BOXES (12000 PARTS/350 KINDS/MONTH)	NC TURRET PUNCH PRESS 1, (42 STATIONS) NC FOLDING MACHINE 1	CONVEYOR	1983	COMBINED PROCESSING OF PUNCHING, SHEARING AND THREADING BY NC TURRET PUNCH PRESS. REDUCTION OF LEAD TIME CAPABLE OF AUTOMATIC OPERATION FOR FULL DAY.
	PANELS OF CONTROL BOX AND AIR CONDITIONER, FRAMES OF AIR CONDITIONER FOR VEHICLE (4000 PARTS/200 KINDS/MONTH)	NC TURRET PUNCH PUNCH PRESS 1 (50 STATION) NC STRAIGHT SHEARING MACHINE 1, AUTOMATIC LASER CUTTING MACHINE 1	NONE DIRECTLY LINKED TO WAREHOUSE		DIRECT OUTPUT OF NC DATA FROM CAD INFORMATION. SHORTENING OF TIME FOR DELIVERING. CAPABLE OF UNATTENDED OPERATIONS BY COMMANDING SCHEDULES ONCE A DAY.

		FEEDER		
MITSUBISHI MOTOR CO.	GEAR AND HUB (150000 PARTS/10 KINDS/MONTH)	FORGING PRESS 1, BILLET SHEARING MACHINE 1, PRODUCT AND BURR SEPARATION DEVICE, QUICK DIE CHANGING DEVICE, BILLET HEATER, HEAT TREATMENT FURNACE		1983	CONSISTENT FLOW LINE SYSTEM FOR SUPPLY OF STEEL MATERIAL TO COMPLETION OF FORGED RAW MATERIAL. SAVING OF MAN POWER.
MURATA MACHINERY LTD.	TRANSPORTATION DEVICE, SHEET METAL PARTS OF TEXTILE MACHINE AND CONTROLLER OF NC MACHINE TOOL (800 KINDS/MONTH)	CNC TURRET PUNCH PRESS 2, CNC WRIGHT ANGLE SHEARING MACHINE 1, PRESS BREAK 2	UNATTACHED CART	1984	CAPABLE OF COMPLETE UNATTENDED OPERATIONS DURING NIGHT SHIFTS. IMPROVEMENT OF PRODUCTIVITY SAVING OF MAN POWER.

Source: K. Iwata, "Recent Developments of Flexible Manufacturing Systems in Japan" (Proceedings of the ICMA Symposium on Flexible Automation in Production Technology, Hanover, East Germany, September 18-19, 1985), pp. 49-60.

Figure 2. FMS-CAD/CAM Development

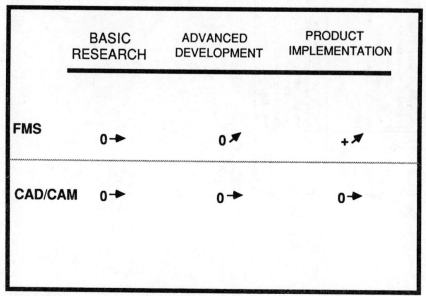

Source: JTECH Mechatronics Panel, *Final Report* (La Jolla, Calif.: Science Applications International, March 1985).

Assembly/Inspection Systems

One area of mechatronics in which the Japanese excel is assembly systems. The Japanese have achieved this by choosing a system design strategy that is deterministic (geometrically driven) – that is, a successful assembly can be accomplished by an open-loop control strategy (generally no sensing or feedback) where the parts are simply pushed together. Quality of product and high yield are direct results of part quality and tooling precision. Through careful product redesign, motions to assemble are restricted to one or two degrees of freedom, thus simplifying the system design. Further, the Japanese have achieved a high level of integration of the product design, function, production technology, and vendor/supplier control.

Part of the product assembly is done by people and the rest by automation. Tasks such as attaching and mating fine wires are done by people. If the wire laying is a structured task (like attaching leads to a chip), then the process is automated.

The interesting thing is the sheer number of new systems that have been implemented since 1980 and the variety of system architecture being explored. Each system architecture appears unique to each company. There appears to be little interest in determining which system design might be optimal across a variety of product lines. System types range from the modular, highly parallel operation, Sony FX units to the Seiko Hoop Integrating Assembly System (HIKS) linear system with an uptime goal of 99.5 percent. Sony and Hitachi are using totally dissimilar architectures to assemble the same basic video cassette recorder (VCR) mechanism. Hitachi uses a distributed system composed of people, robots, and fixed automation whereas Sony uses groups of FX modules and people.

The Japanese also benefit from the fact that their production technology centers can create the necessary system as well as being an integral part of the product-manufacturing system design. In the United States, only a few companies, such as IBM, GE, or AT&T, are mounting comparable efforts. Many companies are certainly capable, but they have chosen the external supplier method to implement systems. If the market dynamics are slow, then this is the most cost-efficient method. Engineering costs for systems developed in production technology centers appear to be twice that of U.S. assembly equipment suppliers. Actually the new Japanese systems are doing things that are more complex than comparable U.S. systems. The lower engineering cost for U.S. systems is because the incremental engineering done for each system is quite small. There is also much dependence on standard modules and standard tooling. In a rapidly changing marketplace, there is a question as to the viability of the U.S. method.

Present Systems

In the late 1970s, a number of Japanese companies independently reached the conclusion that fixed automation assembly systems would not be adequate in the 1980s. This conclusion was based on two needs(5): the need to automate the assembly of products with fine precision parts; and the need to satisfy the marketplace with a wide range of products and with large fluctuations in product volume.

The Hitachi system for assembling tape recorder mechanisms(6) is an example of older type automation. Whereas the Sony FX-I and II Phoenix-10 Assembly Center(7, 8) and the Hitachi Assembly Line for VTR mechanisms(9) are examples of the new systems. The arguments for the Japanese move from fixed automation to a more advanced, flexible automation system can be found in references 5, 7, and 10. Where reference 10 argues the societal-institutional pressures for increased quality and productivity, reference 7 is an excellent case study of how, why, and what one company did in response to the perceived needs. Reference 5 gives a general summary of a number of activities and systems, and Table 3 lists a number of systems scheduled to come on line in 1983.

Professor Sata during his talk at the 1986 Japan-USA Symposium on Flexible Automation(3) states that in Japan people make an assembly error in 1/25,000-1/100,000 operations; that the desired level for quality is ten times better than these numbers; and that the difference is often the sole source for justification. On the other hand, U.S. manufacturers feel that if they could achieve an error rate of 1/25,000 that would allow them to eliminate the cost due to warranties. They typically see error rates of 1-3/100 operations. The Japanese data are quoted for personal computer (PC) board operations and small as well as large mechanical items.

The activities currently taking place can be categorized into three efforts, namely:

1.   Major Trends
                    Higher precision requirement
                    Multikind products with wide ranges in annual volumes
                    Many different system architectures
                            Modular — Sony FX(7)
                            Distributed — Hitachi Assembly Line(9)
                            Continuous Flow — Seiko HIKS(11)
2.   Technology
                    Minimal system complexity (hardware and software)
                    Open-loop control strategy for most assembly
3.   Strategies
                    System design driven by market needs
                    Highly integrated multidisciplinary effort
                    Products extensively redesigned
                    Systems generally hybrids

The following figures from a Sony FX-I system presentation(7) illustrate these issues. Figure 3 shows the relation between the number of product models and production systems for Sony tape recorder mechanisms from 1976 to 1981. Figure 4 shows the assembly process elements and the relative time required for each element operation. The requirements of product design and production requirements are shown in Figure 5. The results of this integrated effort were simplicity in product design (Figure 6) and the unique FX-1 modular assembly system (Figure 7). The FX-1 system consists of an x-y table, a frame from which tools are hung, pallets for parts, and a pallet transporter all controlled by an Intel 8080. One system configuration built with FX modules for assembling the Sony Walkman is in Figure 8. The latest from Sony indicates that this type of system has proved to be too expensive. It appears that Sony is moving to a more distributed system with a lower individual station cost.

The development of an automatic assembly line for video tape recorder (VTR) mechanisms is described in the Hitachi paper (ref. 9). This paper, as well as the paper by Taniguchi(5), describes the Hitachi Asssemblability Evaluation Method (AEM) used to quantify and control product design (this system is currently being marketed in the United States by General Electric).

TABLE 3. EXAMPLES OF FLEXIBLE ASSEMBLY SYSTEMS DEVELOPED RECENTLY.
(LISTED ARE MAINLY SYSTEMS WHICH STARTED OPERATIONS IN 1983)

COMPANY WHERE SYSTEM IS INSTALLED	KINDS OF PRODUCTS	OUTLINE OF SYSTEM		YEAR OF START OF OPERATION	Remarks
		ASSEMBLY EQUIPMENT	EQUIPMENT OF TRANSPORTATION		
TAKASAKI PLANT OF OKI ELECTRIC CO.	CHINESE CHARACTER PRINTER 3 TYPES, 143 KINDS, NUMBER OF PARTS 219, 2000/MONTH	ASSEMBLY ROBOT 49, (6 AXIS ROBOT 21 4 AXIS ROBOT 28) SPECIAL PURPOSE UNIT 21 10 LINES.	AUTOMATIC CART 4, FREE FLOW CONVEYOR	NOVEMBER 1983	BASICALLY 6 AXIS ROBOT, BUT PARTIALLY 4 AXIS ROBOT. FLOOR SPACE 3200m². DEVELOPMENT OF MULTIFUNCTIONAL HAND TO GRASP DIFFERENT KINDS OF PARTS. AIMED AT ON-LINE LINKAGE TO EDP SYSTEM. REDUCTION OF OPERATOR FROM 105 TO 29. REDUCTION OF LEAD TIME TO 60% (LEAD TIME IS 24 HOURS), ASSEMBLY COST TO 1/10, AND RATE OF REJECTION 1/10. INVESTENT 800 MILLION YEN.
RICHO CO.	DEVELOPING MACHINE 4 KINDS	6 AXIS ROBOT 7	MOTORIZED CONVEYOR, UNATTACHED CART AND FORKLIFT ARE USED PARTIALLY	SPRING 1984	INVESTMENT 200 MILLION YEN. PERCENTAGE OF AUTOMATION MORE THAN 30%. PREPARATION OF LARGE AMOUNT OF ASSEMBLY JIGS.

TABLE 3. (cont.)

AWAZU PLANT OF KOMATSU LTD.	PARTS OF CONSTRUCTION MACHINERY, MAINLY ARM AND FRAME ETC. ABOUT 30 KINDS	ARC WELDING ROBOT 7 (RECTANDULAR TYPE), VERSATILE STOCKER 10, COMPLEX NC MACHINE 1.	GUIDED UNATTACHED CART 3	MARCH 1984	FLEXIBLE WELDING SYSTEM. PRELIMINARY AND FINISH WELDING ARE DONE ON MANUAL STATIONS. (ABOUT 20)
KAJI PLANT OF MITSUBISHI ELECTRIC CO.	ELECTROMAGNETIC SWITCH, 7 KINDS NUMBER OF PARTS ABOUT 30	ASSEMBLY ROBOT 4, (4 AXIS) AUTOMATIC PRODUCT INSPECTION MACHINE 1	FREE FLOW CONVEYOR	OCTOBER 1983	AUTOMATIC HAND CHANGER, TACT TIME 1 MIN 30 SEC TO 2 MIN 30 SEC. REDUCTION OF OPERATORS FROM 7 TO 3. LINKED TO PRODUCTION CONTROL COMPUTER.
OZAKI PLANT OF TOYODA MACHINE WORKS CO.	VANE PUMP FOR AUTOMOBILE POWER STEERING 24 KINDS, NUMBER OF PARTS 35	ASSEMBLY ROBOT 15 (5 TYPES), MEASUREMENT, INSPECTION	LINEAR MOTION	APRIL 1983	TACT TIME 45 SEC. REDUCTION OF 20 OPERATORS. AUTOMATIC ASSEMBLY WITH USE OF VISION SENSORS AND PRECISION MEASURING EQUIPMENTS.
	FLOW CONTROL VALVE 6 KINDS	ASSEMBLY CENTER (ASSEMBLY ROBOT 3 BASE FRAME)	ROBOT	APRIL 1983	

Source: K. Iwata, "Recent Developments of Flexible Manufacturing Systems in Japan" (Proceedings of the ICMA Symposium on Flexible Automation in Production Technology, Hanover, East Germany, September 18-19, 1985), pp. 49-60.

Figure 3. Trend in numbers of models and related production systems in Sony Tape recorders

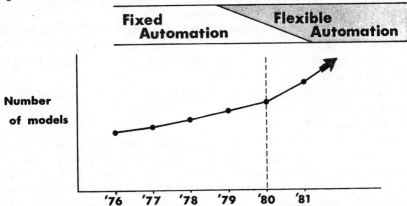

Source: J. Akiyama, "Flexible Assembly Center System—FX-1 System" (Annual Seminar on Robotics and Advanced Assembly Systems, Charles Stark Draper Laboratory, Cambridge, Massachusetts, November 1981).

Figure 4. Assembly process elements

Assembly of the Tape recorder mechanism can be grouped into six elements as shown.

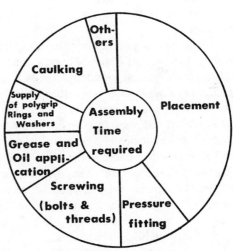

Source: J. Akiyama, "Flexible Assembly Center System—FX-1 System" (Annual Seminar on Robotics and Advanced Assembly Systems, Charles Stark Draper Laboratory, Cambridge, Massachusetts, November 1981).

The Taniguchi paper also describes a Versatility Indicator for evaluating the degree of flexibility of assembly systems prepared by Professor Makino, who is also the designer of the world famous SCARA robot.

Although Sony and Hitachi products are similar, initially the companies chose different system architectures. The Hitachi choice is a highly distributed system composed of robots, fixed automation stations, and people. The Sony system was composed of modules and people. Both systems have highly integrated flexible parts supply and product handling systems. But as noted earlier, Sony now appears to be moving away from the highly integrated module approach.

The earlier fixed automation systems had positioning accuracies of the order of 0.1 mm. The newer systems are capable of positioning accuracies of 0.01 mm (6). (Most assembly systems use an open-loop control strategy and depend on this positioning accuracy and good piece parts to achieve high yields. High-speed, closed-loop vision systems have been implemented for automatic wire bonding machines for I.C.s (5). The extension of these techniques to continuous flow systems is being done by Seiko with its HIKS with cycle times of approximately 1.2 sec(11). To achieve near continuous flow, Seiko has designed an assembly system with an uptime of 99 percent for each ten process steps. The associated reliability of the part feeding units is 99.9 percent. A line can be switched from one product to another in ten minutes. To achieve this Seiko has designed totally new part feeding mechanisms. Small parts are captured in plastic strips that are reeled. Larger parts are captured on "short-braid" strips with about twenty-four pieces on a strip. But, the quality of the piece parts still defeats the 99.9 percent goal.

Each company pursues a different system strategy depending on their product and market place. Nippondenso has three basic strategies. For high-volume lines Nippondenso tends to use continuous flow lines (cycle times approximately 1.0 sec.) integrated to extensively redesigned products. The classic one is the instrument gauge for automobile dashboards (5, 10). With product redesign, four or five components can be assembled into one hundred different product types on a line with a cycle time of one sec that can be switched in one complete machine cycle by a dummy base unit cycling through the system. The line is capable of two hundred model changes per day. Similar work has been done for relays used in automobiles.

For lower volume lines, Nippondenso has developed a family of robots. These robots are used to assemble such things as automobile instrument clusters, air-conditioner modules, etc. For small batch manufacturing like radiator cores, Nippondenso uses adjustable dedicated systems interconnected with flexible parts handling systems.

One of the unique aspects of these activities is that new production technology is developed. For example, Sony, after five years of developing and

Figure 5. Requirements and Measures for flexible automation

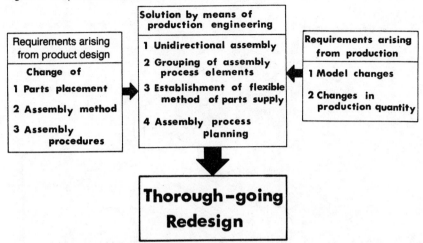

Requirements arising from product design	Solution by means of production engineering	Requirements arising from production
Change of	1 Unidirectional assembly	
1 Parts placement	2 Grouping of assembly process elements	1 Model changes
2 Assembly method	3 Establishment of flexible method of parts supply	2 Changes in production quantity
3 Assembly procedures	4 Assembly process planning	

Thorough-going Redesign

Source: J. Akiyama, Flexible Assembly Center System—FX-1 System" (Annual Seminar on Robotics and Advanced Assembly Systems, Charles Stark Draper Laboratory, Cambridge, Massachusetts, November 1981).

Figure 6. Unidirectional Assembly

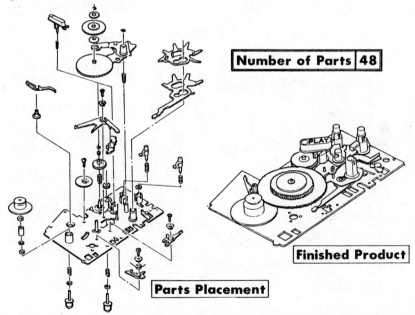

Number of Parts 48

Finished Product

Parts Placement

Source: J. Akiyama, "Flexible Assembly Center System—FX-1 System" (Annual Seminar on Robotics and Advanced Assembly Systems, Charles Stark Draper Laboratory, Cambridge, Massachusetts, November 1981).

Figure 7. Assembly Center

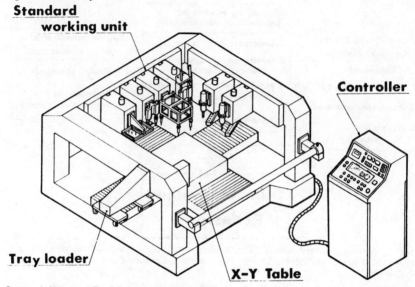

Source: J. Akiyama, "Flexible Assembly Center System—FX-1 System" (Annual Seminar on Robotics and Advanced Assembly Systems, Charles Stark Draper Laboratory, Cambridge, Massachusetts, November 1981).

Figure 8. FX-1 System Layout

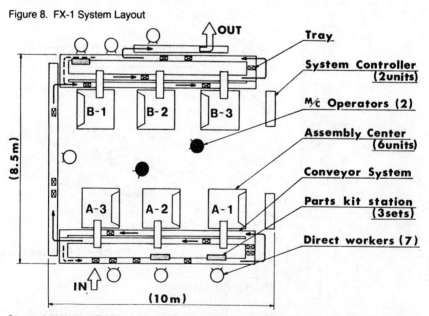

Source: J. Akiyama, "Flexible Assembly Center System—FX-1 System" (Annual Seminar on Robotics and Advanced Assembly Systems, Charles Stark Draper Laboratory, Cambridge, Massachusetts, November 1981).

testing its new systems, offered them for sale late fall 1984. A similar pattern has been followed by Hitachi, Fujitsu-Fanuc, and others. It is part of the reason why so many Japanese robots are licensed in the United States instead of being developed by U.S. industry.

Future Systems

Much research is being done on intelligent systems in Japan. With their experience in integrating product design, manufacturing process, and system design, the Japanese are in a good position to capitalize on these advanced systems. Further, the proven ability of the Japanese for rapid development and implementation of advanced product technology will make them a strong competitor for advanced production technology and systems. Figure 9 summarizes these assessments.

Sensors

Vision Systems — Inspection and Computer Vision

Japanese firms lead in in-house vision applications and have serious development efforts. These firms threaten to dominate vision applications, although U.S. firms hold their own now in several major areas.

R&D in VLSI devices for vision is especially important. Japanese firms lead in VLSI for vision; they have stronger development efforts leading to low cost, high performance vision devices. VLSI devices will have a major impact on vision applications.

Company research centers, not government labs and universities, are developing applications and VLSI in Japan. U.S. labs lead in areas of fundamental vision research, models of biological vision, optical flow, and stereo. The United States has a slight lead in vision systems. In the United States, research is conducted primarily in university laboratories.

Background. Sensory processing is difficult, computationally demanding, intimately involved in intelligent behavior, and requires the deployment of domain-specific models to be practicable. Hence, much of the development of sensing is involved with intelligent machines.

At present, there is enormous activity in vision ranging from chip through innovative algorithm development for three-dimensional vision. Overall, the Japanese are slightly ahead in product development, but they lag in research. Device development includes fast convolution hardware, such as Hitachi's Sobel chip, and entire image processing stations such as Toshiba's TOSPIX 2. These devices are used to reduce to real time well-understood processes that previously took minutes in microcode. Experimental systems based on these devices include motion (U. Osaka), stereo (U. Osaka,

Figure 9. Summary of Relative Japanese/U.S. Status in Assembly System

	Basic Research	Advanced Development	Product Implementation
Deterministic Geometrically Driven Processes	0	>	>
Intelligent Systems	-	-	-
System Architectures	0	>	>
Software Architectures	-	0	0
Smart End Effectors	0	0	0

Source: JTECH Mechatronics Panel, *Final Report* (La Jolla, Calif.: Science Applications International, March 1985).

Toshiba), and photometric stereo (ETL). ETL has emphasized research on matching computed three-dimensional representation (surface patch models and extended Gaussian images) to stored object models (CAD models). In a similar vein, domain-specific knowledge has been used by Hitachi, Fujitsu, and University of Kyoto to guide segmentation of multi-spectral (typically landsat) images.

The Japanese began major development effort in vision for applications early on. Hitachi first reported on PC board inspection in 1973 and on transistor lead bonding in 1974.

Initial applications used simple binary vision. Initially, Japanese firms developed dedicated hardware for applications of binary image processing. Applications have become increasingly sophisticated. To support sophisticated vision with increasing computation power, Japanese firms have invested heavily in development of special purpose hardware for computer vision. Now they are developing VLSI architecture for gray scale vision.

The major efforts in applications and dedicated vision hardware have been in private companies. Hitachi Production Engineering Research Lab, Hitachi Central Research Lab, NEC, Toshiba, Fujitsu, Mitsubishi Research Lab, and Komatsu have been leaders.

The Japanese have had a lead in commercial image sensors as a result of their dominant position in consumer electronics, especially TV. Sony, Hitachi, and Panasonic (Matsushita) have all marketed low-cost, solid-state cameras. Their work in applications was backed up by research in sophisticated vision. In 1971, Hitachi demonstrated an impressive system that duplicated an assembly from drawings.

Considerable impetus was given to vision development in Japanese companies by the Pattern Information Processing System (PIPS) Project. PIPS provided broad industry participation, which aided in bringing about image technology transfer into companies.

Applications. Vision applications provide a contrast between the Japanese electronics giants with their large in-house efforts and the mostly small, start-up U.S. companies with their fragile backing. The applications targets have similarities in mask and reticle inspection in semiconductor manufacturing, IC lead bonding, PC board inspection, and automotive inspection.

Another contrast is between commercial firms with goals to develop products for high-volume, low-cost applications versus military, low-volume, high-cost applications. Commercial and government support of computer vision R&D in Japan has had commercial applications goals. Much computer vision research in the United States has had military support for future applications in mapping, photointerpretation, surveillance, and weapons. Funding for civilian research in the United States has been inadequate.

Japanese participants in vision applications are the electronics giants— Hitachi, Mitsubishi, NEC, NTT, Toshiba, and Fujitsu. In the United States, giant companies have played some role, but a lesser one. GM developed a handful of applications and has a credible research laboratory but has had trouble transitioning systems from research to production. GE has had a substantial research effort, a few applications, and some commercial efforts. IBM has had little research in vision and presumably had traditional applications in lead bonding and mask inspection. TI had some applications in computer vision. Westinghouse, Honeywell, CDC, and Hughes have participated in research and development of military projects like the Auto-Q system for film imagery.

One of the major applications for vision has been in lead bonding. Hitachi developed a system for automated lead bonding of transistor chips in 1974 and automated lead bonding for integrated circuits a few years after. GM, TI, and IBM developed systems at about the same time. A small vendor, View Engineering, developed a visual control for lead bonding which has been successful.

A second area of applications is inspection of masks and reticles for IC manufacturing. Masks are crucially important in IC production because faults in masks are replicated in the product. Binary vision is adequate because masks are inspected in transmission. Inspecting masks is low volume as opposed to inspecting products; hence, computation requirements are not extreme. In the United States, KLA is dominant. In Japan, NJS and Seiko are competitors, while major electronics companies (Hitachi and NEC) have in-house programs. Automated mask inspection is used in only about 50 percent of production, even though this is a standard and cost-effective process.

PC board inspection, both bare and populated boards, has received considerable attention in Japan and the United States. In Japan, Hitachi, Fujitsu, and Toshiba have conducted extensive development efforts in this area. The first system reported was in 1973 at Hitachi; the system was based on a design rule method and was said to have been used in production. By 1981, it was not used in production. Hitachi had developed another system which was used in production. It is difficult to get information about which systems are used in production, how many, and what their performance is. Hitachi reports that it uses inspection systems in production, although it is reticent about saying anything further. In the United States, about five vendor companies have developed systems in the recent past. This is an area of rapid development, especially in inspection systems for loaded boards. Because there are many forms of defects on PC boards, no system appears capable of doing the total inspection job for bare boards. Because inspection of PC boards is inspection of product, computation requirements are much higher than for mask inspection. Because defects on automatically loaded boards are infrequent, reliability requirements for inspection are high.

Inspection of solder joints has attracted some attention. An infrared method was developed by Vanzetti. Hitachi Production Engineering Research Laboratory (PERL) has developed a production system for solder joint inspection. This laboratory sent samples to Vanzetti to test its infrared method and found it inadequate. Based on a personal visit to PERL and a brief discussion of the system, it appears capable only of crude analysis of solder joints by a plane of light 3D method. The system does not seem adequate to determine cold solder joints. A member of PERL stated that cold solder joints are not a problem in wave soldering if the system is operating right; if there are any cold solder joints there are many. The JTECH panel's conclusion is that the solder joint inspection system does only part of the job. The defect rate for solder joints is low, and it is not clear how many defects can be distinguished visually. Solder joint inspection is difficult.

Wafer inspection systems have been developed at Hitachi PERL and at other firms. This is a simple visual problem.

Inspection of diode pellets was demonstrated long ago at Hitachi PERL. Inspection of pellets for drugs has been a real application. Mitsubishi reported commercial classification of fish and fruit using vision. There has been some effort on inspection of hybrid circuits and in-process inspection of products which has proven to be very difficult and not yet within reach.

Industrial OCR is another substantial inspection application. Cognex and GE specialize in reading markings on products, reading characters in instruments, LEDs, and LCDs. There are in-house efforts at major firms. Some applications now under investigation are handling packages and inspecting currency. Japanese firms are concerned with reading addresses, a special problem because of the Kanji characters. A variety of companies have worked on visual input of drawings, with some success. Different domains have different drawing conventions and require development of separate systems. Design automation for electronics has been a special project at Fujitsu. This work has been combined with expert systems for design automation.

Inspecting arc welds is a large market being sought by many Japanese firms. These firms use mechanical tracing of parts, eddy current techniques, and vision. Komatsu uses sophisticated through-the-arc vision and looking at the arc puddle. Arc welding is one of the major vision applications.

Komatsu, a major manufacturer of automated vehicle systems for warehousing, is concerned with visually guided vehicles which could adapt to changing warehouse configurations and navigating around obstacles. Komatsu's current vehicles follow wires in the floor.

Mitsubishi considers visual control important for assembly, particularly in electronics. Vision is regarded as even more important for assembly of mechanical parts.

Project Jupiter, the Japanese effort to develop robots for dangerous work, includes research in vision.

Image sensors have been developed by Sony, Hitachi, and Panasonic (Matsushita). These firms have major consumer product efforts, have developed solid state cameras for the VCR market, and have reportedly introduced them at artificially low prices based on a projected increase in volume. Prices are about $1,000 for 380 × 480 arrays. The U.S. firms which make image sensors include Fairchild and RCA, which market products, and

TI, which has built special systems. These three U.S. firms have had some military sales but do not seem cost competitive, although their camera specs are similar. Much of the competition in the United States is for the general vision module consisting of frame grabber, frame buffer, arithmetic logic unit display, and general microcomputer.

Nonvision Sensor Systems

The Japanese sensor industry is active, with more than three hundred firms supplying specialized sensors of nearly every type. Apart from this activity most of the larger robot manufacturers have their own sensor development groups producing devices specifically tailored to robotic application. The Japanese practice is to divide such sensors into internal and external devices. The former includes all angular and linear encoders that relate to the robot configuration as well as internal temperature sensors to correct for arm thermal expansion effects. All sensors that allow the robot to interact with its task are regarded as external sensors. (Only a small subset of sensor topics, primarily those that relate directly to robotics, will be considered in the following discussion.)

Position and Angle. As is the case with the majority of the robots made today, most Japanese units have incremental optical encoders associated with each drive motor. The motors drive the various degrees of freedom through suitable reduction gearing, often of the harmonic type. Knowledge of the motor revolution, the gearing details, and the arm geometry allows calculation of the end effector position.

A variant of this scheme has been the recent development of small, high-precision, cartesian assembly robots by Panasonic and others. These also employ incremental optical encoders, but they are used in conjunction with high-precision, preloaded, helical ball screws to provide accurate cartesian motion at amazingly low cost — for example, $10,000 for an actuator with 25u accuracy.

Force, Torque and Pressure Sensors. Force and torque sensing, usually implemented by means of silicon strain gauges at the robot wrist, have been demonstrated to be useful information-gathering techniques. Most of this work has been reported in research endeavors, although some U.S. manufacturers, notably IBM, have already incorporated such a capability into production robots. This technique is beginning to be used commercially in Japan. For example, both Kobe Steel and Kawasaki have deburring robots where force feedback information is employed. Fujitsu has developed a precise active-compliance device for precision assembly. But, they found that a SCARA configuration was more economic.

Modest and readily implementable extensions of such schemes can lead to useful capabilities. One example is the simultaneous measurement of both the torque and the normal force exerted by a drilling robot, which provides information on the sharpness of the drill bit. It can be expected that similar techniques will be undertaken by the Japanese in the near future.

A related area is the problem of pressure sensing. Here a highly developed technique is that of using diffused silicon strain gauges integrally fabricated on a thin silicon pressure-deformable diaphragm. Techniques of this kind are well advanced in Japan and fit naturally into programs for "smart sensors" in which both the sensing and information processing are implemented on the same semiconductor chip. Similar work is carried out by U.S. corporations such as Honeywell.

Tactile Imagers. Much has already been written regarding the potential of touch sensors (or "tactile imagers") in robot assembly. Opinion is divided as to how such sensors should best be made. European and most U.S. work has so far favored various resistive sheet schemes in which the local electrical resistance of a suitable sheet of material is modified by the applied pressure pattern. Some believe that a multiplexed capacitor approach is more favorable. Significant work of this latter type has been reported in both the United States and Germany, although the basic idea was apparently first disclosed in a 1979 Japanese patent application.

A number of other schemes have been suggested, although very few have actually been demonstrated. These include piezoelectric effect arrays (which have the disadvantage of lacking a DC response) and arrays of small magnets flexibly mounted above corresponding arrays of multiple permalloy magneto-resistive readout elements. The latter scheme holds the potential of providing both shear and torque information, along with the normal force, but is complex and suffers from the fact that the magnetoresistive effect is very small (only 2 percent total resistance change for a ninety degree rotation of the applied magnetic field). Various optical fiber schemes have also had an airing both in the United States and Japan.

A topic that resurfaces regularly is that of microscopic tactile imagers. Many tactile imaging schemes can in principle be married to some form of silicon VLSI to form a tiny tactile imaging device. Several attempts have already been made (it is neither easy nor inexpensive), but none so far has succeeded. The problem is due in part to economic scale. Silicon microcircuit elements are only inexpensive if fabricated in very large numbers. The need for significant numbers of robots with tiny tactile imagers is not yet apparent. Until such a need is demonstrated, it is doubtful that there will be much Japanese work in this area.

The only tactile imager currently commercially available in the United States is manufactured by the Lord Corporation. The imager uses an array of small, spring-loaded mechanical vanes which interrupt the light beam between an LED and a photodiode at each location of interest. This scheme has the advantage of completely separating the mechanical and electrical features of the system, but the scheme does so at the expense of a complicated sensing arrangement with a large number of separate components.

Most of the preceding approaches have been proposed or developed in the United States. The Japanese have concentrated on simple single degree of freedom torque or force information sensors and have actually implemented them in production lines. Honda, for example, uses robots with simple one-dimensional tactile sensors in automobile windshield insertion. The Japanese will probably hold off from significant high-resolution tactile imager work until there is a demonstration of the utility of such devices.

Speech Sensors. Machine recognition of speech is an important area that is being actively pursued around the world, particularly in Japan. The development of practical speech recognition devices would have a significant impact on robotics and mechatronics. However, speech recognition can be viewed as an add-on technology and will not be discussed here. As NTT and other Japanese leaders develop this technology, it will become increasingly important in mechatronic applications.

Sensors for Navigation. Autonomously guided vehicles, or "smart carts," are becoming important for material transport in factory and warehouse environments. Sometime in the future, these vehicles may also become widely used in semiconductor VLSI clean room facilities. At present, all of the commercially available carts are simple cable (or, alternatively, paint-stripe) following devices. They have no autonomous navigational capability. A significant area of endeavor is to make these carts free ranging, and that requires a navigational sensing capability.

Among a variety of possibilities, one of the most attractive is the use of inertial guidance techniques in conjunction with odometry (integrating off-the-wheel rations). The key element here is a low-cost, low-drift gyroscope. Superb ring laser gyros have been developed in the United States for military programs. Unfortunately, these gyros are far too expensive for factory applications.

Honda has produced a low-cost, gas jet inertial guidance system for automobile navigation called a "gyrocator." This type of technology is tailor-made for smart factory applications. A number of Japanese organizations are now working on the factory cart navigation problem using both laser beam guidance and vibrating beam piezo-vibrator pump (PZT) inertial guidance systems, among other approaches.

Ultrasonics. The biggest area for ultrasonics at the present time is in medical imaging. A conceptually similar area is that of ultrasonic imaging of defects in nuclear reactor pressure vessels and monitoring weld integrity. Mobile robots provide a convenient way to make such measurements on large structures. It may turn out that ultrasonics will play a significant role in local ranging and imaging in assembly and other robotic applications.

Mitsubishi, among others, has significant activity in the ultrasonic sensor and imaging areas.

Other Sensors (The Jupiter Project). Virtually any type of sensor can be used in conjunction with a robotic system. The MITI-organized program on robots for hazardous environments is a good example. Here one can expect that robots for radiation environments will employ scintillation counters, ion chambers, p-n junction radiation detectors, and so forth, all adapted to the specific robotic use. Fire-fighting robots will need smoke detectors, thermometers, optical pyrometers, and chemical vapor sensors. Robots for hazardous environments will also make extensive use of remote video and other links to human guidance.

The last point raises the question of autonomy versus teleoperation for such mobile robots. Although teleoperation is clearly advantageous, there are a number of situations where autonomous operation is mandatory. The work by the Jet Propulsion Laboratory on the Pioneer spacecraft is an example. Other areas where autonomy may also be crucial could involve situations such as traversing a hazardous path where an umbilical cord was impossible while metallic shielding precluded radio communications.

Americans can expect rapid Japanese progress in this area. Successful Japanese developments of this type will have an impact far beyond the obvious technical or financial contributions. Consider, for example, the national pride and international impact when the first human beings are rescued by a Japanese robot.

Sensor Information Processing. The question of how best to handle and use the information from robot sensors is a central issue. Languages such as VAL II and IBM's AML have sensor input capability. Advanced Japanese software systems, such as those provided for the Mitsubishi MELFA series of robots, are also being considered.

The whole area of intelligent industrial robots centers on closed-loop feedback control of the mechanical actuators. How the robot observes its world and how it makes decisions based on these observations are basic questions. This issue is sharply defined in the area of robot control through machine vision and makes contact with many areas of artificial intelligence. Basic U.S. research in these areas is substantially ahead of the Japanese and is likely to remain so for some time (see Figure 10).

Intelligent Modules/Autonomous Machines

"Intelligence" as applied to mechanisms means different things to different people. A simple interpretation of intelligence refers to the replacement of a fixed controller by a program that incorporates logical branching. As microprocessors become smaller, cheaper, and use less power, and as

Figure 10. Summary of Relative Japanese/U.S. Positions in Sensors

	Basic Research	Advanced Development	Product Implementation
Position/Angle Encoders	0 →	0 →	0 →
Force/Torque/ Pressure Sensors	0 →	0 →	+ ↗
Tactile Imagers	- →	- →	- →
Proximity/Range Detectors	0 →	0 →	0 →
Smoke/Chemical/ Radiation	0 →	0 →	0 →
Navigation Sensors (low cost)	0 →	+ ↗	+ ↗
Sensor Information Processing	< →	- →	0 ↗

Source: JTECH Mechatronics Panel, *Final Report* (La Jolla, Calif.: Science Applications International, March 1985).

they increase in speed and complexity to the level of Motorola's 68000 range of 32 bit to 10 MHz machines, so more and more functionality is assumed by a controlling computer. Disk drives and other computer peripheral equipment are now dubbed "intelligent" according to this interpretation. The incorporation of powerful controlling microprocessors into mechatronics has been a logical step. Progress is rapid both in the United States and in Japan with no discernible leader.

Microprocessor control allows better modeling of external events and "disturbances," built-in test and diagnostic capabilities, information pooling (as in the popular FOF proposal), and sensory processing. Microprocessor control represents a step along the continuum that stretches from adaptive control, through microprocessor control, to artificial intelligence.

Mechatronics spans the union of mechanical and electrical engineering and emphasizes a multidisciplinary integrated approach to product and manufacturing system design. There is considerable activity in Japan aimed at the development of increasingly intelligent machines, but only a fraction of that activity is specifically aimed at mechatronics. Best known among the other projects are

The Fifth Generation Project that hopes to propel Japan into world leadership in computing
- The Jupiter Project that aims at flexible, sensor-based, robot control with emphasis on hazardous environments
- The Language Translation Project that aims at usable machine translation between Japanese and English with automatic relational data base entry

The Fifth Generation Project marks a major commitment to software by the Japanese, who have traditionally been regarded as strong in hardware development but weak in software. Significantly, the Fifth Generation Project represents a major leap forward in software practice in Japan. Traditionally, software has been written in assembler or in Fortran. The languages chosen for the Fifth Generation Project are LISP and PROLOG. This commitment to advanced software systems represents two important commitments by the Japanese:

- AI is viable. The Japanese have reached this consensus and have begun development.
- AI is the basis of future software systems. An early example of this trend can be seen in "intelligent" aids for VLSI design.

The Fifth Generation project can already take credit for the following:

- It has been a learning exercise for industry. There is now a much keener awareness of what AI can achieve.
- The project has enabled large numbers of AI programmers from industry to be trained. U.S. companies have tried to promote AI efforts by hiring programmers straight from college. These programmers have little understanding of the disciplines and requirements of industrial programming. U.S. companies have also hired programmers from other companies without adding to the total pool of talent. The PIPS Project of the 1970s was considered to be a scientific failure in the United States; but it achieved the goal of placing thousands of well-trained image-processing personnel in industry. Many were trained in U.S. universities.

The applications of "intelligent mechanisms" in mechatronics include

- Hazardous environments. Through the Jupiter project and other efforts, Japan is pulling away from the United States.
- Warehousing. There is no strong effort in this area in Japan. The United States and Japan appear approximately equal.
- Intelligent design aids. Japan started from a position behind the United States. However, the growing concentration on advanced software and the strong base of expertise provided by the PIPS project are enabling the Japanese to pull away. Examples include VLSI design systems, systems that can produce finished machine drawings of circuits and other linear data from hand-drawn sketches, and interactive CAD systems for building and plant layout.
- Natural language interfaces. Japan is starting from behind the United States. There is no equivalent of ATN-based products such as LIFER. However, through national direction that combines the power of universities such as Nagao's group in Kyoto with companies such as Toshiba, the Japanese appear to be pulling away. They are concentrating initially on translating abstracts of technical papers.
- Robot programming. The Japanese have only recently produced programming languages such as IBM's AML, Automatix's RAIL, and Unimations's VAL n. The Japanese have never developed an analogue of Stanford University's AL. Recently, AL has been adopted as a standard in Japan to run on VAX-like computers. A key to higher level languages building on AL is spatial reasoning and compliance. The Japanese have organized several workshops on these issues. Nevertheless, it is safe to rate Japan as being behind and staying behind.
- Speech input. The Japanese have assumed a position of leadership in speech input. They seem to be pulling away. Chips and recognition systems can now be purchased at modest prices from several Japanese corporations.
- Dynamic scheduling. The situation in Japan appears to be on a par with that in the United States and is staying that way.

Figure 11 summarizes these assessments.

Software for Mechatronics

Japanese efforts in mechatronics have been concentrated almost entirely on hardware. Software had historically received low priority, but there are signs that this is changing(1,3). For example, the highly publicized project, Flexible Manufacturing System Complex Provided With Laser, made virtually no effort to coordinate or manage the development of software. In fact, it has been reported that the Ministry of Finance was upset about the

Figure 11. Applications of Intelligent Machines in Mechatronics in Japan Relative to the United States

Application	Status / Change
Hazardous Environment	0 ↗
Warehousing	0 →
Intelligent Design Aids	- ↗
Natural Language Interface	< ↗
Robot Programming	- →
Speech Input	+ ↗
Dynamic Scheduling	0 →

Source: JTECH Mechatronics Panel, *Final Report* (La Jolla, Calif.: Science Applications International, March 1985).

amount of money spent on software development in previous projects; and as a result, this FMS project was not even allowed to include software in its budget. What happened was that each company on the project was responsible for developing its own software and simply "padded" its hardware budget to cover some software costs. Thus, the FMS with Laser project developed as little software as possible, and that was mostly assembly language code. The system had no geometric models for producing NC tapes. NC programs were written manually and at a very low level. Little programming was done in APT. The strategy was to build flexible hardware first and worry about the software later. This is perhaps an extreme case, but for it to happen at all on a project as large and prestigious as FMS with Laser indicated the historical attitude toward software.

There are many software development systems currently in use for automation systems throughout Japanese industry. But, for the most part, these are not considered advanced systems by U.S. standards. For example, Toyoda Machine Works, Japan's second largest machine tool company, uses geometric modeling for NC program development for turned parts only. The company plans to extend this capability to milled parts in the future. Currently Toyoda uses an automated scheduling system similar to the IBM CAPOSS system.

A more advanced system is the FMS system at the Yamazaki Machinery Work, which uses the MAZATROL tool software system for turned parts. The software development environment here allows an operator to input the geometry of the part, put up a graphics display of the part, and prompts him or her with various menus for relevant information. The display then simulates the cutting sequence, shows the cutter pathways, and outputs the program to a milling tool to make the part. There is also a new MAZATROL system for milling which was in use earlier than the comparable General Electric GE2000 system. Yamazaki also uses the CAD/CAM system on an IBM 4341 computer.

The most impressive Japanese software development project that has come to the attention of the JTECH panel is the Software WorkBench (SWB) factory of Toshiba Fuchu(1). The SWB factory consists of about two thousand programmers sitting at individual workstations in a large one-room building. The factory specializes in process-control software for systems used in steel mills, nuclear power plants, and flight guidance. The development of software in this factory environment, using rigid software engineering principles for a narrow problem domain, has produced some remarkable results. It is claimed that the output is much higher than the output for similar code in the United States. In addition, the SWB factory achieves a reuse rate of about 65 percent, which means that for every one thousand lines of code delivered, six hundred fifty lines are lifted from previously written programs. This is unheard of in the United States. Finally, the code is of extremely high quality. The unsubstantiated claim is that the Toshiba code comes with a ten-year warranty. Any bug discovered within ten years will be fixed at no charge to the customer.

Universities

Some of the most advanced work is being done in the universities. For example, the GEOMAP CAD modeling system developed at Tokyo University has the ability to automatically generate NC data from models for hole cutting, face milling, and contour milling. The system also generates robot programs in VAL. GEOMAP contains about two hundred thousand lines of FORTRAN code. The system's geometric modeling part is similar to the

PADL2 system developed at the University of Rochester. GEOMAP has been supported by about thirty companies, but, so far, it remains a university research project. There is no indication that GEOMAP has been used in industrial production.

There are fifteen public universities with computer science departments in Japan, each of which has approximately fifty students. The private universities admit several hundred computer science students per year. This is a small number by U.S. standards.

Fifth Generation Project

The Japanese efforts in software development may be considerably advanced by the recently initiated Intelligent Robotics project as well as by the highly touted Fifth Generation Computer Project. On the Fifth Generation Project, however, it appears that software is not the primary emphasis. The effort so far has been in developing the hardware for an artificial intelligence workstation that can perform logical inferences at one hundred to one thousand times as fast as presently possible. Much emphasis is being placed on a natural language interface.

PROLOG has been chosen as the language for this project. Many U.S. computer scientists feel that a more logical choice would have been LISP. It has been suggested that one of the primary reasons for using PROLOG was that it would distinguish the Fifth Generation Project from U.S. artificial intelligence research, which is virtually all done in LISP. The JTECH panelists generally thought, however, that PROLOG was an unfortunate choice because of the relative scarcity of software written in PROLOG, the fact that few computer scientists are trained in PROLOG, and the relative scarcity of documentation and textbooks on PROLOG.

In any case, there probably will be little or no impact of the Fifth Generation Project on mechatronics because there is no indication that robotics or automated manufacturing software is high on the list of candidates for Fifth Generation Project application software. However, there is some indication that the Japanese are planning to use ADA extensively for applications in mechatronics. This is because they believe that most computers in the future will have an implementation of ADA. However, this remains to be seen because production-quality ADA compilers are not yet ready. In any case, such plans do not indicate any lead on the part of the Japanese over the Americans.

Next Generation Application Software Project

This project is focused on development of production software for the whole process of manufacturing including assembly, CAD/CAM, and control. The project has already begun with a two-year survey which was scheduled to be completed by the end of March 1985 when a proposal for a national software project will be developed. There is no indication of what the magnitude of the new project will be. The study is being chaired by Professor Yoshikawa of Tokyo University and is under the direction of the Agency for Industrial Science and Technology, which is one of the branches of MITI.

Robot Planner and Off-Line Programming

The Japanese are active in the Computer-Aided Manufacturing—International (CAM-I) Robot Planner Project. CAM-I's proposed work statement for a contract to develop the robot planner was written by Dr. Norio Okino of Hokkaido University. This robot planner will be an off-line programming system that will define robot motions for multiple robots and environments. It will include the possibility of moving objects. The planner will have a simulator and interactive graphics system to facilitate the human-machine interface and provide for program verification. The planner will be independent of any specific robot, producing output similar to cutter location (CL) data, which can be postprocessed into specific robot instructions. The planner also will be computer independent, written in FORTRAN or C under a Unix operating system. This system will attempt to have a convenient interface to CAD data so that robot programs can be generated automatically (for certain specific tasks such as arc welding or spot welding) from the dimensional data in the CAD data base. For example, the path of an arc welding robot can be determined from the intersection of two planar parts with the angle of the welding rod defined from the normal vectors of the two surfaces. The system will also provide for intelligent responses to sensor inputs and will have convenient interfacing to FMS systems.

The CAM-I effort is relatively small, less than $1 million, which translates into something around 10 human/years of programming effort. This is probably too little to produce a very large advance in the state of the art, but it is quite possible that the companies bidding on this project will put their own money into the effort. The development of such a system could have great commercial value, and the company which does the work will have a distinct competitive advantage despite the fact that the results of this work will be shared by all of the participants in the Robot Planner Project. There are many U.S. firms represented in CAM-1, so this effort is far from being an exclusive Japanese project. However, the contractor selected to produce the software will probably be a Japanese firm.

Japanese Research Compared to U.S. Research

The Japanese are three to five years behind the leading edge of software for robots compared with the most advanced work in the United States. The robot programming goals of CAM-I are somewhat advanced over U.S systems, which are already in operation in the U.S. Air Force-sponsored machine control logic (MCL) system or its derivatives of McDonnell-Douglas, Grumman, and GCA. But MCL systems have been in existence for more than two years, and the CAM-I project has begun and is now located in Arlington, Texas. The Japanese have nothing on the market comparable to the Westinghouse VAL-II system, the IBM AML language, the Grumman MCL System, the McDonnell-Douglas Computer-Vision, or General Electric CALMA robot programming system. Japanese published research does not reveal work equivalent to the experimental robot programming environments being developed at the National Bureau of Standards, Purdue, MIT, Stanford University, Carnegie-Mellon, and elsewhere. The Japanese are aware of these more advanced systems, they understand the basic principles involved, and they intend to pursue these issues vigorously. Most of the technical leaders in Japanese software research laboratories have been educated at the best institutions, such as Edinburgh, MIT, Stanford, and Carnegie-Mellon.

The Japanese are less behind in CAD and machine tool programming systems. The General Electric CALMA system, Computer-Vision, Evans and Southerland, Autotrol, CADDAM, Catia, and a host of other systems developed and marketed in the United States are more advanced than competing Japanese products. There are, however, several areas where Japanese systems seem to have some competitive advantage. MAZATROL machine tool controllers have interactive operator interfaces with graphics displays that compare favorably with products available in the United States. Also, the Tokyo University GEOMAP work is equivalent to, or better than, comparable efforts in the United States.

Although the United States appears to have a significant lead in most areas of software development for mechatronics, particularly in high-level languages and systems software development, Japan is achieving some remarkable results in the implementation of software engineering for specific applications. In the case of the Toshiba Software Workbench Factory, the Japanese have not only closed the gap but are far ahead. The SWB factory is a uniquely Japanese phenomenon. Although the SWB factory environment would probably not be acceptable to the U.S. worker, the productivity of this installation is far superior to comparable U.S. software houses. The implication is that the U.S. lead in software is substantial but by no means decisive. The software factory concept may enable the Japanese to overcome their relatively poor position in software research and system development.

The relatively small number of computer science graduates in Japan is another factor that will slow the Japanese down, but their use of software factories to produce workable code may enable them to overcome their shortage of formally trained computer scientists. Certainly, the current U.S. lead in software research and development is no reason for complacency. The Japanese have finally recognized the importance of software and are now making great efforts to excel in producing good manufacturing software.

There is every indication from the research literature that the Japanese know how robot and machine tool software should be written. There appears little likelihood that the development of Japanese mechatronics will be retarded for long by a temporary lag in software research.

Precision Mechanisms

Status of Japanese R&D

Precision mechatronics is divided into three areas: high-precision robots, semiconductor device fabrication, and computer peripherals. The word *precision* is used here in keeping with current practice but is not particularly well-defined. Better terms are *accuracy* (for absolute error), *resolution* (for fractional error) and *repeatability* (for absolute error in relocation). Precision is sometimes used interchangeably for any of the preceding terms, but most frequently refers to accuracy.

The development of precise, intelligent, mechanical-electronic systems lies at the core of many emerging technologies. Accurate mechanical motion is at the $\sim 1u$ level or better, as evidenced by optical storage discs and VLSI camera autoregistration systems, while fundamental physical research is at the $\sim 1A$ level. The trend toward higher electromechanical precision, together with its electronic control, will be a continuing and increasingly important theme.

High-Precision Robots

High-precision robots can be used in demanding assembly tasks. Examples of such tasks are the assembly of magnetic disc drives, optical disc drives, videotape transports, optical communication elements, hybrid semiconductor circuits, and a wide variety of small electromechanical systems. At present, all of the high-precision robots are made in Japan. One example is the remarkable $\sim 5u$ accuracy and $\sim 1u$ repeatability achieved by a preproduction Fujitsu arm. A repeatability of $\sim 5u$ has also been claimed by Seiko for some of its smaller assembly robots. By way of comparison, the most precise U.S. robots currently exhibit an accuracy of ~25u.

The SCARA geometry, a purely Japanese development, is finding increasing use in precise robotic assembly. The invention of this arm was motivated by the practical consideration that in many tasks it is advantageous if the manipulator is very stiff in one direction, the direction of part insertion during assembly, while maintaining acceptable compliance in the two perpendicular directions. This led to the highly cost-effective SCARA design, which is now being actively exploited by virtually all Japanese assembly robot vendors. By contrast, few U.S. vendors currently manufacture SCARA arms, although several sell imported Japanese units.

Early work in precision assembly tasks was exemplified by the development of the Remote Center Compliance (RCC) device at Draper Lab. However, although passive RCC devices are available in the United States, sophisticated industrial work has recently been reported in Japan. For example, Fujitsu has demonstrated an active two-dimensional, compliance-controlled actuator for use in the assembly of magnetic disc drives. This is the same actuator that has been reported in press releases as writing three Japanese characters on a grain of rice.

Comparable two-dimensional actuators were developed at Draper Laboratory as early as 1972 but did not find commercial applications. In 1984, IBM reported a two-dimensional "planar fine positioning" device, conceptually quite similar to Fujitsu's and capable of related applications. The development of small, very precise actuators of this general type most likely will be a growing activity, particularly in connection with the future production of very small assemblies.

Newer work at Draper has achieved systems capable of assembling mechanisms with clearances of the order of 50 millionths of an inch in closed environments of Class 10 cleanliness or better, with size of particulates controlled to 0.3 microns or better(12). Related work on a much larger scale has been reported by the Carnegie-Mellon Robotics Institute. This involved the construction of a computer-controlled RCC device that exhibits software controllable compliance but without the feature of high-speed, two-dimensional feedback. Instrumented, but still completely passive, RCC devices have also been produced by Draper Lab.

The excellent performance of Japanese high-precision robots is not primarily attributable to superior angular (or linear) position encoder performance, but rather to painstaking and original mechanical design and construction. The robots are usually constructed by a group which is closely connected with the needs of the precision application, which has a direct and beneficial bearing on the design process.

The Japanese have been among the leaders in improving electric motor performance through the development of brushless techniques, AC servo motors, coreless motors, and related developments. Improvements have been incremental and cumulatively significant, particularly in the areas of improved reliability and reduced maintenance costs. (Essentially all precision robots are driven by electric motors. Even for large, high-power robots, electric motor drives are making steady inroads on hydraulic systems.)

Permanent magnet motors are particularly attractive in small sizes of the type employed in high-precision mechanisms. Here the most significant advance is the recent development of the neodymium-iron-boron permanent magnet materials. The Japanese have done ground-breaking work in this area, and Sumitomo is the acknowledged world leader with its NEOMAX material. Not only does this provide twice the energy of cobalt-samarium, but it does so at a much lower, (perhaps one third), cost per unit weight. This translates into a factor of six in the critical "flux per buck" figure of merit.

A further point to be made is that the development of better magnets leads to lighter electric motors of the same torque. Improvement in motor performance therefore carries with it a large premium in terms of overall actuator performance.

This is an example of basic and original Japanese materials research leading to a significant technological improvement. The closest U.S. work on magnetics is probably that of the GM Research Lab, although the majority opinion is that Sumitomo holds a significant lead.

There are a number of basic considerations and constraints concerning high-precision robots. One is that for any given robot design the tracking error scales like $L[5]$, where L is the linear dimension of the system. This indicates that small robots should be used for small, precise applications, and several Japanese vendors are supplying small, high-precision robots. (The only miniature robots manufactured in the United States are very low precision units, primarily intended for hobby or instructional purposes.)

A similar result relates to speed. It can be shown that the energy required for a given actuator motion scales like $T[-3]$, where T is the total time of execution. This indicates that significant speed improvements for a given actuator design are costly in terms of energy. This of itself is not important, but the associated temperature rise can be a significant problem. (This is particularly true for NEOMAX, which has a Curie temperature of only 130 degrees.) This again ultimately argues, through thermal and scale-effect considerations, for small, high-precision robots for small, high-precision tasks.

The whole area of actuator design for small, precise motions is an open one that can be expected to become increasingly important, particularly if smaller and smaller elements and systems are to be fabricated. Electromagnetic elements may not be the only basic actuators of interest for such applications. One example is the Japanese work reported on the use of nickel-titanium "Nitinol" shape-memory alloys for robotic actuators. Another is the Hitachi development of very large multipole layer interleaved stacks of piezoelectric elements to provide an entirely electrostatic wide range mechanical drive capability. Such approaches could prove significant for numbers of future precision applications.

Remarkable work on miniature two-dimensional "walking" piezoelectric actuators has also been reported by IBM Zurich. Although this work was actually carried out in connection with fundamental physics research on vacuum tunneling microscopy, the work may find applications in other areas concerned with micromanipulation. (This class of device is related to the well-known PZT inchworm actuators, although carried out in two dimensions.)

Structural stiffness and rigidity are important factors in robots and in high-precision devices. Here the development of high-strength, lightweight composites, such as monofilament carbon reinforced plastics, is an emerging area of great potential. A number of robot manufacturers in the United States and Japan are experimenting with such materials. Mitsubishi, Shinmeiwa, and Hitachi have all reported the construction of complete carbon filament resinous polymer (CFRP) arms. This also is expected to be an area of increasing activity. The user of stiffer, lighter materials raises the lowest mechanical resonant frequency of the arm, while the tracking error scales like the square of reciprocal of that frequency.

Similar remarks can be made with respect to large direct-drive motors for "gearless" robots. These have the potential to produce high-speed, highly accurate robots without the backlash and cyclic nonlinearities exhibited by reduction gears. One U.S. manufacturer, Adept, is already manufacturing such a robot, and a significant U.S. research effort is underway at both CMU and MIT, among other places. In Japan, two such arms have already been reported by ETL Tsukuba, while Mitsubishi, Shinmeiwa, and Yokogawa-hokushin have all developed preproduction direct-drive arms.

Sony FX-I, FX-II, and Phoenix-10 systems cannot be described as general purpose robots. However, they are exceedingly efficient devices and have yielded impressive accuracy ($\sim 15u$) in continuous high-speed production use. The underlying strategy of providing separately controlled precision motions of both the workpiece and the insertion device is applicable to a wide range of small assembly tasks.

Precision Mechanisms for Semiconductor Device Manufacture

Semiconductor devices can be divided into silicon VLSI and all others (III-V, II-VI, modulation band-gap, optoelectronic, etc.). The silicon devices are the dominant items both in terms of numbers and commercial value. Gallium arsenide devices, particularly in modulated band-gap realizations, are exhibiting the highest speed performance in both logic and radio frequency (RF) applications, while a variety of compound and heterojunction semiconductors find widespread use in optoelectronic areas. The basic fabrication steps are similar for all these devices and will be discussed with reference to silicon VLSI because this is the dominant technology.

Semiconductor device fabrication, except for the physical transport of wafers between the various processing stations, is not an area that naturally lends itself to the introduction of general purpose machines. This is because the process depends on the repeated application of a small number of highly specialized basic steps—for example, oxidation, photoresist spin on, lithographic exposure, etching, cleaning, ion implantation, diffusion, etc. In a typical case, device fabrication involves ~ 120 steps achieved by suitably and repetitively cycling through the ~ 10 basic processes.

Semiconductor device fabrication is the most demanding and complex mass produced item made today. The price of entry for a new state-of-the-art silicon VLSI plant is currently in excess of $100 million and rising rapidly as device dimensions continue to shrink. This is an area in which Japan is making a tremendous investment and is bidding to become the dominant VLSI producers.

Among all of the difficult issues involved in this technology, four problem areas stand out: lithography, pattern transfer, inspection, and cleanliness. Mechatronics has significant bearing on three of these four topics.

The Japanese VLSI industry has been successful in spite of the fact that it does not hold a significant technological edge in any of the basic fabrication processes. This success lies in the Japanese superior inspection, cleanliness, and production controls that have resulted in consistently higher yields. These production controls apparently have less to do with machine technology than with the fact that Japanese VLSI plants have dedicated engineers assigned to the factory floor and sometimes to individual machines.

All VLSI photolithographic hardware involves an extensive mechatronic component. Modern projection step-and-repeat printers, for example, employ complex autoregistration and autofocus techniques that provide a fractional-micron mask reregistration capability in each ~ 1 cm^2 field in a time of ~ 1 second. These techniques will be stressed to their limit as feature sizes continue to shrink. The Japanese, with their competence in high-precision engineering (they probably already make the best high-resolution electron microscopes in the world), can be expected to be strong contenders in the photolithographic area. In view of the very high cost of these machines, price/performance will be a decisive factor.

Since my original report was written for the JTECH mechatronics panel in March 1985, great turmoil has taken place in this field(13). Nikon

Precision is now advertising(14) that it will be offering 0.5 micron resolution in its production steppers in 1990 based on a 1986 R&D optics capability of 0.6 micron.

As mentioned at the outset, there is only one area in semiconductor device fabrication that seems to lend itself to the use of general purposes machines – the physical transport of wafers between the various processing stations. At present, such transport is primarily by hand-carried boxed cassettes. One idea is to automate transport. This was done some years ago by Hitachi at its Musashino VLSI plant using small "smart carts." (Veeco and FMS in the United States announced a similar smart cart products, while OKI completed a VLSI plant using an unconventional linear motor wafer transport system.) However, Hitachi is reported to have discontinued the use of the carts and returned to hand carrying. This may be for the previously mentioned reason that little is to be gained in plant cleanliness by totally automated wafer transport until the inspection problem is solved and people are removed from the fabrication areas.

A halfway measure exists in which cassette-to-cassette wafer processing stations are linked by individual robot transport systems. This poses little in the way of technical problems because any electric powered robot can be configured to produce less contamination than a person, but this does not solve the general problem. One final area is the issue of automatic wire bonding. The surge in acquisition of offshore semiconductor facilities in the 1970s was primarily driven by the need for low-cost labor. This trend has reversed in the 1980s with the development of high-speed, completely automated wire bonders. Machines of this type use computer vision and pattern recognition for accurate parts and contact-pad recognition and location, coupled with high-speed wire bonding heads. The state of the art is an incredible seven bonds per second, and it is generally considered that the best machines are those produced by Hitachi. To date, these machines have not been for sale.

This technology has important potential in connection with that of miniature hybrid microcircuit assembly with particular significance for the rapidly growing field of lightwave communication. More than likely, optoelectronics will remain a hybrid semiconductor technology for many years because the light sources and optical detectors have different semiconductor material requirements. It follows that lightwave systems will probably be hybrid, and the automated fabrication of these hybrid systems will become an important activity. A concomitant feature of these systems, particularly in "pigtail" configurations, is that they also require highly accurate automatic mechanical alignment of the optical fibers and the semiconductor optoelectronic elements. This whole area is a natural one for advanced miniature precision mechatronic assembly. Toshiba-Seiki has targeted this area of the production of precise miniature robots specifically designed for miniature semiconductor assembly.

Mechatronics in Computer Peripherals and Related Areas

The cost per function of semiconductor elements has dropped by more than a factor of 10[4] in the last twenty years, while precision electromechanical devices declined in price much more slowly. Even in mechanical areas the pace has been quickened in the last few years due to the introduction of a high degree of automation in production.

In the high-precision areas of computer printers, U.S. manufacturers are maintaining a position of parity in spite of aggressive Japanese competition. The situation in precision mechatronics for entertainment is well known. Only Japanese tape transports are used in U.S. VCRs, and these transports come from just three Japanese manufacturers.

A similar situation is now developing in both the video and digital-audio entertainment optical disc area. Domination of low-cost production in this high-precision (~ 2u tracking) technology will lead to a corresponding control of the developing interactive computer-video disc and large data base area. The status of Japanese work in precision mechatronics is summarized in Figure 12.

Standards

The Japanese Industrial Standards Committee was established in 1949 as a part of MITI. It employs 94 people and has 154 additional people working for it but paid by other organizations. At the end of 1981, the committee had published about 7,700 standards in the fields of industrial and mineral products. A search of this list shows 2,046 standards listed under mechanical engineering, many of which deal with machine tools. The following standards deal specifically with industrial robots:

B0134	Glossary of terms
B0138	Symbols
B8431	Standard form for indicating characteristics and functions
B8432	Measuring methods for characteristics and functions
B8433	General code for safety
B8434	Identification symbols and colors for operator controls

Figure 12. Relative Japanese/U.S. Positions in Precision Mechatronics

	Basic Research	Advanced Development	Product Implementation
High Precision Robots	0 ↗	+ ↗	> ↗
Mechatronics for Semiconductor Fabrication	- →	- ↗	0 ↗
Computer Peripherals	0 →	0 ↗	0 ↗
Optical Discs	0 →	+ ↗	+ ↗
Improved Motors	+ →	+ →	+ →

Source: JTECH Mechatronics Panel, *Final Report* (La Jolla, Calif.: Science Applications International, March 1985).

There is a fundamental difference between the United States and Japan with respect to standards. Under the direction of the government, Japanese companies cooperate to form product standards. Companies are not threatened with antitrust actions and, in fact, are encouraged to cooperate to capture the market in specific areas. Families of products with interchangeable parts are one way of achieving this goal.

The Japanese have been active in the International Standards Organization Technical Committee. They have submitted many articles on safety and classification on the subcommittees on Numerical Control of Machines, Robots, and Requirements for Standards to Enable System Integration.

The Japanese Industrial Robot Association (JIRA) has established a committee on the standardization of robot language with Toshio Sada of Tokyo University as director. A recent paper by Tamio Ari of Tokyo University outlines a proposed standard robot language called STROL. This work is a preliminary academic project, but it does reveal a thorough knowledge of work on robot programming languages in the United States and Europe.

The CAM-I robot programming language project claims to be attempting to develop a standard robot language. However, the size of this effort is probably too small to achieve a good off-line programming system. There seems to be little likelihood that a standard robot language will emerge from this project.

There are many U.S. efforts to develop standards for robots. In fact, there is so much activity in this area that there is an obvious need for coordination. A committee called the Industrial Automation Planning Panel was established in an attempt to provide this coordination role, but it has been unsuccessful. The Robot Industries Association and the National Bureau of Standards have contracted with a private company to generate a comprehensive report on what committees are currently working toward robot standards and what coordination is required. This effort is complex because standardization in robotics is intertwined with other areas. The most important example is the GM manufacturing automation protocol (MAP) protocols. The MAP protocols are being extended to include the application layer for numerical control machines and robots. There are three such efforts including IE 1393A, MIFAS, CCITT.4 and CCITT.6.

Japanese Mechatronics Literature

One of the key issues the JTECH panel was asked to comment on was the availability of open literature in this important research area. Given that the most interesting work is done by industry rather than government laboratories, the work is only reported on in Japanese professional journals, which are not routinely translated into English.

In addition, Japanese academic societies hold biannual or annual meetings, and participants are provided with the abstracts of the meeting. These abstracts are frequently handwritten; they are not reproduced in regular journal publications. The abstracts contain current and useful information, but they are obtained through privately held sources. In this sense, the meeting abstracts are regarded as semiopen. In the Japanese high-tech community, seminars and conferences are organized to pool and disseminate research information. Meetings are usually attended by the invitees only, and the conference proceedings are printed in Japanese with most manuscripts being handwritten to allow entry of the latest information. Some of the more formal technical information contained in these proceedings eventually works its way through the appropriate professional journals published in English, but with a typical delay of six to eighteen months.

Japanese industries participate in the national R&D projects under a research association type of arrangement. The reports from these projects are disseminated first in the technical committees composed of member companies. The edited reports reach the public domain at a much later time.

Unfortunately, it will be difficult for non-Japanese readers to benefit even from such delayed reports because of the shortage of translators and the lack of a machine translator. Some U.S. universities have started intern programs with Japanese companies. The intern period, usually one year, is financially supported by the Japanese company. But, the basic training and orientation, including at least ten weeks of intensive language instruction, are supported by the university. The most notable of these programs is probably the MIT/Japan Science and Technology Program. In its first year (1984), the program placed eight students in Japan. Eight students were placed in 1985 and nineteen in September 1986.

The principal society publications on mechatronics are

- JIRA, *Robot Monthly*, and *Robots in the Japanese Economy*
- Robotics Society of Japan (1983 +), *Journal of the* Robotics Society of Japan
- *Transactions of the Society for Instrument and Control Engineering (SICE)*
- *Journal of the* Japan Electrical Society
- *Journal of the* Japan Information Processing Society
- *Journal of the* Japan Machinery Society

SUMMARY

Mechatronics is important for three reasons. First, it provides the integration of mechanical and electronic engineering important for the next advancement in manufacturing systems. Second, mechatronics provides part of the intellectual argument that all manufacturing functions must be highly integrated in order that the entire manufacturing system be optimized as a system instead of the present locally optimized functions. Third, mechatronics provides a focus for manufacturing engineering education.

REFERENCES

1. See Brandin, D. et al., *JTEC Panel Report on Computer Science in Japan* (La Jolla, Calif.: Science Applications International, December 1984, JTEC-TAR-8401.

2. Iwata, K., "Recent Developments of Flexible Manufacturing Systems in Japan" (Proceedings of ICMA Symposium Flexible Automation in

Production Technology, Hanover, East Germany, September 18-19, 1985), pp. 49-60.

3. Sata, T., "Development of Flexible Manufacturing Systems in Japan," (Proceedings of Japan–USA Symposium on Flexible Automation, Osaka, July 14-18, 1986), pp. 21-26.

4. Seminar on Robotics and Advanced Assembly Systems, CSDL Fifth Annual Seminar, Cambridge, Massachusetts, November 6-8, 1984, pp. 2(a), 52-54.

5. Taniguchi, N. J., "Present State of the Arts of System Design on Automated Assembly in Japan" (Paper presented at the Fourth International Conference on Assembly Automation, October 1983).

6. Hashizume, S., Matsunaga, M., Sugimoto, N., Miyakawa, S., and Kishi, M., "Development of an Automatic Assembly System for Tape Recorder Mechanisms," Research and Development in Japan, 1980[11]. Awarded the Okochi Memorial Prize.

7. Akiyama, J., "Flexible Assembly Center System—FX-1 System" (Presentation made at the Charles Stark Draper Laboratory, Second Annual Three-day Seminar, Robotics and Advanced Assembly Systems, Cambridge, Massachusetts, November 1981).

8. "Sony Compact Assembly Center (AC) Phoenix-10" (Material provided to the Charles Stark Draper Laboratory, Fourth Annual Three-day Seminar, Robotics and Advanced Assembly Systems, Cambridge, Massachusetts, November 1983).

9. Ohachi, T., Miyakawa, S., Arai, Y., Inoshita, S., and Yamada, A., "The Development of Automatic Assembly Line for VTR Mechanisms" (Paper presented at the Fifteenth CIRP International Seminar on Manufacturing Systems, Amherst, Massachusetts, June 1983).

10. Aoki, K., "High Speed and Flexible Automated Assembly Line — Why has Automation Successfully Advanced in Japan?" (Paper presented at the Fourth International Conference on Production Engineering, Tokyo, August 1980).

11. Kaneko, K., and Tatsuji, S., "A Newly Developed Unit Feeder Used in the Analog Quartz Watch Assembly System" (Paper presented at CIC, 1984).

12. Rourke, J. M., and Seltzer, D. S., "Precision Automated Assembly in a Clean Room Environment" (Paper presented at the Ninth Contamination Control Working Group Meeting, October 8-10, 1985); also published as CSDL Report P-2622 (October 1985).

13. "Big Worries Over Small GCA," *New York Times*, January 19, 1987, p. D1-3.

14. Nikon Precision advertisement, *Electronic News* January 5, 1987, p. 64.

DISCUSSION SUMMARY

Cultural factors affect the United States and Japan in the field of mechatronics. In Western culture, the emphasis is placed on the scientific breakthrough in the laboratory; in Japan the step-by-step refinement process on the production floor is more prevalent. The Western mind wants to make the unknown into the known, while the Japanese takes the known and makes it into the useful. Work attitudes also play a role. In Japan, teamwork and group identity are stressed. In the United States, each worker has his or her own career goals, and when they conflict with a company's demands the worker will often look elsewhere for employment. This individualistic work attitude often makes it difficult to target improvement.

In Japan, the limits of what robots can do are generally recognized. In the United States, many companies are interested in robots because these companies believe robots can easily solve their problems. This is not true. One must thoroughly know the product and the production system before considering robots. The U.S. belief that what the customer wants is always right has resulted in automatization systems which are often "overspecified" and not competitive. In the United States, companies will often have a back-up system or inspection, which is an overinvestment and wasteful duplication of resources in the eyes of the Japanese. The Japanese believe that if there is a problem, fix it *now*. The Americans rely on fall-back systems and do not worry if there is a problem unless it becomes severe.

The impact of automatization on blue collar workers is overemphasized, and one participant predicted that there will be an increasing effect on *all* workers. An appropriate national response should be formulated to protect mechatronics, or else it could suffer the same fate as the U.S. semiconductor industry. On the positive side, in certain areas such as systems software, the United States is maintaining its position under Department of Defense encouragement.

Following this segment, discussion was opened to questions from the audience. The first question sought to clarify the concept of technological advancement and an earlier statement that "simpler is better." A member of the panel responded that one strives for simplicity, but that there is a trade-off between cost, maximum simplicity, and maximum reliability. Another panelist stressed that there is no one best answer or approach to a technological problem. Unless one tries "bold and daring" things, however, one will not obtain the same results as if one had been timid. He gave an example in which a firm tried to build the "factory of the future" and failed. Enough was learned from the failure to lead to succeeding generations of projects. Simplicity was stressed as a basic tenet of Japanese culture; by reducing the number of components in a system, one can reduce the likelihood of failure. The success of IBM computers, where people can use them without actually knowing how complex they are, is an example of such success in simplicity.

In the United States, companies who need mechatronics technology will generally write the specifications for what they want and then have the item produced by an outside supplier. The problem arises when specifications cannot be adequately written or the problem cannot be described. For advanced systems, Japanese companies have in-house technology production centers which work to meet the special needs of the company. These centers are advantageous for several reasons. Such in-house teams can be very creative in finding new approaches to problems. The teams also have the benefit of capturing the collective experience of the people working on a given problem.

The crucial issue is how to improve overall plant management. A facet of this is the decision on whether to produce something internally or from an outside source. Ultimately the question is one of competitiveness. There is a need for more production management centers (PMCs), which U.S. companies lack in sufficient numbers. The problem is what to do with PMCs once a project is completed. The alternative, having ongoing PMCs, requires four "deep pockets" and a long-range view that few U.S. companies possess.

Is a national response to the challenge posed by other nations in mechatronics possible? To agree on any one recommendation would be difficult; the real need is to sensitize the public about the issues. The public is not aware of what it means to manufacture a product. It was suggested that there be protocols drawn up for various sectors and that the whole issue of incentive need be addressed. Incentives could be used to avoid large-scale displacements as the U.S. economy progresses.

Many of the panelists felt that the U.S. government should be taking some action, specifically in accordance with the Stevens-Wilder Act, which allows for research in this area. Additional seed money should go to nonprofit organizations to launch programs dealing with technology. The panelists wondered what would have happened if several years ago the U.S. government had pinpointed the mechatronics industry for development. The United States has lost about six years in which skills could have been sharpened and technology developed if the U.S. government had pinpointed the mechatronics industry for development several years ago.

The question is how to utilize technology for future improvements. Mechatronics is not a science; instead, it is the industrial achievement of various technologies, such as production procedures, designed to enhance the efforts of engineers on the "shop floor."

6

Computers and Communications

M. Iwama and F. R. Magee

During the past thirty years, Japan has benefited significantly from technology that has flowed from the United States to Japan. During this period, the Japanese have selected technology to build upon in a coordinated fashion. The Ministry of International Trade and Industry (MITI) has been responsible for locating technology with significant commercial value and negotiating for its use in Japan, while preventing Japanese industry from bidding up its price(1). During the years, Japan has used these technologies to form the basis of its modern products(2) and commercial success(3). Concurrent with its commercial success, Japan has significantly increased its research and development (R&D) efforts. These efforts have resulted in a healthy international competition that has resulted in faster technological progress.

We will first review the basic flow of technology to Japan that has resulted in the production of modern products in the computers and communications areas, followed by an assessment of the contemporary Japanese research programs and their impact on modern technologies, giving examples in selected areas. The flow of technology from Japan to the United States is then assessed and shown to be rapidly increasing. Finally, suggestions are made to foster the maximum mutual benefit from the technology exchange.

BASIC TECHNOLOGY FLOW FROM THE
UNITED STATES TO JAPAN

Table 1 gives a summary of some of the key technologies(4, 5) Japan has acquired from the United States that have significant impact in the areas of computers and communications. In fact, the basis of modern electronic equipment was developed in the United States (that is, the transistor and integrated circuits). This technology has been utilized with great commercial

Table 1. Basic Technology Flow from the United States to Japan

Common Technology	Computer Technology	Communication Technology
Transistor (1947)	First generation (1946) (electronic)	Telephone (1876)
Integrated circuit (1957) microprocessor ram (early 1970s)	Second generation (1959) (transistorized)	Negative feedback amplifier (1927)
Quality control engineering (1920-1940)	Third generation (1960s) integrated circuits	Digital communication (1937) Laser (1958)
Systems Engineering (1920s)	Compilers (early 1950s) Higher level languages Fortran (1956) Algol (1958) Cobol (1960)	Electronic switching (1960) Satellite trans (Telstar) (1962) Fiber transmission (1970s) Mobile cellular radio (1972)

Sources: Prescott C. Mabon, *Mission Communications: The Story of Bell Laboratories* (Murray Hill, N. J.: Bell Laboratories, 1975); and *The New Encyclopedia Britannica*, 15th ed. (1984).

success in Japan, particularly in the area of consumer electronics. In addition, modern quality control engineering has its roots in the United States and has been successfully applied in Japan. This has resulted in some of the highest quality equipment available in the world. The United States has also led the way with planning skills by developing systems engineering as a practice. Typical results have included the application of fundamental limits, such as information theoretic limits to planning technology development and application.

In addition to the common technology which has been applied, modern computer technology was developed in the United States. The first electronic computer, known as the ENIAC, was developed in 1946. This was predated by the Harvard Mark 1 in 1944, which was an electromechanical machine, and in fact, all computers have roots in the Oriental abacus of five thousand years ago. Early electronic computer work was rapidly followed up by compilers in the early 1950s, which allowed programming without using machine language. Modern programming languages rapidly followed — for example, Fortran, Algol, and Cobol.

Modern communications technology also has its roots in the United States. In fact, modern communications were touched off by the development of the telephone in 1876. This invention was rapidly deployed throughout the United States, but long distance transmission required further developments, such as the negative feedback amplifier (1927). The era of modern digital communications was ushered in with the development of pulse code modulation in 1937. This was rapidly followed by the laser (1958), which led to the development of fiber transmission systems in the 1970s. Further significant developments included electronic switching (1960), which has allowed major feature enhancement and will allow the implementation of integrated services digital network (ISDN), and Satellite Transmission (1962), which has helped the rapid spread of economical long distance transmission to most countries. Finally, mobile cellular radio telephone is rapidly increasing communications options and, with technology improvements, may lead to a truly portable personal telephone.

Japan has quickly and effectively applied these and other technologies to develop the capabilities for commercial success. Over time, this has resulted in a significant trade imbalance ($49.5 billion in 1985 [6]) with the United States. Although this imbalance had started in basic industries such as the steel industry, it has now spread into the high-technology areas which have been the strength of the United States. Figure 1 shows the trend in telecommunications equipment trade between the United States and Japan(7). Although a breakdown of the computer equipment trade with Japan was not specifically available, it is known that the United States is running a trade deficit with the Far East (including Japan) in the order of $3 billion per year. This deficit is primarily in equipment such as printers and video display terminals.

Figure 1. Trends in U.S.-Japan Trade in Telecommunications Equipment

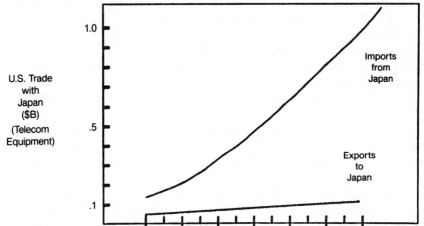

Source: 1986 U.S. Industrial Outlook, U.S. Dept. of Commerce International Trade Association

Given the large base of U.S. technology upon which Japan has built and the latter's large trade surplus, many wonder how it is that Japan is contributing to the U.S. technological base. This chapter will show how, through the eyes of U.S. engineers, Japan is now developing significant technology which is being fed back to the United States. This is occurring because Japan has significantly increased its spending on R&D. MITI-sponsored research projects helped focus R&D efforts in designated technology areas. The focus areas the Japanese have chosen and how they impacted significant commercial areas will be discussed. Then some detailed examples of areas that are in direct competition for technological leadership will be described.

JAPANESE IMPACT IN KEY TECHNOLOGY AREAS

The expansion of Japanese R&D has produced Japanese contributions and created a competitive environment with the United States. Figure 2, from a JTECH report(8), illustrates differences in definition of R&D between the United States and Japan. Specifically, if the break between basic research, advanced development, and product development is viewed in terms of likelihood of leading to a marketable product, the Japanese do not generally undertake a research project unless there is about a 50 percent chance of market entry. On the other hand, U.S. researchers commonly undertake research projects not necessarily with specific application in mind. This is consistent with a common perception of limited basic research results coming out of Japan. More of Japan's R&D emphasis is on projects with a specific commercial orientation. In Figure 3, the view of relative time spans to a possible product is shown. Again, it is clear that a longer term horizon is generally taken in the United States. For purposes of this discussion, the division between research and development will be as marked in Figure 2.

It appears that Japan approaches its R&D effort in a highly focused manner through a cooperative effort between Japanese industry and MITI. Specifically, MITI selects key (high commercial potential) focus areas and funds R&D in those areas. Japanese companies contribute significant additional resources to these efforts, and the results of these efforts are shared among the companies participating in the efforts. Table 2, from a JTECH report(8), shows the key focus areas for which MITI has funded research and lists the time span of the effort and the amount of money invested by MITI.

This chapter uses the data in Table 2 as the basis for assessing how these programs affect given areas and where new results can be expected. The following two subsections discuss where these programs are likely to impact and give examples of how competition has developed in specific areas.

Figure 2. Definitions of U.S. and Japanese R&D

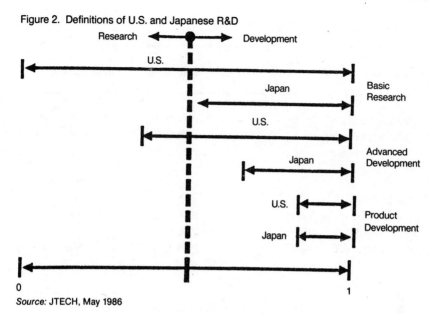

Source: JTECH, May 1986

Figure 3. Time Spans of U.S. and Japanese R&D

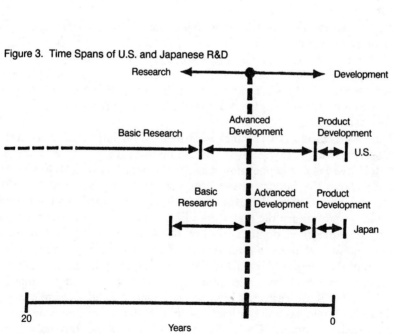

Source: JTECH, May 1986

Table 2. Japanese Technology Focus Areas

Technology	Time Span	Funds Invested
Semiconductors, VLSI, etc.	1981-1990	$275M
Photonic Technologies	1979-1985	160M
Photonic information processing	1979-1985	70M
Sigma software development	1985-1989	120M
Fifth generation computers	1979-1991	270M
Supercomputer development	1981-1989	200M
Interoperable data bases	1985-1992	150M

Impact in Communications

The Japanese R&D effort in communications was recently analyzed by a panel of U.S. experts. In the resulting JTECH report, the panel did a detailed assessment of Japanese focus areas and their impact on key areas of communications. In addition, the panel included an assessment of the impact of the Nippon Telephone and Telegraph Information Network Service (INS) trial now being completed in Mikata as an experiment in innovative network services(9).

Figure 4 gives the JTECH Panel assessment of the impact of these MITI programs on switching systems(8). As can be seen, these programs are expected to have a major impact almost across the board on switching systems. Figure 5 shows the impact of the programs on transmission systems(8). Again, major impact can be expected, although the semiconductors and photonics programs are the major ones likely to cause the impact because most of the other areas do not apply in transmission except for operations, administration, and maintenance. As a third example, Figure 6 shows an assessment of the programs' impact in the customer premises area. Here the primary impact is made by semiconductors and is followed in importance by the INS trial. Of the customer premises equipment listed, facsimile is the one in which Japan has a major lead due to its high level of domestic use to support their language. Facsimile is a technology the Japanese have developed, and it accounts for almost all manufacturing. Based on these three figures, it is clear that the focus areas will have major commercial value in communications.

Figure 4. Japanese Programs Impacting Switching Systems R&D

System \ Program	Circuit	ISDN/INS	Packet	Broadband
Semiconductors (VLSI, etc.)	Major Impact	Major Impact	Major Impact	Major Impact
Photonics	Some Impact	Some Impact	Some Impact	Major Impact
Software Development (SIGMA)	Major Impact	Major Impact	Major Impact	Major Impact
Fifth Generation Computers	Major Impact	Major Impact	Major Impact	Major Impact
Super-Speed Computers	Major Impact	Major Impact	Major Impact	Major Impact
Interoperable Databases	Insignificant Impact	Some Impact	Insignificant Impact	Insignificant Impact
INS Trial	Some Impact	Major Impact	Major Impact	Some Impact

○ Insignificant Impact   ⊕ Some Impact   ● Major Impact

Source: JTECH Panel Judgment

Figure 5. Japanese Programs Impacting Transmission Systems R&D

System \ Program	Lightwave	Submarine Cable	Multiplexers and Subscriber Loop Carrier	Digital Radio
Semiconductors (VLSI, etc.)	Major Impact	Major Impact	Major Impact	Major Impact
Photonics	Major Impact	Major Impact	Major Impact	Insignificant Impact
Software Development (SIGMA)	Some Impact*	Some Impact*	Some Impact*	Some Impact*
Fifth Generation Computers	Insignificant Impact	Insignificant Impact	Some Impact*	Insignificant Impact
Super-Speed Computers	Insignificant Impact	Insignificant Impact	Some Impact*	Insignificant Impact
Interoperable Databases	Insignificant Impact	Insignificant Impact	Some Impact*	Insignificant Impact
INS Trial	Major Impact	Insignificant Impact	Major Impact	Some Impact*

* For OA&M   ○ Insignificant Impact   ⊕ Some Impact   ● Major Impact

Source: JTECH Panel Judgment

Figure 6. Japanese Programs Impacting Customer Premises System R&D

Program \ System	Telephones	Voice/Data Terminals	Facsimile	KTS & PBX
Semiconductors (VLSI, etc.)	●	●	●	●
Photonics	○	✪	●	●
Software Development (SIGMA)	○	✪*	✪*	●
Fifth Generation Computers	○	✪*	✪*	●
Super-Speed Computers	○	○	✪	●
Interoperable Databases	○	✪	○	✪
INS Trial	●	●	●	●

* For OA&M   ○ Insignificant Impact   ✪ Some Impact   ● Major Impact

Source: JTECH Panel Judgment

Examples of Japanese Impact in Communications

In order to determine the effectiveness of these Japanese research programs and assess the resulting technology interdependency between the United States and Japan, we now can take a more detailed look at photonics in relation to lightwave transmission systems. Figure 7 shows how lightwave transmission systems have progressed over the last ten years. This has been a very rapid progression with a continual increase in the effectiveness of the system as measured by the product of the bandwidth times the repeater spacing. This has been marked by a constant competition between the United States and Japan with the United States generally in the lead until recently. Now Japan is at par with the United States. This intense international competition has likely resulted in a significant increase in the

speed of the development of the technology. Furthermore, the exchange of results through talks, papers, and conferences fosters this speedup. Figure 8 shows lightwave systems which have been demonstrated as of 1986 by AT&T and Japan. The United States currently holds the lead for the highest bandwidth systems; however, Japan holds a small lead for systems with the largest span between repeaters. This Japanese lead is caused by their progress in high power lasers. This is clearly a technology where great progress is being made in parallel by the United States and Japan.

Figure 7. Lightwave Progress

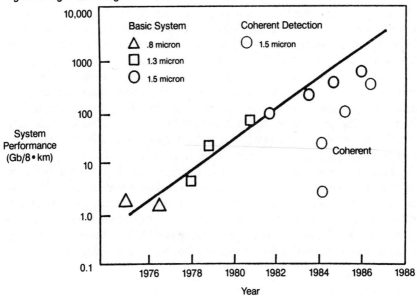

Figure 8. Lightwave Systems Today

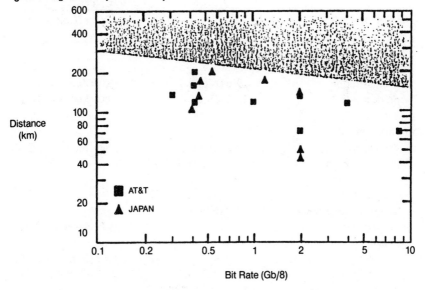

The systems referred to in Figures 7 and 8 depend on underlying technological advances for their rapid improvement. Table 3 summarizes some key developments in the area of lightwave signal detectors. As the detectors become more sensitive, the spacing of the repeaters can be increased and thus the system can be more economical. In addition, the detectors must be responsive to higher data rates in order to increase the bit rate system. This table provides information that shows the competitiveness of the products and highlights differences between the approach of Japan and the United States. Using germanium avalanche photodiode as an example, it was first developed in the United States but was abandoned shortly thereafter(10) due to some problems caused by inherent properties of germanium. The Japanese continued working with the material and with some refinement produced a practical design which has since demonstrated high reliability. In other work based upon indium phosphorous material, there were significant advances in the United States resulting in high sensitivity photodetectors; however, Japan has beaten the United States in marketing commercial devices which are now available from Fujitsu and NEC.

Table 3. Key Developments in Long-wavelength Detectors

Development	JAPAN Year (Company)	UNITED STATES Year (Company)
InP planar pin		
- demonstration	1980 (NTT)	1981 (Forrest-AT&T)
- production	1985 (Hitachi)	1983 (McCoy-AT&T)
Germanium APD		
- demonstration	1973 (Fujitsu)	1966 (Melchior-AT&T)
- practical design	1981 (Fujitsu-NTT)	-
InP planar APD		
- sam structure proposed	1979 (NEC)	-
- sensitivity improvement demo	-	1981 (Forrest-AT&T)
- hole trapping discovered	-	1982 (Forrest-AT&T)
- quaternary interface	1982 (KDD)	1983 (Campbell-AT&T)
- commercial devices	1986 (Fujitsu, NEC)	-

Another perspective from which to compare the Japanese approach to communications to that in the United States is to compare the relative approaches to network services. To make this comparison, the INS trial in Japan being conducted by NTT (9) is contrasted to the U.S. ISDN Trials (11) being conducted by the Regional Operating Companies and AT&T. As is summarized in Table 4, a key difference in the two approaches is that the United States is approaching network services primarily as a new technology that is being tested, while Japan is emphasizing early customer feedback on new services. This is consistent with the Japanese emphasis on the commercial value of their work. As a consequence of this difference in approach, Japan was able to assess customer impact by getting early customer feedback in September 1984; U.S. trials got started in late 1986. The U.S. trial systems will be fully developed digital systems supporting CCITT standards. Japan utilized current technology where necessary to get an early start, and thus its network services do not fully support the CCITT-specified standard interfaces, nor are they totally digital. Another difference in approach is that the U.S. trials have been emphasizing the use of a single large customer for each trial while the Japanese trials have multiple volunteer smaller customers. This difference is natural because the U.S. approach has the appearance of letting the customer figure out how to apply the technology; this approach requires a customer with significant resources. Japan has

Table 4. Network Services/ISDN Approach Comparison

	JAPAN	UNITED STATES
Approach to services	customer-need driven	technology driven
	trial customers early with current systems	based on CCITT standards
Application	volunteer customers emphasis on information retrieval	single large customer finds own use
Dates	start Sept. 1984	start late 1986
Goals	obtain customer reaction determine social impact confirm technology	technology development verification of standards
Service provided	64 KBPS digital broadband (video) high-definition television	integrated voice/data basic access primary rate access

approached the problem by emphasizing the provision of services, such as information retrieval and high-definition television, customers could use. Thus, the United States can learn from the results of the early Japanese application of these services (taking cultural differences into account).

Impact in Computers

In 1984, another JTECH panel assessed Japan's status in computer technology (12). The report gave an overall assessment of Japan's position relative to the United States in computer technology. Table 5 shows the results of the panel's assessment of Japan's position at the time of the report. The table shows the Japanese were doing relatively well in product engineering but were further behind the closer the assessment got to basic research. Since the report, Japan has made progress as a result of its research projects.

Examples of Japanese Impact in Computers

Japanese results in the device area tend to be at the leading edge; the Japanese have made and are continuing to make significant basic contributions to technology. One technology in which they have moved ahead very quickly is dynamic random access memory (DRAM). Figure 9 depicts the progress in development and production of DRAM, an important element in computers between 1976 and 1986. The DRAM technology, which was pioneered by INTEL (1976) with 16 Kbit random access memory, now shows the Japanese taking a clear lead in technology by demonstrating a 4 Mbit DRAM at the 1986 International Solid State Circuits Conference. Japan has been very successful in the device area and leads the field with production techniques using superior clean rooms and mask production techniques. This has led to generally higher yields than in the United States and has ironically driven out INTEL, a pioneer, from the DRAM business.

Despite the Japanese edge in semiconductor technology, the current focus of Japanese technology which is likely to have the most impact in the computer area is the widely discussed Fifth Generation Computer Project. This project is heavily documented in English (14, 15, 16, 17), although much of the reporting so far has been in terms of setting goals and direction. Based upon personal discussions (18), the authors have developed a partial assessment of the impact of Japanese computer technology as illustrated in Table 6. The most direct impact is device technology, but other results are also starting to be felt. One area is the development of the personal sequential inference workstation. This machine is unique because it is a desktop system with an 80 Mbite main memory. The implications of having such a largemachine on the desktop are not well understood, but it is expected to have significant implications. Another area of impact is the improvement of

Table 5. Assessment of Japan's Capabilities in Computers by Category

Category	Basic Research	Advanced Development	Product Engineering
Software	far behind the U.S. and slipping quickly	behind in development of prototype software and losing ground	ahead of the U.S. in the development of applications code and holding position
Artificial intelligence & human-machine interface	far behind the U.S. and losing ground	behind and holding position	behind and holding position
Processor architecture & computer organization	far behind the U.S. and losing ground	on par with the U.S. and gaining ground	ahead of the U.S. and gaining ground
Communications	far behind the U.S. and losing ground; software-behind and holding position	hardware-even and holding position; software-far behind but catching up	hardware-ahead and gaining ground

Source: JTECH.

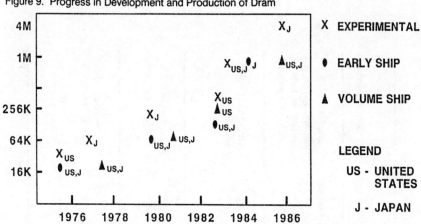

Figure 9. Progress in Development and Production of Dram

Source: "Annual Technology Issue," *IEEE Spectrum* (January issues for years 1976–1986).

Table 6. Current Japanese Impact on U.S.
Computer Technology

Direct	Indirect
Devices	stimulate activity
Fifth Generation	in U.S. and Japanese
project results	industry
PSI workstation	alert world to artificial
man-machine	intelligence potential
(natural language)	information exchange
interface	through NSF interns
parallel architecture	
experiment	

the man-machine interface. This will have significant impact in making computers more readily available to all. Finally, the experiments with parallel architecture have been discontinued, thus showing that this area may not be as fruitful as had been hoped.

In terms of indirect impact, the Japanese have clearly stimulated the competitive spirit and caused the start-up of new work in the United States. In a lengthy article in the *Proceedings of the IEEE*, K. G. Wilson calls the United States to action to meet the Japanese challenge (19). Such a reaction has been commonplace and will undoubtedly help accelerate technological improvements in computers. In addition, progress in artificial intelligence has alerted the world to its potential and increased its application(16). Finally, Japan has opened up its Fifth Generation Project to National Science Foundation interns, thereby facilitating the exchange of research results.

TECHNOLOGY FLOW FROM JAPAN TO THE UNITED STATES

Given that Japan is highly competitive with the United States in a number of areas (particularly in devices), there is much to learn from the Japanese. This exchange of information can be clearly demonstrated, and the current high level of Japanese participation in the International Solid State Circuits Conference is frequently cited as an example(8). Because devices are an area where the Japanese have taken strong leadership with effective commercial results, this type of exchange is as expected.

In order to see what degree of impact the Japanese are having in research-oriented publications, the authors examined the Japanese contributions in the *IEEE Transactions on Computers* and the *IEEE Transactions on Communications*. Specifically, we investigated the rate at which Japanese-authored publications are referenced in these journals, because this is an indication of how much others rely on work by the Japanese. Figure 10 shows the results of this count. During the twelve-year period 1974-1986 for which the count was made, the *IEEE Transactions on Communications* went from one reference per four articles to almost one reference per article. This significant growth was paralleled by a somewhat slower growth in Computer Transactions from one reference per five articles to about one reference per two articles. The growth in the computer area can be expected to accelerate as the results of the Fifth Generation Computer Project become more widely utilized. This has clearly demonstrated how Japanese results are being utilized in the United States at an ever increasing rate.

Another way to see how the Japanese are assuming an ever increasing role in computers and communications is to observe Japanese participation in CCITT standards activities. Table 7 gives a summary of both U.S. and Japanese participation in CCITT in terms of taking leadership positions. As can be seen, the Japanese have started to take more leadership positions than their U.S. counterparts in CCITT standards activities. This indicates that the Japanese have given standards a high priority and that the Japanese are contributing in a significant way. Although language differences may have partially limited their participation in real-time discussion, they have been quite active in terms of attending, making written contributions, and taking leadership roles.

Figure 10. Japanese Surname References per Published Article

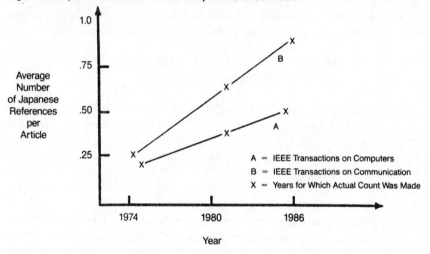

Table 7. U.S./Japanese People in Leadership Positions at CCITT Plenary Sessions

Year	Number of Study Groups	Chairpeople		Vicechair	
		U.S.	Japan	U.S.	Japan
1976	20	3	1	4/47	3/47
1980	15	2	1	6/57	7/57
1984	15	2	1	8/54	10/54

CONCLUSIONS

This paper has shown how the technological relationship has grown between the United States and Japan through the eyes of R&D engineers in the United States. Although this relationship started as one in which the United States was primarily licensing technology to Japan, the relationship has grown to the point where there are many areas in which the two countries are highly competitive in making research and development contributions. Particularly with respect to devices, Japan leads in many areas. The United States is now benefiting from Japanese results in terms of learning about technological advances as well as obtaining high-technology products.

Now that Japan has reached a level where it is making technological contributions that can significantly benefit the United States, it must make a larger effort to learn about them. This will require an increase in people going to Japan to participate in research projects just as the Japanese have done in the United States. An increase in study of the Japanese language as well as an increase in study of Japanese language journals will also be necessary. Initiating these types of steps, as the Japanese have done, must now occur in order to get full benefit on a reciprocal basis. Such efforts will result in a long-term beneficial relationship for both the United States and Japan.

REFERENCES

1. "Japanese Research and Technology Policy," *Science* (July 18, 1986):296-301.

2. Kobayashi, K., *Computers and Communication: A Vision of C&C* (Cambridge, Mass.: MIT Press, 1986).

3. "High Technology, Clash of the Titans," *The Economist* (August 23, 1986).

4. Mabon, Prescott C., Mission Communications: The Story of Bell Laboratories, (Murray Hill, N. J.: Bell Laboratories, 1975).

5. *The New Encyclopaedia Britannica*, 15th ed. 1984.

6. "Japan's U.S. R&D Role Widens, Begs Attention," *Science* (July 18, 1986):270-272.

7. U.S. Department of Commerce, International Trade Association, *1986 U.S. Industrial Outlook* (Washington, D. C.: U.S. Government Printing Office, 1986).

8. Turin, G. et al., *JTECH Panel Report on Telecommunications Technology in Japan* (La Jolla, Calif.: Science Applications International Corporation, May 1986).

9. Takahashi, T., and Okimi, K., "A Report from Mikata-INS Model System Experimental Site," *IEEE Journal on Selected Areas in Communications* no. 3 (May, 1986):376-383.

10. Wieder, H. et al., *JTECH Panel Report on Opto- and Microelectronics* (La Jolla, Calif.: Science Applications International Corporation, May 1985).

11. Mitchell, O. M., "Implementing ISDN in the United States," *IEEE Journal on Selected Areas in Communications* no. 3 (May 1986):398-406.

12. Brandin, D. et al., *JTECH Panel Report on Computer Science in Japan* (La Jolla, Calif.: Science Applications International Corporation, December 1984).

13. "Annual Technology Issue," *IEEE Spectrum* (January 1976-1986).

14. Motooka, T., ed., *Proceedings of the International Conference on Fifth Generation Computer Systems* (Tokyo, October 19-22, 1981).

15. Motooka, T., ed., *Proceedings of the International Conference on Fifth Generation Computer Systems* (Tokyo, November 6-9, 1984).

16. Rigas, H. et al., "Artificial Intelligence Research in Japan," *Computer* (September 1985):83-90.

17. *International Developments in Computer Science* (Washington, D. C.: National Academy Press, 1982).

18. Stone, Harold, personal discussion at IBM Thomas J. Watson Research Center, September 12, 1986.

19. Wilson, K. G., "Science, Industry, and the New Japanese Challenge," *Proceedings of the IEEE* 72, no. 1 (January 1984):6-18.

DISCUSSION SUMMARY

The technology industry in Japan has gone from absorbing information to one of parity with the U.S. industry. In the four areas of computer capabilities — software, artificial intelligence, processor architecture, and communications — Japan is behind the United States in basic research and advanced development. Japan is ahead in the actual manufacturing of products. One major factor presented during the discussion is that U.S. firms, in many instances, fail to have the foresight to see what technology is important and have not been willing to invest enough time and effort to bring technology to reality. Japanese companies have stayed with much of that same technology and perfected it, which results in the development of useful products.

Japanese firms focus on manufacturing products with whatever technology is currently available, with emphasis on serving customer needs and using feedback to further develop the technology. U.S. researchers, on the other hand, tend to fall in love with technology. The U.S. approach is to wait for all of the technology to become available before performing field trials.

It was stated that because Japan is no longer a "poor" country, having obtained much assistance from the United States and Europe for many years, it is now time to become more responsible to the world economy and invent more resources in basic research. What happens in the next ten years will be vital to the stability of the world's markets. Japan must expand its expenditures and create new markets.

The next area to be developed is centered around new information technology. Japan's researchers dream of developing simultaneous automatic interpretation telephone technology. Yet it was pointed out that no single country can achieve such a goal. There will need to be global collaboration. In the ideal situation, all countries would be cooperating with each other to create the basic knowledge and technology. When the level of technology is close to practical manufacturing, private enterprise could then compete within the market.

Unfortunately, this scenario is quite unrealistic. The hard reality facing the United States is that the research and development telecommunications trade imbalance will continue in Japan's favor in the foreseeable future, despite deregulations, reduction of barriers, etc. The presentations suggested a few ways the U.S. technology industry could become more competitive with the Japanese industry. First, given that the United States responds well to a crisis that threatens the safety of the country, this situation must be viewed as a major technological threat facing the country. People in the U.S. technology industry must be willing to learn from Japan because Japan has recently reached a level where it is making contributions to the field that can benefit the United States. This will require more Americans going to Japan to work as well as an increase in the study of the Japanese language and culture.

It was felt that Japan also has opportunities to help alleviate the perceived one-way flow of technology from the United States. One step that can be taken is for Japanese companies to invite U.S. firms to participate in MITI-sponsored consortiums or to request U.S. employees to work in the research and development departments in firms in Japan.

Trade barriers on both sides need to be reduced. A bilateral flow of information is crucial in order to maintain healthy relations between the two countries. If this does not occur, the political climate will continue toward protectionism, particularly with a Democratic Congress. The dollar value of the trade deficit between the countries is of importance in the short run, but successful trade agreements, such as the semiconductor agreement, and efforts to share information will reduce the incentive for protectionist measures. In conclusion, the greater flow of technology will, in the long run, be beneficial to both countries and economies. It will be a mistake if the United States and Japan do not work with one another and with all other countries in the world.

7

Biotechnology

Arthur Humphrey

This chapter is based on a three-week visit to Japan which included chairing the U.S. delegation to the Second Conference to Promote Japan-U.S. Joint Projects and Cooperation in Biotechnology at Lake Biwa, September 27-30, 1986, visiting a number of Japanese biotechnology companies and institutes in connection with the conference, and abstracting material from a very thorough report on "Biotechnology in Japan" by Herman W. Lewis which appeared in *ONRFE Scientific Bulletin* 10, no. 128 (1985):3, and a second report on "Biotechnology in Pharmaceuticals: The Japanese Challenge" by M. D. Dibner that appeared in *Science*, no. 229 (September 20, 1985):1230-1235. This chapter is colored by my experience in biochemical engineering for nearly a year in the Institute of Applied Microbiology at Tokyo University and the personal reports I have received from my former Japanese students and colleagues as a result of that experience.

INTRODUCTION

The United States and Japan are clearly the world leaders in biotechnology. The U.S. leadership stems from the strong U.S. position in basic science that underpins cell fusion and recombinant DNA technology and from the identification of interesting and potentially useful products of genetic engineering.

Over the decades, Japanese scientists and engineers have clearly demonstrated their ability to develop superior processes utilizing fermentation technology. The Japanese dominated the amino acid and nucleoside/nucleotide fields by developing large-scale fermentations as well as by applying immobilized enzyme and cell technology. The ability of Japanese scientists to work with microorganisms to identify and produce new metabolites is unsurpassed.

Because of their long tradition in fermentations, Japanese scientists readily mastered the new technology of genetic engineering and have quickly entered into process scale-up studies. There is no question that Japanese bioprocess technology will soon match if not surpass that of the United States.

During the past decades, information concerning Japanese technology has been slow in coming to the West, largely because of difficulties of communication related to the infrequency of contact and the language barrier. In order to restrict the scientific flow of information to the West, researchers only needed to publish in Japanese. Unfortunately, such a policy limited the development of international reputations for some of the Japanese scientists and many young Japanese scientists no longer ascribe to the policy of publishing only in Japanese. They frequently will publish key results in English language journals, or in the case of Japanese journals, these researchers add English as well as Japanese language abstracts.

Japanese research is clearly more applied than its U.S. counterpart. Japanese industry derives much of its strength from close association and cooperation with scientists and engineers of the applied science faculties of many Japanese universities. Scientists in the Japanese universities frequently undertake projects that are target oriented with industrial overtones in contrast to the generalized approaches usually followed by scientists in the United States. This directness of approach in technology development seems to permeate all facets of Japanese science today.

SOME REASONS FOR JAPAN'S FOCUS ON BIOTECHNOLOGY

Biotechnology is the most recent high-technology area of commercialization the Japanese government is trying to stimulate through public and private sectors. A number of factors contribute to this focus: limited national natural resources (I would observe in passing that when my daughters attended elementary school in Japan they repeatedly heard their teachers state that "people are Japan's greatest resource and only high people productivity would make up for this lack of natural resources"), existence of a highly literate and skilled middle-class society, the emergence of new smokestack competitors in Asia, and Japanese vulnerability to oil shortages.

Biotechnology is an especially attractive role candidate in new high technologies for Japan to pursue in the future. Fermentation, the foundation on which cell culture and genetics can be built, has roots in the Japanese economy that go back nearly one hundred years. The manufacture of sake (rice wine), miso (bean paste), and shoyu (soy sauce) are fermented products that have played and still do play a major role in the cultural and economic life of the Japanese. All the imperial universities had, as the national universities now have, schools of agriculture with departments of agricultural chemistry or applied microbiology where intense programs of fermentation technology existed. Graduates of these departments became important industrial leaders, and a large cadre of trained scientists in fermentation evolved.

Following World War II, when most of Japan's industry was destroyed and new industries were needed to replace them, the United States encouraged Japan to produce antibiotics, the wonder drugs that evolved during the war. Strains of penicillium along with penicillin production knowhow were provided to the Japanese, and within a brief period of four years nearly seventy companies were founded to produce penicillin. Virtually the entire 1942 class of the Department of Agricultural chemistry (Tokyo University) became officers in these new companies of which only four survive today. Through intensive screening methods and innovations in large-scale fermentation, particularly computer control techniques, the Japanese antibiotic companies grew to challenge U.S. and European companies in worldwide sale and manufacture of antibiotics. In passing I would note that it was the Ajinomoto Company that took the first significant step in applying computers to direct digital control of fermentations. It was also another fermentation company, Kyowa Hakko, that evolved a method of producing glutamic acid through cultivating microorganisms in an environment that produced "leaky" cells. Similar developments rapidly followed in nucleic acid fermentations and enzymic transformations. Today, Japan dominates world markets in amino acids, nucleic acids, and certain enzyme products as a result of these developments.

When microbial genetics – that is, purposeful mutation of efficient strains to obtain even higher producers – became an important area of research, it was given high priority by the Japanese antibiotic companies. This intensive genetics research led to the discovery of the "R factors," transferable gene elements in bacteria that confer antibiotic resistance. It turned out that the "R factors" were in fact plasmids, the key gene agent in recombinant DNA technology. Consequently, Japan was poised with the necessary skilled work force to vigorously commercialize biotechnology opportunities. Is it any wonder, therefore, that the Ministry of International Trade and Industry (MITI) should make biotechnology one of Japan's major priorities?

THE U.S. AND JAPANESE OUTLOOKS
ON BIOTECHNOLOGY

Estimates for the annual bulk sales of biotechnology products by the year 2000 (see Table 1) suggest an activity of somewhere between $30 and 110 billion. Various estimates from companies and governmental agencies within the United States suggest that more than half of this will come from

U.S. companies. Of this around $30 billion of annual sales will come from new biotechnology products in the medical (pharmaceutical) field. A recent estimate from the Japanese Bio-Industry Development Center predicts $60.7 billion in biotechnology product sales in Japan by the year 2000. Of this the center predicts that $12.8 billion will come from pharmaceutical sales. These estimates represent a significant portion of the total market. They certainly suggest a very strong commitment by Japan to commercialize future biotechnology opportunities.

Historically, the Japanese pharmaceutical industry has been characteristically different from that in the United States (see Table 2). First, Japanese pharmaceutical firms are smaller than U.S. firms. There are eleven U.S. pharmaceutical firms with annual sales of more than $1 billion per year. In Japan, there is only one company (Takeda Pharmaceutical) with annual sales of more than $1 billion. In the past, the U.S. companies were responsible for introducing twice as many new drugs as did their Japanese counterparts. This is no longer true. Japanese pharmaceutical firms are now spending 50 percent more of their sales dollars on research than comparable U.S. firms

Table 1. Estimates For Annual Bulk Sales of Biotechnology Products by the Year 2000 (millions of dollars)

Item	Sales: Low Estimate	Sales: High Estimate
Medical products	7,000	45,000
Chemical products	5,000	25,000
Agricultural products	3,000	9,000
Food feed	3,000	4,000
Associated equipment & engineering systems	10,000	24,000
Total	28,000	107,000

Source: A. E. Humphrey, "The Challenge of Biotechnology to the Chemical Engineering Profession," *Chemical Engineering Progress* (December 1984): 7-12.

Table 2. Comparison of U.S. and Japanese Pharmaceutical Industries and Involvement in Biotechnology[a]

Category	United States	Japan
Population (millions)	234.5	119.2
Gross national product	$3.3 trillion	$1.2 trillion
Domestic pharmaceutical market (world rank)	$21.3 billion (1)	$13.4 billion (2)
Number of pharmaceutical companies with sales of more than $1 billion[b]	11	1
Total pharmaceutical sales of ten largest pharmaceutical companies[c]	$16.7 billion	$6 billion
Pharmaceutical sales as percent of total sales[d]	50.1	74.1
Number of new pharmaceutical products introduced		
1961-1980	353	155
1981-1983	24	41
R&D expenditures as percent of sales[d]	6.8	9.2
Scientists and engineers in industrial R&D[e]		
Total number	573,900	272,000
Percentage of work force	0.58	0.50
Government-funded research in biotechnology		
Total	$520 million	$60 million
Percentage of basic research	>98	<50
Targets of funding in biotechnology	Basic research	Basic research, scale-up industrial projects, government laboratory facilities, manufacturing technology

[a]All data for 1983 unless noted.
[b]Pharmaceutical sales only.
[c]Total world pharmaceutical sales in 1983 were approximately $60 billion.
[d]Average of top ten companies.
[e]All industries, 1977 data.

Sources: Lewis, Herman W., "Biotechnology in Japan," ONFRE Scientific Bulletin 10, no. 2 (1985): 11-68; and Lewis, Herman W., "Biotechnology in Japan," ONFRE Scientific Bulletin 10, no. 3 (1985): 91-105.

are. As a result, between 1981 and 1983, Japanese firms introduced 70 percent more new drugs than U.S. pharmaceutical companies did. This translates to at least a six-fold greater productivity by the Japanese (as measured by the number of drugs introduced).

THE SECOND U.S.-JAPANESE CONFERENCE ON COOPERATION IN BIOTECHNOLOGY

On September 27-30, 1986, at Lake Biwa, Moriyama, Shiga, Prefecture in Japan, the Second Conference on Cooperation and Joint Products in Biotechnology was held. It was significantly different in two ways from previous conferences: half of the participants (nineteen from Japan and fifteen from the United States) were young scientists, some in their early thirties, and the openness and intimacy of the meeting allowed representatives from both countries time to get to know each other, discuss research results, exchange ideas, and lay plans for collaborative projects in biotechnology.

The differences in approaches taken by the two scientific communities became abundantly evident as the meeting progressed. Papers presented by U.S. participants were generally very theoretical with little sense of immediate application. In contrast, most of the papers presented by the Japanese participants were target oriented with strong industrial overtones. This directness of approach to biotechnology development by the Japanese was evident in all facets of the conference.

Examples of such presentations by the Japanese participants included information by Professor Atsuo Tanaka of Kyoto University on problems of plant cell tissue culture on a pilot scale; Dr. Minowada's description of the extensive human hematopoietic cell lines available from the Fujisaki Cell Center of Hayashibara Biochemical Laboratories; the summary by Professor Hideaki Yamada of processes developed at Kyoto University for the production of a variety of biologically useful compounds by coupled enzymatic reactions; the disclosure by Professor Isao Urabe of Osaka University that DHG-PEG-NAD (an enzyme/cofactor system covalently coupled through a polyethylene glycol linker molecule) could function on an industrial scale as a NADH-regeneration system; the summary of process development studies underway for the production of L-phenylalanine (the key component of the artificial sweetener aspartame) at various Japanese companies; and Professor Akira Kimura's presentation on gene cloning work with industrial microorganisms at Tokyo University.

In previous years, information such as that exchanged at the Lake Biwa conference was slow in coming to the West primarily because of difficulties of communications related to the infrequency of contact and the language barrier. Particularly among the young scientists, there need no longer be a language barrier as most young Japanese biotechnologists fluently speak and read English. What is now needed is to build on the relationships and understandings that are emerging from such contact and to use them in the most effective way to ensure the rapid development of biotechnology to the benefit of both countries. Clearly, however, the Japanese are far better at technology transfer between academia and industry than their U.S. counterparts are, or at least it would appear so. Scientists in the United States need to learn from their Japanese colleagues in this regard.

JAPANESE STRATEGY FOR
DEVELOPING BIOTECHNOLOGY

Japanese government programs in biotechnology have emerged from five main sources: the Science and Technology Agency (STA) through the Prime Minister's Office and the Council of Science and Technology, the Ministry of International Trade and Industry, the Ministry of Agriculture, Forestry, and Fisheries (MAFF) the Ministry of Education, Science, and Culture (MESC), and the Ministry of Health and Welfare (MHW).

The total Japanese government spending for biotechnology by these agencies and ministries was approximately $65 million in 1985. This compares to nearly $650 million in the United States for generic (basic) research in biotechnology and approximately $6.5 million in "downstream" bioprocessing research. Japanese scientists claim that the U.S. expenditure in biotechnology research is ten times that of theirs, while the U.S. biochemical engineering community claims that the applied biotechnology research in Japan is ten times that of the United States. Neither claim is technically wrong; however, neither claim is quite correct. The Japanese do not need to do much basic research in biotechnology because most of the U.S. research is essentially instantaneously available to Japanese scientists through professional society meetings and through computer-accessed journals. In the case of the claim by U.S. technologists of more Japanese applied research, what little there is through governmental agencies in the United States is beginning to pale in the light of the many state programs to support biotechnology centers. For example, the recently announced program for the state of Michigan could almost equal the whole Japanese government spending for biotechnology in terms of annual dollars budgeted. The key, however, is not in dollars allocated but rather in the organization and focus of the research and how efficiently the technology is transferred to industry for commercialization. My impression is that Japanese researchers do this significantly better than do U.S. researchers, and therein is the equalizer if not the advantage. Let us look specifically at the Japanese government organization of biotechnology support.

STA

The Council of Science and Technology is advisory to the prime minister, much like the White House Office of Science and Technology Policy. The council has eleven members and is chaired by the prime minister, with STA serving as the secretariate. The STA's major responsibility for biotechnology is the promotion of recombinant DNA research. This includes problems in safety as well as development technologies. The STA has the responsibility for coordinating research done in the national P4 facility in Tsukuba Science City. By contract to the Institute of Physical and Chemical Research (RIKEN), a public corporation that conducts advanced scientific research, STA is supporting research in development of bioreactors, development of an automated system for searching for biologically active substances, and development of new technologies relating to molecular genetics.

MITI

The MITI program for the next decade has targeted three fundamental technologies for support. One of these is biotechnology. MITI has also identified nine "big projects" for governmental support, one of which involves renaissance of aquifers in which biotechnology plays an important role. Similarly, in the energy projects and the energy savings projects, biotechnology through biomass and biofuel cell research will be supported. The specific MITI biotechnology program promotes three areas: fermentation, large-scale tissue culture, and recombinant DNA technology.

MITI has established the Research Association for Biotechnology (RAB) to facilitate interaction in biotechnology research among government, industry, and academia. RAB is a consortium of fourteen companies selected by invitation to stimulate and advise research in the three areas of biotechnology research. MITI allocates approximately $5 million per year for RAB's research budget. MITI also sponsors sixteen national institutes; one institute, the Fermentation Research Institute, is engaged in research on the utilization of nitrogen fixation by microorganisms.

MESC

This ministry has responsibility for supporting basic research in universities and national institutes throughout Japan. The ministry's annual budget is nearly $1.4 billion. Just how much goes for biotechnology is difficult to ascertain. Under the ministry's purview are the National Institutes for Biological Science, Basic Biology, and Genetics. Also, its funding of basic research in the national universities involves nine different institutes at seven national universities with missions related to biotechnology. Also under MESC is the Japan Society for the Promotion of Science, which supports cooperative research, fellowships, and exchange programs for researchers. The International Center at Osaka University for Industrial Fermentation gets part of its support from this ministry.

MAFF

This agency is reported to spend in excess of $10 million per year in biotechnology. This includes research in photosynthesis, biomass utilization, and the development of new biological resources through cell fusion and gene transplant. This activity does not appear to be coordinated with the MITI biotechnology plan or with other ministries; rather, the MAFF biotechnology program is strictly mission oriented.

MHW

This ministry has little responsibility for biotechnology research except as a concern for human safety. Its support for biotechnology research is almost solely confined to the safety of recombinant DNA technologies.

Essentially, therefore, three agencies — STA, MITI, and MAFF — represent the bulk of government support in biotechnology. Although the MITI plan has received a lot of international attention, its program in biotechnology is not a coordinated national plan. A similar statement could be made for U.S. biotechnology research, which is supported by numerous governmental agencies such as the National Institutes of Health, the National Science Foundation, the Department of Agriculture, the Department of Energy, the National Bureau of Standards, the Department of Defense, etc. No coordinated national plan exists except in the area of human safety with reference to recombinant DNA technologies, for which an interagency committee does exist. The key differences between biotechnology research in Japan and in the United States is that research is more applied in Japan and the work more directed toward industry's immediate needs. There also appears to be better cooperation between academia and industry in Japan.

KEY OBSERVATIONS

1. The promotion of biotechnology by MITI has focused international attention on biotechnology in Japan. However, the MITI plan is not a coordinated national plan. Other Japanese agencies, such as the Science and Technology Agency, Ministry of Education, Science, and Culture, Ministry of Agriculture, Forestry, and Fisheries, and the Ministry of Health and Welfare, whose constituencies are involved in biotechnology have not designated biotechnology as a priority area. This could happen in the near future.

Should a truly coordinated and integrated national plan for biotechnology emerge, then Japan could achieve a significant edge in the international race for commercializing biotechnology. To date this has not happened.

2. The MITI program promotes three specific biotechnology areas: fermentation, large-scale tissue culture, and recombinant DNA. These areas are deficient in that they do not address the problems of establishing a knowledge base in the behavior of protein molecules, particularly with respect to recovery, purification, and maintenance of specific activity of complex biomolecules during downstream bioprocessing.

3. MITI has established the Research Association for Biotechnology to facilitate interactions in biotechnology research among government, industry, and academia. RAB is a consortium of fourteen companies that subsidizes and plans cooperative research in the three areas targeted in the MITI biotechnology research plan.

4. Guided and subsidized in part by MITI and MESC, the Japanese Association of Industrial Fermentation has established a center at Osaka University to promote training, international cooperation, personnel and information exchange, and studies of special interest to biotechnology. This center appears to be more oriented toward extending the sphere of influence in biotechnology beyond Japanese borders, more especially to Southeast Asia, than helping the Japanese biotechnology industry.

5. Unlike the United States, Japan has virtually no newly established biotechnology companies. However, because of its strong tradition in fermented foods and pharmaceuticals, a large number of the traditional companies have joint projects with comparable U.S. firms. In these partnerships it would appear that the U.S. partner is doing the basic research and the Japanese partner the applied research.

6. MITI is attempting to facilitate the introduction of biotechnology into companies in need of revitalization. Thus, some Japanese companies in the chemical, textile, paint, and construction companies are becoming engaged in biotechnology activity. These companies, however, appear to be having difficulties in finding profitable outlets for the biotechnology research results.

7. Research carried out in Japanese universities is much more applied than in the United States. This is particularly true for research in genetics, which is for the most part very applied. Further, this research is carried out in university departments with an applied focus, such as Departments of Fermentation Technology, Departments of Applied Microbiology, and Departments of Agricultural Chemistry. These departments have close ties with industry, thereby encouraging many industrial employees to spend one- or two-year residencies in a university.

8. The Japanese regard the microflora in their soil as a natural resource and, therefore, have aggressively added to their culture collections from soils throughout Asia. As a consequence, the Japanese have developed a cadre of technical help skilled in the art of microbial screening that is readily adaptable to genetic engineering and associated screening techniques.

9. Most university and industrial laboratories involved in biotechnology research in Japan are well equipped with state-of-the-art equipment. For example, the biotechnology laboratories at the Takeda Chemical Company are certainly comparable with those at SmithKline, Beckman, and French. The biotechnology pilot plant facilities at Tokyo University's Institute of Applied Microbiology are quite comparable to the LORRE facilities at Purdue University. The only observable differences between the United States and Japanese laboratories are that comparable laboratories in Japan seemed to have about twice the technical support staff of those in the United States.

10. *Overall*, biotechnology research in Japan is comparable to that in the United States in terms of effort, equipment, and knowledge base. The focus in Japan is more applied than that in the United States. Japan appears to have a larger cadre of biotechnologists skilled in the art of screening techniques that can be directed to supporting applied research in genetics. Japan is poised to achieve a national program and purpose in biotechnology, something that is not happening in the United States, particularly in the applied aspects of biotechnology.

As biotechnology moves forward and more critical discoveries are made, it is important that close cooperation between scientists and engineers in these two societies is fostered. Frequent joint conferences, short visits by senior scientists, postgraduate and graduate student exchanges, and joint projects will help to aid both countries in bettering their scientific communication and aid the rapid commercialization of needed biotechnology for the world as a whole and developing nations in particular.

SELECTED BIBLIOGRAPHY

Dibner, M. D. "Biotechnology in Pharmaceuticals: The Japanese Challenge." *Science* 229 (September 1985):1230.

Lewis, Herman W. "Biotechnology in Japan" *ONRFE Scientific Bulletin* 10, no. 2 (1985):11-68.

_____ "Biotechnology in Japan," *ONRFE Scientific Bulletin* 10, no. 3 (1985): 91-105.

National Academy of Sciences. "Chemical and Process Engineering for Biotechnology." *Research Briefings*. Washington, D.C.: National Academy Press, 1984.

Office of Technological Assessment. *Commercial Biotechnology: An International Assessment*. Washington D.C.: Government Printing Office, February 1984.

"Proceedings of Biotechnology: 1st Symposium on Research and Development Project of Basic Technology for Future Industries." Tokyo, December 1983.

"Proceedings of the 2nd Conference to Promote Japan/U.S. Joint Projects and Cooperation in Biotechnology." Hotel Lake Biwa, Moriyama, Shiga, Japan, September 27-30, 1986.

"Research and Development of Life Sciences in Japan." *Science and Technology in Japan* (April-June 1983).

DISCUSSION SUMMARY

On the overall competitive balance between the United States and Japan in pharmaceuticals produced by biotechnological means, the United States has been the leader in discovering and applying the technology, but future products will not be developed solely in the United States. Although there has been an upsurge in new drug introductions by Japanese firms in the past several years, these are products of traditional technology. In light of the rapid progress by Japanese firms in recombinant DNA technology, the first wave of all-Japanese products made with new technology can be expected on the market in the early 1990s.

The industry's pattern of development in the United States has actually created opportunities for large foreign firms, like the Japanese drug companies, to quickly become active in the field. In the late 1970s, small U.S. companies recognized the importance of basic biotechnology discoveries made in U.S. universities. In order to test and market these discoveries, these companies sought tie-ups with large firms that had the resources to fund these costly and time-consuming procedures. By licensing foreign sales rights to the products, small U.S. firms generated the necessary cash flow to develop other products. This also gave large foreign firms instant access to the new field, and Japanese businesses actively established their own research facilities.

The lack of formal structure between academic institutions and businesses in the United States allows businesses to tailor an arrangement to the individual needs and conditions of a particular university. The Japanese system is more rigid and in some ways more restrictive, but performs well enough.

The greatest difference between the educational resources of the two nations is in the postdoctoral area. While postdoctoral programs are very strong in the United States, they are almost nonexistent in Japan. This is one reason why so many Japanese postdoctoral researchers are working in this country. Although Japan has tried to alleviate the deficiency by training postdoctoral researchers in the United States, foreign-trained researchers often have difficulty in making an impact on Japanese research when they return. Because the researchers are usually young and the university and private laboratories are structured on a seniority basis, these researchers are unable to obtain funding and launch their own research activities. This pattern of being buried under senior researchers is slowly changing. Given that these young Japanese researchers will make the basic discoveries of the future, cooperation between younger scientists of the two countries is the key to a cooperative future.

The channels for transfer from the United States to Japan are well developed. In addition to tapping into the large pool of journals and other literature, Japanese companies have used three approaches: licensing, joint ventures, and placing scientists in federal research facilities. The flow of biotechnology in the opposite direction, however, is still immature. The establishment of basic research and development facilities in Japan by Merck and Upjohn Pharmaceuticals is an encouraging sign. It was hoped that U.S. firms would take advantage of Japan's expertise in manufacturing and well-trained labor pool.

It was lamented that Japan does not have a satisfactory postdoctoral education system, although the Japanese Ministry of Education was considering offering grants to Japanese to go abroad and to fund foreign research activities. Japanese professors cannot be hired as consultants, and they are under social pressure not to establish their own company to commercialize their ideas. This is in stark contrast to the U.S. situation. To compensate for this, Japanese universities invite companies to send personnel to work with a professor and defray some of the cost of research equipment.

In Japan, a firm has no qualms about putting a great deal of money into the training and development of a researcher because of the lifetime employment system. Because it is relatively easy and common for U.S. researchers to switch employers, a Japanese firm may hesitate to provide adequate financial support or put them in key positions, making a delicate balance difficult to achieve.

One of Japan's great strengths is the fact that it pays great attention to foreign research activities, particularly those of the United States. Several examples were given of how a basic discovery made in the United States is put on a back shelf until a Japanese firm discovers a use for it. The United States needs to respond to this challenge in some organized fashion, perhaps using the Microelectronics and Computer Technology Corporation joint industrial research organization as a model. Another example showed that in 1984 no significant research activity in protein engineering and X-ray crystallography was taking place. But six months later, MITI had established a

30 billion yen protein engineering program in cooperation with approximately seventeen Japanese companies. Although this showed admirable responsiveness and cooperation, it was wondered if this program would be truly effective and efficient.

In regard to the regulatory environments of the two countries, it was noted that Japanese companies have followed the lead of U.S. firms in performing clinical trials in Europe where the requirements are less strict. However, the Food and Drug Administration's guidelines were much stricter than those of Japan's Ministry of Health. Nevertheless, even if only a slight change is made in the experiment or industrial biotechnology process, a completely new and separate government approval is necessary in Japan. There are Japanese who are as concerned about the impact of biotechnological research and products as Jeremy Rifkin, head of the Washington-based Foundation on Economic Trends, who has forced several government agencies to reconsider their research and testing guidelines for biotechnology. There was a loud outburst of public concern after Tokyo approved experiments with single cell proteins, so loud that Tokyo reconsidered. The United States and Japan should agree on a common set of guidelines to promote development and cooperation. Deliberate release of biotechnologically altered organisms is the flashpoint in the United States. The Japanese are even more concerned about such experiments.

The Japanese papers presented at the Lake Biwa conference tended to be focused on a single real problem, such as design, scale-up, and control of bioreactors or applications of specific enzyme-coupled reactions. In contrast, the U.S. papers tackled theoretical problems that might occur.

Are there any long-term problems with small U.S. biotechnology firms linking up with large foreign drug firms? Is it possible that these links will eventually allow the large foreign firm to force the small firms out of the market? According to Dr. Goeddel, Genentech is concerned about this possibility and has therefore decided against licensing its technology to any foreign firm or inviting foreign research personnel into its laboratories. It has sales and marketing agreements, but tries to hold onto its technology. This is not so with other U.S. firms. For example, Merck and Kyowa Hakko agreed to an amino acid venture some time ago. Merck no longer produces amino acids, which is food for thought.

Bioethics is a lively topic in Japan. There is great concern in Japan about deliberate release of biotechnologically altered microorganisms and the long-term implications of the industry's growth. However, there seems to be no real debate about bioethics in universities or government agencies. Instead, the subject seems to come up in small private groups. On the other hand, if it does become a problem, it is easier to sell a national priority in Japan than it is in the United States.

Is the United States taking a more pragmatic, long-term view of the impact of biotechnology, or is the United States simply rushing blindly ahead? Are Americans more accepting of the implications for genetic counseling, etc.? Perhaps interdisciplinary studies and university courses on bioethics contribute to greater U.S. concern about the subject. It appears that Japanese universities do not offer such courses or programs of study. Furthermore, the strong loyalty of an employee to his or her company may blind private researchers to any negative implications of biotechnology research. In general, it appears that bioethical considerations are not institutionalized in Japanese business or society.

Are Japanese companies willing to accept foreign researchers? Audience comments felt that they might be considered a disruptive element and would require special accommodative efforts by Japanese researchers. The panel cited a National Science Foundation survey of Japanese attitudes toward foreign researchers, and the result was a resounding yes in favor of having more foreign researchers in Japanese laboratories. It was felt that language would not be a problem because most Japanese researchers, particularly the younger ones, were relatively proficient in English. How to successfully integrate the outsider into the Japanese laboratory's structure was viewed as a more difficult problem. Japanese scientists who studied abroad and returned home would eventually have an impact on these attitudes. As these researchers rise to senior positions in private and public organizations, Japan may open up to a greater extent to foreigners.

On the other side of the coin, the panel was asked if many U.S. researchers would be willing to travel abroad to do research in the more structured, hierarchical Japanese facilities. Even if English was used in the laboratory, Americans would still find it difficult to take care of everyday tasks in Japan. Differences in food, housing, and other customs may make it difficult to adjust. The panel responded that this was a very valid consideration. If the foreign experience was viewed as a marketable asset — if it would improve a researcher's chances of getting a promotion or finding a better job — then there would be no lack of Americans willing to go abroad. Therefore, it is equally important to work on U.S. attitudes toward sending research personnel overseas. The panel mentioned that one solution may be to ask U.S. corporations to sponsor one or more researchers to go abroad and work in a foreign laboratory. This concern about U.S. attitudes was broadened to include the general U.S. view toward foreign research. The not-invented-here (NIH) syndrome blinds the U.S. business and scientific community to the valuable work that is going on in other countries. An attack on this broad attitude was also deemed necessary.

As an indication that Japan is attempting to integrate its research activities with the international community, Dr. Ulmer explained his participation in Tokyo's Human Frontiers Research Program. The program consists of three five-year phases with up to 30 percent foreign participation. Two of the current projects — bioelectronics and nonlinear materials — are led by Americans, of which he is one. As a project head, Dr. Ulmer goes to Japan twice a year for several weeks and can send a postdoctoral fellow to work at RIKEN. He said that Tokyo also plans to set up research facilities with foreigners in mind, perhaps providing special housing and living services.

The audience commented that although this was a significant break with Japan's previous practices, the Human Frontiers project employs only fifteen foreign researchers from several countries. Compared with the approximately three hundred Japanese researchers at the National Institutes of Health alone, this effort seems very modest, so modest, in fact, that it will be unable to deflect congressional action should the Hill decide that the technology flow is too far out of balance. The panel and the audience pointed to the just-passed Stevenson-Wydler Amendment, which gives directors of U.S. government research facilities the authority to deny access to foreign researchers unless the foreign government offers reciprocal access to its laboratories, as a warning to the U.S. and foreign research communities that new attitudes and greater cooperation are vital. Therefore, the panel agreed that there are not only many opportunities for the United States and Japan to cooperate in biotechnology, but that such cooperation may be vital to the health of the overall bilateral relationship.

8

Science and Technology Policy in Japan

Yoshimitsu Takeyasu

In this chapter, I will discuss science and technology policy in Japan. First, let me review briefly the history of scientific and technological policy in Japan since 1945. Shortly after World War II, science and technology were strongly emphasized. Emphasis was placed on the transfer of technology from overseas and on the modernization of industries. There was little room to promote either original science or technology. However, by the late 1950s, the Japanese economy had recovered and actually experienced a period of growth. Accordingly, greater emphasis was placed on efforts to promote Japan's own science and technology, and for this purpose, the Science and Technology Agency was established in 1956. Three years later, the Council for Science and Technology was organized as an advisory body to the prime minister, who would be able to play a role in the timely recommendation of guidelines for long-term policies.

The council's science and technology policy guidelines have been implemented in a series of phases. The first phase, during the 1960s, stressed the development of a fundamental research system, and the number of undergraduates studying in the scientific and technological disciplines increased. From the late 1960s to the early 1970s, the second phase marked the beginning of such diverse research and development (R&D) projects as the space program and nuclear power reactor development. In the early 1970s, the third phase was devoted to dealing with pollution, which had, by then, become a major social and environmental issue. The fourth phase, in the late 1970s, was marked by intense work carried out on energy-related R&D projects such as the development of alternative energy sources and energy conservation.

Next, I would like to comment on the improvement of industrial technology since World War II. In order to promote industrial technology development through the modernization of industrial facilities, the government has financed industrial investments from government institutions and encouraged the introduction of new technologies in key industries. Ultimately, it is up to industry to improve its own technology. For example, shipbuilding and steelmaking were Japanese industries that had been internationally competitive, but they were also involved in joint research projects with academia.

Nippon Telegraph and Telephone Public Corporation, formerly a state-run enterprise but now a private corporation, also pursued joint research with industry and by constantly applying those results has succeeded in raising the level of industrial technology in that field. The Japanese National Railways has also advanced industrial technology with its railroad successes, such as the Shinkansen-Bullet Train.

In the new fields of development such as nuclear power, space programs, and ocean studies, governmental organizations were established to promote development with the cooperation of the private sector. The Japanese government also promoted R&D in fields that were beneficial to the general public, such as alternative energy sources and energy conservation particularly after the oil crises.

In the area of direct aid to industry, research subsidies have been granted since the 1950s, but they were intended only to stimulate private research; therefore, the amounts were relatively small, and in recent years, these subsidies have been reduced annually.

For the past twenty years, the percentage of research investment borne by the government, including funds for commissioned work and subsidies, has been around 1 percent of the total research expenditures by various industries. This is a small percentage when compared to expenditures of around 20 percent to 30 percent by the United States and European countries.

Generally speaking, the government's role in financing R&D investment has been, and still is, quite a minor one. Direct subsidies are extremely limited. The improvements made in Japanese scientific and technological standards are not the end result of large government subsidies, but are basically due to the vitality of the industries themselves.

My next topic is the present trends in science and technology policies in Japan. In entering the 1980s, Japan has already overcome two oil crises in the 1970s and has grown more confident economically. In order to further vitalize the economy and accomplish future growth throughout the country, all sectors recognize the importance of science and technology. The move-

ment for economic and social development through the advancement of
science and technology and new technological innovation is strong and growing.

The private sector has put more effort in R&D, and those research funds
have increased rapidly. The total amount of research funds spent in Japan,
reflecting the large increase in private sector research funds, rapidly increased to 7 trillion yen in fiscal year 1984, or 3 percent of the total Japanese
national income, which was approximately even with the United States and
European countries.

In response to inquiries from the prime minister, the council issued its
latest report in 1984, which presented the basic policies for science technology promotion for the next ten years. In principle, Japan's present science
and technology policies are based on this report.

According to the recommendation of the council, the government decided
in 1986 on the General Guidelines for Science and Technology Policy which
indicated Japan's fundamental science and technology policies for the up-
coming four or five years. The basic guidelines as described in this document are the following three points:

1. Strengthen basic research and promote original science and technology;
2. Develop science and technology while emphasizing specifically international contributions; and
3. Encourage harmony between science and technology, and human
society.

Along with these three points, it was decided that a basic plan for R&D
advancement should be drawn up, and sixteen important R&D fields would
be designated for growth and special attention. This was the first time since
the end of World War II that the cabinet decided on a science and technology policy based on a consensus by the ministries and agencies. Presently,
the restoration of sound government finances, by minimizing the dependence on government bonds within a few years, is the most important government guideline. Although expenditures have been rapidly reduced, defense
and international joint-cooperation obligations require spending increases.
Given this financial situation, there is concern that it might be difficult to expect any immediate large budget increases in support of science and technology. Therefore, the present science and technology policy development
is constrained by either across-the-board budget reductions or by the allocation of funds according to project priority. All ministries and agencies are
troubled by this prospect and are taking great pains to improve project ef-
ficiencies.

Despite the gloomy financial outlook, Japan has already made a start toward realization of the basic objectives of the general guidelines. The necessity of strengthening basic research was mentioned in the previous policy proposals of the council, but this is the first time it has been put forth as the most important item in the science and technology policy.

About ten years ago, the National Science Foundation released the Gellman Report, which analyzed the main innovations throughout the world case by case. This report indicated that the number of Japanese innovations had increased, but that many of these innovations were improvements on existing technology and that epoch-making "breakthrough" innovations were very few. In recent years, experts in all fields have become aware of the necessity of strengthening basic research to promote future technological innovation. There is a general consensus within Japan that it should move in the direction of a stronger basic research base. I would like to refer to some examples of these efforts.

First, research funds for universities have increased each year. The Japanese government has also provided special funds to national research institutes for basic research.

In addition, new research systems have been initiated to promote basic research. Among these, the Exploratory Research for Advanced Technology (ERATO), which was started in 1981 by the Research Development Corporation of Japan, is now promoting research in eight projects. MITI's Research and Development Project of Basic Technology for Future Industries which started the same year as ERATO, is also promoting research on future basic technologies with the cooperation of the private sector.

In October 1986, the Institute of Physical and Chemical Research launched the international frontier research system as another new system. Japanese and foreign researchers will now conduct advanced fundamental research in two research fields. Moreover, of the six team leaders, two positions have been assumed by U.S. researchers.

The advanced and complex levels of research that are carried out today accentuate the importance of research and information exchanges across borders and among organizations. It is understood that through these kinds of exchanges, it is possible to plan for more efficient and effective use of funds, skills, and other research resources. With this is mind, the completion of measures for recent research exchange promotion have been planned. For example, the budget for carrying out joint research between national universities and the private sector has been expanded yearly, and funds for the establishment of a joint research center for the national universities have been requested in the 1988 budget. Also, all ministries and agencies are actively pursuing joint research between government research laboratories and the private sector. In addition, the Law for Facilitating

Research Exchanges was enacted in 1986. Through this law, joint research and other research exchanges between government and the private sector are expected to be greatly facilitated.

I understand that the United States is also intensifying policies for the promotion of joint research between the government and the private sector with a view to the promotion of technology transfer mainly to the private sector. Also being emphasized is the promotion of the establishment of centers for joint research between the private sector and universities and other cooperative promotion among industry, academia, and government. I think that the U.S. experience can also be a good reference for Japan.

Also, with the emphasis on basic research, the roles of universities and national research organizations have become more important. For this reason, discussion is continuing on the research systems of universities in the Provisional Commission for Educational Reform, and the council is investigating the roles of the national research organizations from the mid- to long-term point of view.

Next, I would like to touch on Japan's efforts to promote international research exchanges and on Japan's contributions to the international community. The role that Japan should perform in the international community has been growing steadily in recent years. Although the Nakasone government is promoting the adjustment of the Japanese economic structure, it is also necessary for science and technology to be more internationally open, and substantial efforts in this direction are evident in many scientific fields in Japan. The rate at which Japanese dissertations are cited in major foreign technical journals has increased and is now higher than that of any other country.

Progress is also being made in the compilation of English language data bases of Japanese technical literature, and overseas on-line data supply systems have started operating in October 1986. With the cooperation of the United States and West Germany, this system is scheduled to be expanded next year. Additionally, development is underway to create a machine that can translate Japanese into English. This system is expected to be ready for practical use sometime in the near future.

International exchanges of researchers are growing rapidly. Trends show that the number of Japanese researchers abroad and the hosting of foreign researchers in Japan are both increasing. Looking at the exchange situation by country, the number of researchers abroad and foreign researchers in Japan are nearly equal in total. But in the exchanges between Japan and advanced countries, Japanese researchers abroad greatly outnumbered those in Japan. This difference is quickly being rectified, but I am hoping with all my heart that researchers from the United States and the other advanced countries would look to Japan and actively participate in research in Japan.

Japanese must make greater efforts to create an environment where overseas researchers can visit and carry out substantial research activities in Japan.

The number of foreign exchange students are also expected to increase. Presently, fifteen thousand foreign exchange students are studying in Japan; 10 percent are from the economically advanced countries. This number is much less than the three hundred thirty thousand studying in the United States, but it has been growing in recent years. The aim of Japanese policy is to have one hundred thousand exchange students by the early twenty-first century.

Although the employment of foreign researchers at national universities has been allowed, the Law for Facilitating Research Exchanges will make it possible to work within a national research organization. Measures to gain reciprocal gratis or reduced fee for the use of patent rights and the waiver of damage compensation rights are also under consideration. Through these measures, obstacles to the promotion of international exchanges and cooperation are being removed.

However, international cooperation is also necessary within the framework of science and technology cooperation agreements. The number of these agreements concluded between Japan and other countries and the number of cooperation subjects agreed upon are growing each year. In particular, cooperation with the United States is carried out within the framework of many cooperation agreements in such areas as energy- and nonenergy-related fields.

In order to increase these types of international exchanges and cooperation programs, it is necessary to ensure and maintain adequate funding levels. More specifically, the Japanese government is making special efforts to provide sufficient budget for researcher's foreign travel expenses, particularly those who are employed at the national research organizations and national universities.

Lastly, I would like to introduce the Human Frontier Science Program. We Japanese are faced with an array of serious problems: exhaustion of non-renewable energy and other valuable resources, the accompanying demands on the environment, population explosion, the aging of society, and so on. In addition to finding fundamental solutions to these serious problems, there are great expectations for the development of energy- and resource-efficient "soft" technology. A key to these solutions is the elucidation of the functions of living organisms, a field that is expected to reveal a wealth of new scientific and technological developments. It is necessary for Japan to conduct comprehensive basic research in biotechnology, particularly through international cooperation. By putting substantial emphasis on this field, Japan hopes to make substantial contributions to the international community. It is for these reasons we are conducting conceptual investigations of the Human Frontier Science Program, which we hope can be executed with active international cooperation. Because the program is still in the conceptual stage, it is mainly under the purview of the Council for Science and Technology. This ambitious program will emphasize the essential elucidation of the higher-order functions of human beings and other organisms, including an analysis of the mechanisms of the brain, the nervous system, the immune system, and biological material transport systems. Japan is also studying the prospects of expanding basic research in this field through research subsidies and research schemes. Naturally, it is important that other countries of the world share in the results of this research. The Human Frontier Science Program will be structured around long-term international programs. We sincerely hope the United States and other advanced countries will join our research efforts as our investigations proceed.

In conclusion, Japan is promoting basic research and making substantial efforts to contribute to the world community. The development of basic research and the expansion of contributions to the international community through science and technology are intimately related. In order to raise the level of basic research and fulfill its research goals, it is necessary to enhance the number of international exchanges. Of course, laboratories carrying out high-level research in excellent environments will encourage lively international exchanges; consequently, more interactions and greater contributions to the world are anticipated. These kinds of developments and exchanges are already being carried out in Japan in several fields.

There are still differences that will require further understanding, including domestic systems, customs, languages, and budget constraints. Yet in spite of these differences, I think that Japan's science and technology developments and policies are heading in a new direction, and we would like to see it continue in this direction.

Of particular importance is the need for all concerned to modify their attitudes. From now on, Japan must attach more importance to cultural originality and cultivate new science and technology in that environment. Science and technology should be used for the greatest benefit of all humankind, not just for Japan. Although overcoming these attitudes will require much time and effort, it is extremely vital that they be changed. I sincerely believe that Japan has now started to move in this direction.

Table 1. Country-wide R&D Expenditures and Number of Researchers

Country	Fiscal Year	Total Research (billion)	Expenditures % of Gross National Income	Number of Researchers (thousands)
Japan	1980	4,684	2.35	
Japan	1981	5,364	2.58	
Japan	1982	5,882	2.71	
Japan	1983	6,504	2.85	
Japan	1984	7,177	2.99	380 (FY 1985)
U.S.	1985	25,424	2.94 (FY 1984)	740
West Germany	1985	4,233	3.17 (FY 1984)	130 (FY 1981)
France	1984	2,582	2.38 (FY 1982)	90 (FY 1983)
U.K.	1983	2,372	2.65 (FY 1981)	100 (FY 1981)

Table 2. Transitions in Japan's Science and Technology Budget (100 million)

	1982	1983	1984	1985	1986
Science and technology-related budget	14,479	14,562	14,776	15,253	15,990
(Percent change from previous FY)	(3.6)	(0.6)	(1.5)	(3.2)	(4.8)
Total budget (ordinary expenditure budget)	326,210	326,195	325,857	325,854	325,842
(Percent change from previous FY)	(1.8)	(-0.0)	(-0.1)	(-0.0)	(-0.0)

Table 3. Basic Research Expenditures (100 million)

Type of Organization	Type of Research	Japan (1983)	U.S. (1983)	FRG (1981)	France (1979)	U.K. (1975)
Government research organizations	basic	957	3,919	1,946	1,029	785
	application, development	5,715	20,373	2,876	4,342	3,016
Universities	basic	5,638	14,333	3,762	3,165	1,453
	application, development	4,635	10,070	1,327	352	74
Private sector	basic	2,827	6,947	1,420	544	428
	application, development	45,255	152,594	24,288	13,295	8,893
Total	basic	9,422	25,199	7,128	4,738	2,666
	application, development	55,605	183,037	28,491	17,989	11,983
Population (millions)		119	234	62	54	56

Source: OECD statistics.

Table 4. The State of International Exchanges of Researchers by Country

Country	Japanese Researchers Dispatched Abroad			Foreign Researchers Received in Japan		
	1980	1983	83/80	1980	1983	83/80
United States	12,468	15,271	1.22	1,565	2,591	1.68
United Kingdom	1,556	1,906	1.22	355	778	2.19
France	1,685	1,702	1.01	149	256	1.72
West Germany	1,523	1,724	1.13	176	301	1.71
Others	2,348	3,098	1.21	412	974	2.36
Advanced Western countries	19,580	23,701	1.21	2,657	4,900	1.84
Others	3,569	5,356	1.50	7,713	24,002	3.11
Total	23,149	29,057	1.28	10.370	28,902	2.78

Source: Japanese Ministry of Justice

Table 5. Number of Foreign Exchange Students
in Japan (as of May 1)

1975	1979	1982	1985
5,573	5,933	8,116	15,009

Source: Japanese Ministry of Education, Science,
and Culture

9

The Emergence of Value-Creation Networks in Corporate Strategy

Mel Horwitch

The emergence of so-called strategic alliances signifies a general shift in the practice of strategic management. Corporate strategy is now entering what I call a "postmodern" phase. Strategy is not only more and more global in its orientation; it is also increasingly concerned with higher-value objectives. The purpose of this chapter is to discern the meaning of the advent of strategic alliances within the context of the current transition of strategic management as a whole. A basic position of this chapter is that the increasing number of strategic alliances between the United States and Japan is at least partially a reflection of the more general characteristics of postmodern strategy.

This chapter is organized into three parts. First, there is a brief overview of the current state of the strategic management field. The next part then discusses modern technology strategy and its close relationship with strategic alliances. The final part presents a generic model of a large corporation that has spun a complex web of alliances and offers some conclusions and assessments regarding the meaning of strategic alliances for modern strategic management.

POSTMODERN STRATEGY AND
STRATEGIC ALLIANCES

Strategic management has now become what I call "postmodern." The composition of this kind of strategy needs to be understood from a number of perspectives, as presented in Figure 1. Let us first review postmodern strategic management from a historical perspective. In the immediate post-World War II period until about the late 1960s, the field of strategy was dominated by the general management tradition. The emphasis was on the

Figure 1. The Composition of Postmodern Strategic Management. Copyright Mel Horwitch.

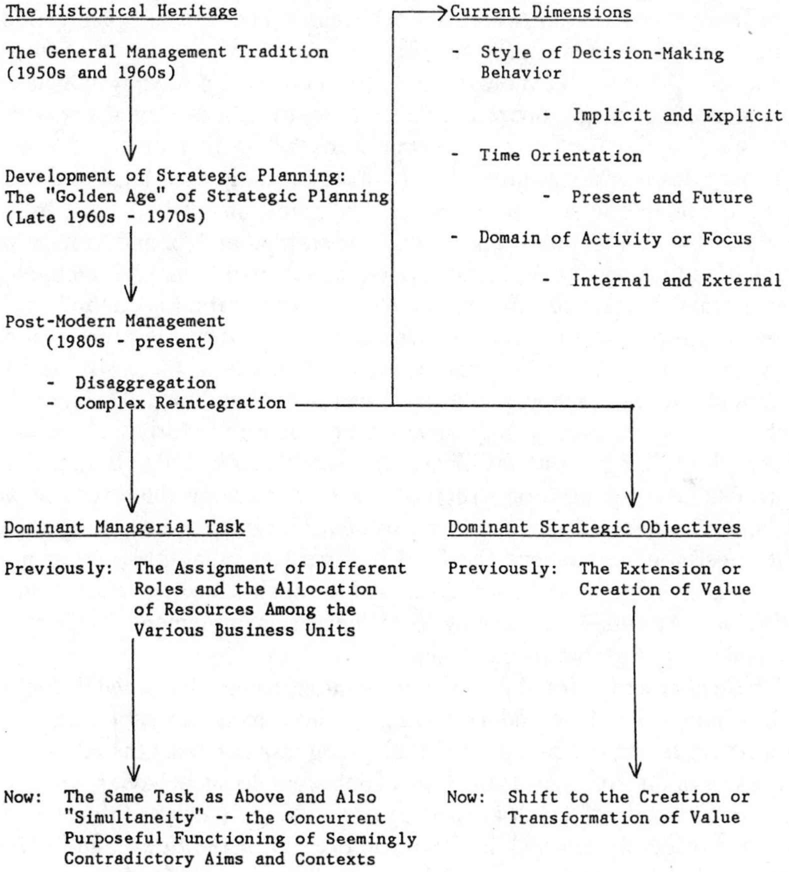

The Historical Heritage

The General Management Tradition
(1950s and 1960s)

Development of Strategic Planning:
The "Golden Age" of Strategic Planning
(Late 1960s - 1970s)

Post-Modern Management
    (1980s - present)

    - Disaggregation
    - Complex Reintegration

Current Dimensions

- Style of Decision-Making
  Behavior

    - Implicit and Explicit

- Time Orientation

    - Present and Future

- Domain of Activity or Focus

    - Internal and External

Dominant Managerial Task

Previously: The Assignment of Different
             Roles and the Allocation
             of Resources Among the
             Various Business Units

Now: The Same Task as Above and Also
      "Simultaneity" -- the Concurrent
      Purposeful Functioning of Seemingly
      Contradictory Aims and Contexts

Dominant Strategic Objectives

Previously: The Extension or
             Creation of Value

Now: Shift to the Creation or
      Transformation of Value

primacy of broad-based and sensitive leadership and a view of strategy that went beyond economic objectives to include the contribution of the firm for its employees, stockholders, and the community at large. Of particular concern under this tradition was how strategy can infuse an organization with "value" or "organizational purpose." The skills to accomplish this goal were "general" attributes that could possibly be used in any industrial setting.[1] The general management tradition was followed by a "golden age" of strategic planning. This phase was rich with development of analytical methodologies for strategic purposes. A whole support service sector, made up of business schools, strategic consulting firms, and information and data collection and analysis firms, emerged to develop and extend this kind of strategy. Strategic management became a profession, a formal management function, and a staff activity.[2] Strategy became differentiated and decoupled from operations. Under the weight of rising overhead, a sluggish response to new market conditions, the growing importance of new concerns such as global competition, technology, and the increasingly acknowledged significance of seemingly operational or line matters, a profound revision of strategic planning took place.[3] Postmodern strategy then emerged.

From a historical viewpoint, this new era partially went back and rediscovered valuable lessons from the general management heritage. In particular, the importance of people, leadership, and broad values was emphasized. Also, the dramatic experience of small-firm, high-technology entrepreneurialism and other factors led to a new emphasis on the benefits of decentralized, small, and flat organizational structures. A process of disaggregation began. At the same time, the benefits of large size and the economics of scale, scope, and analysis were not abandoned. The analytical techniques became less grandiose and more focused. Moreover, a process of complex reintegration took place, where emphasis included fluid and network-like interorganization structures — such as strategic alliances — as well as better and varied use of the traditional hierarchical corporate form.[4] With postmodern strategy, the field became less monolithic, more pragmatic, more eclectic, and more grounded in specific business operations or industries. Attention was turning to such areas as implementation, culture, technology, and global competition.

These characteristics of postmodern strategy can be discerned by looking at its dimensions. Postmodern strategic management is a subtle and ever-present trade-off, balancing act and blending task involving the interplay of three sets of dimensions: (1) the style of decisionmaking behavior, which can be termed "explicit" (such as formal) or "implicit" (such as informal); (2) the time orientation, which is either the present or the future; and (3) the domain of activity or focus, which is either internal or external. Postmodern management also often requires the concurrent blending of seemingly opposite aspects of strategy, such as vigorous disaggregation in order to capture the benefits of flat organizations and an entrepreneurial zeal, and complex reintegration to exploit the advantages of economies of scale and scope. I call this characteristic of postmodern strategy *simultaneity*, the simultaneous incorporation of diverse and possibly seemingly contradictory elements in order to achieve a larger set of strategic objectives.

Finally, the dominant objectives of strategy are changing. In the 1970s, extending and mining a product line via market-share dominance, for example, were as important as creating new products and services. With the arrival of postmodern management the shift is away from the extension of value and toward the creation and transformation of value. Strategic moves that heighten differentiation and value, such as increasing the importance of internal research and development or entering into joint ventures to design and create new products, assume higher priority. This important shift in objectives is a major cause for the elevation of technology as a strategic variable and the creation of "new linkages" by corporations for technology development.

TECHNOLOGY STRATEGY AND
STRATEGIC ALLIANCES

The use of strategic alliances for technology development purposes is part of the more general elevation of technology to a strategic variable in technology-intensive firms in all the advanced economies, which itself reflects the broad transition to postmodern strategy. Therefore, understanding of modern technology strategy is often critical for comprehending the strategic role of interorganizational linkages. In fact, technology strategy can be viewed as a kind of "leading indicator" for pinpointing key trends in strategy generally. For example, technology strategy is part of the growing concern for creating and maintaining increasingly higher value-strategic actions. Technology strategy also focuses on the design and implementation of novel kinds of structures. Technology strategy confronts continuously the critical trade-off between the benefits of large-scale-oriented economies of size, scope, and synergies and the benefits of small-scale-oriented individual or decentralized entrepreneurialism, flat organizations, and fast response to users and the market. A key part of technology strategy also involves the challenge of creating the requisite set of "new linkages" with organizations external to the firm. Finally, in developing a way to put these and possibly other elements together technology strategy must cope with the probable need to concurrently manage inherent contradictions for the long-term strategic success of the enterprise.[5]

The recognition of technology as a top-level and strategic concern for a corporation and its elevation to a strategic variable were due to the convergence of many of the same historical forces that by the 1980s had created the need for postmodern strategic management as a whole. By that time, the full impact of such historical trends – including the negative reaction to strategy planning, the success of the small high-technology firm, the increasingly strategic importance allocated to technology by foreign competition (particularly the Japanese), the related rise in status of manufacturing as a strategic weapon, and the supportive relevant thinking and research in the fields of strategic management and the management of technology – was visible, widespread, and powerful. Technology strategy had emerged as an important and pace-setting management activity in the corporation.

The key characteristics of technology strategy that flowed during the 1980s were quite different from the distinguishing features of private-sector technological innovation that existed through the 1970s. In that earlier era, private-sector U.S. technological innovation was fragmented and could logically be viewed as comprising two paradigms or ideal types: Mode I – small high-technology firm entrepreneurialism; and Mode II – large-scale corporation, industrial research and development (R&D).[6]

By the early 1980s, as technology became increasingly strategic, the boundary between the two major forms of private-sector technological innovative activity – small-firm and large-corporation innovation – began to fade. This blending of these previously distinctive modes is a salient feature of modern technology strategy[7] and a clear reflection of broader postmodern management trends. The previous separation of large- and small-firm technological innovation no longer holds. Out of this fundamental blending, modern technology strategy has emerged. Now a complex array of trade-offs, relationships, and linkages has to be managed.

In order to better understand this new situation, a conceptual framework is helpful and is presented in Figure 2. Large, modern technology-intensive corporations are making technology strategy decisions along three dimensions: competition versus cooperation (competitive strategy); internal versus external development (domain); and traditional large corporation, industrial R&D versus decentralized entrepreneurial units (structure). Achieving the appropriate set of multiple trade-offs and locations along these dimensions is one of the major tasks in technology strategy today.

The practice of technology strategy is increasingly pervasive. The extent and dimensions of modern technology strategy and the key role strategic alliances play in its execution can be seen as a diverse array of technology-intensive industries, including the personal computer industry, which experienced a prototypical evolutionary development from a large number of small firms to competition among fewer large players (Table 1 and Figure 3); the permanently turbulent medical diagnostics industry (Table 2); the revitalized manufacturing technology sector (Tables 3 and 4), the immediately strategic biochemical industry (Figure 4), and the still-unformed-but-already-linked optoelectronics industry (Tables 5 and 6).[8]

Figure 2. Elements of Modern Technology Strategy. Copyright Mel Horwitch.

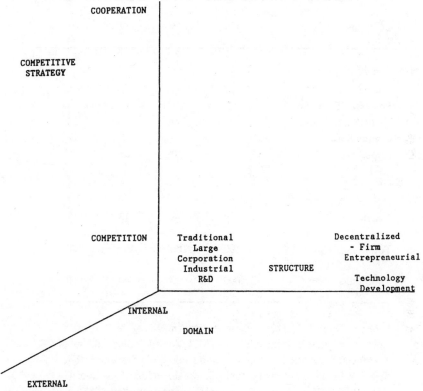

Source: Various issues of *InfoWorld* in 1983 and 1984

Table 1. Market Share of the U.S. Personal Computer Industry (by dollar sales)

Company	1976	1978	1980	1982
MITS	25			
IMSAI	17			
Processor Technology	8			
Radio Shack		50	21	10
Commodore		12	20	12
Apple		10	27	26
IBM				17
NEC			5	11
Hewlett-Packard			9	7
Other	50	28	18	17
Total	100	100	100	100
Total units	15,000	200,000	500,000	1,500,000

Sources: Gary N. Farner, "A Competitive Analysis of the Personal Computer Industry" (Master's thesis, MIT, Alfred P. Sloan School of Management, May 20, 1982), p. 18, and Deborah F. Schreiber, "The Strategic Evolution of the Personal Computer Industry" (Master's thesis, MIT, Alfred P. Sloan School of Management, May, 1983), p. 7.

Figure 3. A Selected List of Linkages in the Personal Computer Industry, 1983–1984

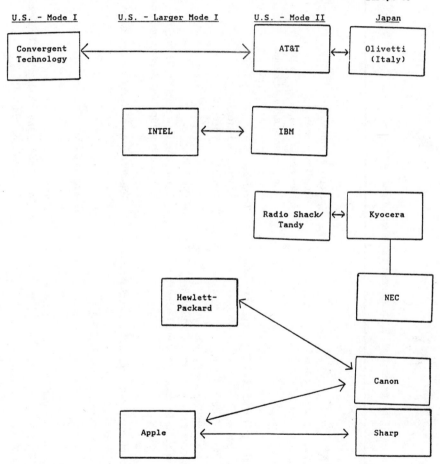

Table 2. Technology Linkages in the U.S. Diagnostic Ultrasound Industry

GEC, Ltd.
Acquired Picker
Acquired Cambridge Instruments
Licensee of SRI and Hitachi

General Electric
Bought technology from Electra-Physics (Litton) and
    hired Litton people.
B-scan product modified by Xonics
Linear array developed by Yokogawa
Phased array developed by Analogic Corporation
Mechanical sector developed by Second Foundation

Johnson & Johnson
Acquired Technicare (Ohio Nuclear, Unirad, Scientific
    Advances, Battelle)
Acquired Irex (joint venture with Hoffrell)

Philips
Acquired Rohe Ultrasound (sold Kretz equipment)
Licensee of Matsushita
Supplied by Hoffrell

Diasonics
Start-up from Searle
Acquired Varian
Licensee of Hitachi
Joint development with Hitachi

Toshiba
Supplied to Litton
Hired Litton people

Hoffrell
Licensee of University of Pittsburgh
Licensor to Philips and Cambridge Instruments
    (Picker)
Joint venture with Irex (Johnson & Johnson)

Fischer
Acquired EMI

Unirad
Acquired by Ohio Nuclear and Technicare
    (Johnson & Johnson)

Siemens
Sold Diasonics equipment in Europe
Acquired Searle's line
Licensee of Matsushita

SmithKline
Started as a joint venture with General Precision
 Corporation
Acquired rights to mechanical sector from Indianapolis
 Center for Advanced Research
Licensee of Mediscan (licensed Xerox)
Formed SKI and sold 80 percent to Xonics

Squibb
Acquired ATL (Licensee of University of Washington
 and SRI)
Acquired ADR (Start-up from Unirad)

Xonics
Owns 80 percent of SKI (SmithKline)
Developed product for GE

Litton
Spawned GE and provided B-Scan
Spawned Toshiba; original licensee of Toshiba

Searle
Spawned Diasonics
Acquired by Siemens

Source: John Friar and Mel Horwitch, "The Emergence of Technology Strategy," *Technology in Society* 7, nos. 2-3 (Winter 1985/86): 156.

Table 3. Market Share: U.S.-Based Robot Vendors 1980-1983

Company	1980	1981	1982	1983
Unimation	44.4	43.8	32.1	22.8
Cincinnati Milacron	32.3	32.2	21.0	16.2
DeVilbiss	5.5	4.2	7.4	6.7
Asea, Inc.	2.8	5.8	8.7	7.2
Prab Robots, Inc.	6.1	5.3	4.2	4.2
Cybotech	-	-	4.9	4.2
Copperweld Robotics	3.3	2.3	2.3	1.8
Automatix	0.4	1.9	4.2	7.6
Advanced Robotics Corp.	1.9	0.5	3.5	3.2
Mordson	0.8	1.6	2.5	2.5
Thermwood	-	0.6	1.6	1.4
Bendix	-	-	1.4	2.3
GCA Industrial Systems	-	-	1.0	2.9
IBM	-	-	0.7	3.0
GE	-	-	0.9	1.1
Westinghouse	-	-	0.4	1.5
U.S. Robots	-	-	0.6	1.5
Graco	-	-	0.6	1.5
Mobot	0.9	0.4	0.8	0.8
GM/Fanuc	-	-	1.5	3.0
American Robot	-	-	-	0.6
Textron	-	-	-	0.3
Nova Robotics	-	-	-	0.3
Control Automation	-	-	0.1	0.3
Machine Intelligence	-	-	-	1.1
Intelledex	-	-	-	0.6
Other	1.7	1.3	1.5	1.7
	100.0	100.0	100.0	100.0

Source: L. Conigliaro, *Robotics Newsletter*, no. 9 (1982).

Table 4. Interfirm Linkages in the U.S. Robotics Industry, 1983

Strategic Management

Licensing Agreements		Joint Ventures		Mergers & Acquisitions	
Licensee	Licensor	Joint Venture	Parents	Subsidiary	Parent
Kawasaki Heavy Ind. (Japan)	Unimation	Unimation	Condac, Pullman Corp.	Unimation	Westinghouse
RN Eurobotics (Belgium)	Arab	GMF Robotics, Inc.	General Motors, Fanuc	PAR Systems	GCA
Can-Eng. Mfg. (Canada)	"	Cybotech	Renault, Randsburg Industries	U.S. Robots	Square D. Corp.
Murata Machinery (Japan)				Copperweld Robotics (formerly Auto-Place)	Copperweld Corp.
Binks (U.K.)	Thermwood	Int'l. Machine Intell.	Machine Intelligence Yaskawa		
Cyclomatic Ind.	"				
Didde Graphics Co.	"	Graco Robotics	Graco Inc., Edon Finishing		
DeVilbiss	Trallfa (Norway)				
Nordson	Taskawa (Japan)				
Admiral Equip. Co.	"				
Bendix					
Automatix	Hitachi (Japan)				
General Electric	"				
Interred	"				
Graco	Nolaug (Norway				
United Technologies	Nimak (W. Germany)				
RCA	Dainichi Kiko (Japan)				
I.B.M.	Sankyo Seiki (Japan)				
General Electric	DEA (Italy)				
"	Volkswagen (W. Germany)				
Westinghouse	Olivetti (Italy)				
"	Hisubishi Electric (Japan)				
"	Komatsu (Japan)				
Lloyd Tool and Mfg.	Jobs Robots (Italy)				

Source: David Schatz, "The Strategic Evolution of the Robotics Industry" (Master's thesis, MIT, Sloan School, May 1983).

Table 5. Participants in the Optoelectronics Industry

Type of Institution	1978	1984
Integrated computer or communications company	AT&T Bell-Northern Research IBM	AT&T NEC Fujitsu
Transmission systems supplier or non-telecommunications integrated company	Hewlett-Packard Texas Instruments RCA ITT	Boeing Electronic Company Sumitomo
Vendor	Galileo Electro General Optronics Spectronics Times Fiber Valter	Hitachi Galilco Electro General Optronics Spectronics Times Fiber Valtei
Multifirm research programs	MITI	MITI Battelle Memorial Institute

Source: Anne T. Fox, "Strategic Decision-Making in a Global Technology-Intensive Environment: A Case of the Optoelectronics Industry" (Master's thesis, MIT, Sloan School of Management, June, 1986), pp. 26-30.

Table 6. Strategic Position of Major
Optoelectronics Firms

Company	1986	1995
AT&T	high	medium
NEC	high	high
Fujitsu	high	high
Sumitomo	low	medium-low
Boeing	low	medium-low

Source: Anne T. Fox, "Strategic Decision-
Making in a Global Technology-Intensive
Environment: A Case of the Optoelectronics
Industry" (Master's thesis, MIT, Sloan School
of Management, June, 1986), p. 94.

Figure 4. Relationships Between U.S. and Japanese Biochemical Companies

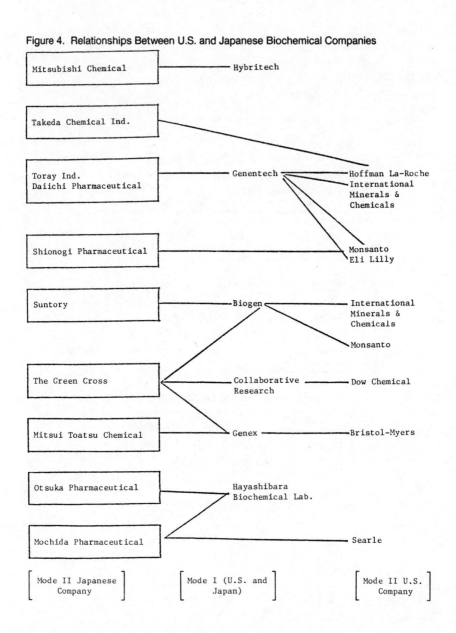

In biotechnology, for example, the postmodern aspects of technology strategy are clearly evident. Linkages are being established between Mode I and II firms in the United States and between Mode I, Mode II, and multiorganization endeavors in Japan. Japanese firms are also entering into important research, licensing, and marketing agreements with U.S. and European firms in order to establish and maintain shares of world leadership in the emerging biotechnology sector. A few Japanese firms and other institutions also have equity in U.S. biochemical firms. This trend is seen in Figure 4.

Technology strategy can even be documented in an industry that does not yet truly exist, the optoelectronic communication switching and computer industry. In fact, the advent of modern technology strategy in this industry is probably the most dramatic manifestation of technology's strategic importance. Optoelectronics still consists mostly of intensive R&D efforts by a host of U.S. and foreign firms and some government-sponsored programs. It is still more a vision based on assumptions and extrapolations of technical and market trends. Even without viable and accepted products, however, technology strategy is being vigorously practiced.[9]

To pinpoint this industry is a particularly difficult task. The Japanese Optoelectronic Industry and Technology Development Association defined the general optoelectronic field as one "targeted at an affective use of various characteristics of light, such as high frequency, space information processing and phase information processing capability."[10] A leading expert at Bell Laboratories defined the industry as including devices that emit or detect light, rather than using light simply for illumination. The foundation of this industry was the invention of the laser in 1960 at Bell Laboratories. The laser made possible the generation of a pure and strong light signal. Optical technology in theory offers several intriguing potential advantages over traditional electronic technology, having greater "bandwidth" and speed capacity for the transmission of information, possessing electronic immunity and thereby avoiding electronic tapping or jamming, and employing lighter and smaller transmission media using optical fiber instead of copper. Some of these characteristics have already led to a growing and increasingly commodity-like fiber optics market for long distance telecommunications and information transmission.

There is also the potential for higher value uses of optical technology when fused with electronics and related technologies and used in information processing and telecommunications. The use of optics in such a fashion would accelerate the processing rates and capacity. Ultimately, optical technology could be used inside telecommunications switching equipment and computers to replace electronic integrated circuits, other semiconductors, and computer wiring. At least in theory, this kind of innovation could lead to mass markets for advanced video and information services and to a huge demand for a host of new products, including optically integrated chips (the so-called "optical chip"), the optical computer, and photonic telecommunication switches. It is this potential sector, the use of optics in electronics, computers, and telecommunications switches, on which I will focus, not on long distance transmission.

By the late 1970s, the possible application of optoelectronics in computing and telecommunications devices was already recognized. Bell Laboratories was researching integrated optoelectronics; dozens of other U.S. research laboratories were spending a total of about $50 million on optoelectronics; and the Ministry of International Trade and Industry (MITI) in Japan established in 1978 a joint $90 million optoelectronic research project with thirteen companies. Also, several companies and small firms were exploring segments of this field.

By the mid-1980s, however, the set of industry participants had changed. A dual structure had emerged with three major Japanese computer companies heavily committed to optoelectronics as well as several other firms, mostly small ones, still staking out niches. Table 5 shows this evolution. In order to understand better this change and the strategic decisions being taken, I will discuss two important and contrasting firms, AT&T and NEC.

AT&T has been the clear leader in optoelectronics research. In 1985 at Bell Labs, out of a total of 18,000 employees and 120 laboratories, about 225 scientists and parts of 6 laboratories (3 wholly dedicated) were working on phonetics research. At that time, Bell Labs spent a total of about $45 million annually on optoelectronics, $25 million on research, and $20 million on development. However, Bell Labs' efforts in optoelectronics are rather unfocused and fragmented, thus reflecting the broad and science-oriented research tradition of that organization. In 1985, its optoelectronics research budget had 33 percent allocated to lasers, 33 percent to detectors, switches, and bistable optical devices (for optical computing), and 33 percent to systems. But meanwhile, the nature of competition had changed.

NEC is a formidable rival to AT&T in optoelectronics. Ten percent of NEC's sales are invested in R&D (2 percent more than AT&T) with about 10 percent of that allocated to optoelectronics (about $50 million in 1985). Optoelectronics R&D has grown about 10 percent annually since 1980. Optoelectronics R&D is consciously structured according to three categories: basic research, device research, and applications research; and the research activities are given priorities within each category. Applied research is linked closely to production and the market. NEC is already committed to produce efficiently small optoelectronics devices and is scheduled to dedicate a plant in 1988 that will produce optoelectronic devices, the first plant of its kind in the world. Clearly, NEC is much more explicitly strategic, coordinated, and integrated in its commitment to optoelectronics than is AT&T.

Other Japanese firms are also strongly involved in developing an optoelectronics capability, including the computer company Fujitsu, which has a general strategy of entering the high growth segments of telecommunications, and the cable firm Sumitomo, which is a leading producer of optical fiber and semiconductors. This company has also made a strong commitment to optoelectronics as part of its overall strategy to move into high-technology and international markets. Sumitomo is targeting high-value components such as optoelectronics modules. In the United States, Boeing also has R&D activity in optoelectronics. The firm established the Boeing Electronics Company in 1985 as part of a strategy to diversify somewhat out of aerospace. In 1986, Boeing also created an optoelectronic research laboratory in its High Technology Center. This laboratory has received about $20 million in funding, or about 20 percent of the center's total budget (which, in turn, represents about 25 percent of Boeing's overall R&D allocation). Boeing's activities are more focused than either AT&T or NEC.

It is extremely hazardous to perform an assessment of the corporate strategies in this industry, where practically no truly significant products have been marketed. Still, certain trends and evaluations can be done. As seen in Table 6, Anne Fox, in her comprehensive analysis of this industry, concluded that both NEC and Fujitsu would maintain their high strategic position during the next decade, that Sumitomo and Boeing would improve moderately, and that AT&T would decline somewhat in relative strategic position due especially to its lack of explicit priority setting within optoelectronics and the absence of strategic coordination and integration. Clearly, AT&T has excellent technology but not necessarily superior technology strategy.

Multifirm activities are also an important aspect of the optoelectronics industry. In Japan, the nine-year, $90 million MITI joint research program on optical measurement and control systems, which started in 1979, still exists with thirteen companies participating. In 1981, MITI also formed the Optoelectronics Research Laboratory to conduct basic research on optoelectronics devices for short-haul uses. MITI is also funding optoelectronics R&D at NEC, Fujitsu, Hitachi, Toshiba, and Mitsubishi. These firms, along with Sumitomo and three others, are also participating in the MITI optoelectronics laboratory. NEC is working with several Japanese materials and chemical firms and a U.S. firm on optoelectronics R&D. In the United States, an optoelectronics research consortium was established by Battelle Memorial Institute in 1985 and had seven corporate sponsors, Boeing, Hewlett-Packard, ITT, Allied, Litton, AMP, and Dukane. Each firm contributed $600,000 for three years of research. Battelle ideally is aiming for sixteen corporate members and a $12 million program. The U.S. Department of Defense also funded $20 million for optoelectronic research in 1985.

The remarkable aspect of the optoelectronic communication switching and computer industry is how strategic it is even before there are significant products on the market. A massive long-term R&D commitment is in place, a global perspective dominates, evaluations of long-term strategic capabilities and advantages are carried out, and a web of new linkages already exists. Amazingly, technology strategy and a postmodern condition have preceded the actual establishment of an ongoing industry.

The most general lesson to be derived from this cross-industry discussion of technology strategy is that a similar pattern of strategic decisionmaking seems to have emerged, mostly without regard to the specific industry. Technology itself has become an increasingly important strategic concern in stereotypically high-tech sectors such as personal computers, ultrasound medical diagnostic equipment, biotechnology, and optoelectronics and in seemingly mature industries such as manufacturing technology. Moreover, the coexistence of multiple internal structures (such as industrial R&D and venturing), of large and small firms, of multifirm research efforts, and of new kinds of linkages is found in all of these industries, whether they are established (manufacturing technology, personal computers, and ultrasound), new (biotechnology), or not yet truly in place (optoelectronics).

John Friar and I studied the technology strategy of a set of firms from those ninety-seven U.S.-based Fortune 500 companies that had spent at least $80 million on R&D in 1982.[11] Several methods for technology development and acquisition were identified, as seen in Table 7. Technologies developed in the industrial R&D laboratory or in entrepreneurial subsidiaries repre-

Table 7. Technology Development and Acquisition Approaches

Internal
   1. Technologies developed originally in the central R&D lab or division
   2. Technologies developed using internal venturing, entrepreneurial subsidiaries, independent business units, etc.

External
   3. Technologies developed through external contracted research
   4. External acquisitions of firms primarily for technology-acquisition purposes
   5. As a licensee for another firm's technology
   6. Joint ventures to develop technology
   7. Equity participation in another firm to acquire or monitor technology
   8. Other approaches for technology development or acquisition

sent the fruits of internal techniques of development. The remaining techniques are considered to be the external methods of technology development or acquisition. In both a review of the *Wall Street Journal Index* citations and in-depth surveys, we found for the 1978-1983 period an increase in the general variety of approaches and a significant increase in the use of each individual method of external technology acquisition (Tables 8 and 9). Companies that have strong in-house research capabilities have been using, at the same time, more of and a greater variety of external sources.[12]

THE NEW STRATEGIC CONFIGURATION OF LARGE TECHNOLOGY-INTENSIVE CORPORATIONS: THE EMERGENCE OF COMPLEX GLOBAL NETWORKS

The importance of strategic alliances in technology strategy can also be demonstrated by briefly reviewing the strategic configuration established by three representative large corporations: the linkages with a biotechnology focus of the Swiss-based pharmaceutical company, Hoffman La-Roche; se-

Table 8. Technology Development Activity of Sixteen Firms, 1978 and 1983[a]

Approach	1978	1983
1. R&D lab	-	1
2. Internal venturing	0	4
3. Contracted research	1	7
4. Acquisition of firms	10	18
5. Licensee	5	9
6. Joint venture	1	16
7. Equity participation	0	8
8. Other (market another's product)	5	14
Total	22	77

[a]Number of publicly reported major instances of technology strategy activities.

Source: Wall Street Journal Index, 1978, 1983.

Table 9. Directional Change in Relative Significance for the Eight
Approaches for Ten Companies, 1978-1984

Approach	+	0	-
1. R&D lab industrial R&D	0	5	5
2. Internal venturing	4	6	0
3. Contracted research	2	8	0
4. Acquisition of firms	6	3	1
5. Licensee	4	5	1
6. Joint venture	5	5	0
7. Equity participation	3	6	1
8. Other (market another's product)	3	7	0

+   increase in relative significance
0   no change in relative significance
-   decrease in relative significance

Source: Personal interviews.

lected strategic alliances formed by the Japanese electronics giant, NEC;
and the constellation of external relationships established by the U.S.
automobile-maker, General Motors. The modern interorganizational structures associated with these three firms are presented in Figures 5, 6, 7, and
Table 10.

As seen in these charts and tables, similar patterns of strategic linkages
have occurred in spite of the fact that these firms possess different histories,
cultures, and national origins and that they compete in industries with sub-
stantively different characteristics. All three firms are now clearly at the
center of a hub of a vast and complex network of relationships. The functions of these networks are clearly multiple. They include simply extending
value of ongoing business activity and, increasingly, creating new value or
radically transforming current value. Also, it is worth mentioning that the
kinds of participants in these webs of linkages are extremely diverse. Large
firms, small firms, multifirm consortia, and governmental agencies or
programs are all represented.

The actual types of linkages identified are also quite varied. They include
licensing agreements, marketing or research contracts, acquisition, and
minority equity holdings. With regard to this last type of linkage, for ex-

Figure 5. Hoffman La-Roche: Selected Linkages with Biotechnology Focus

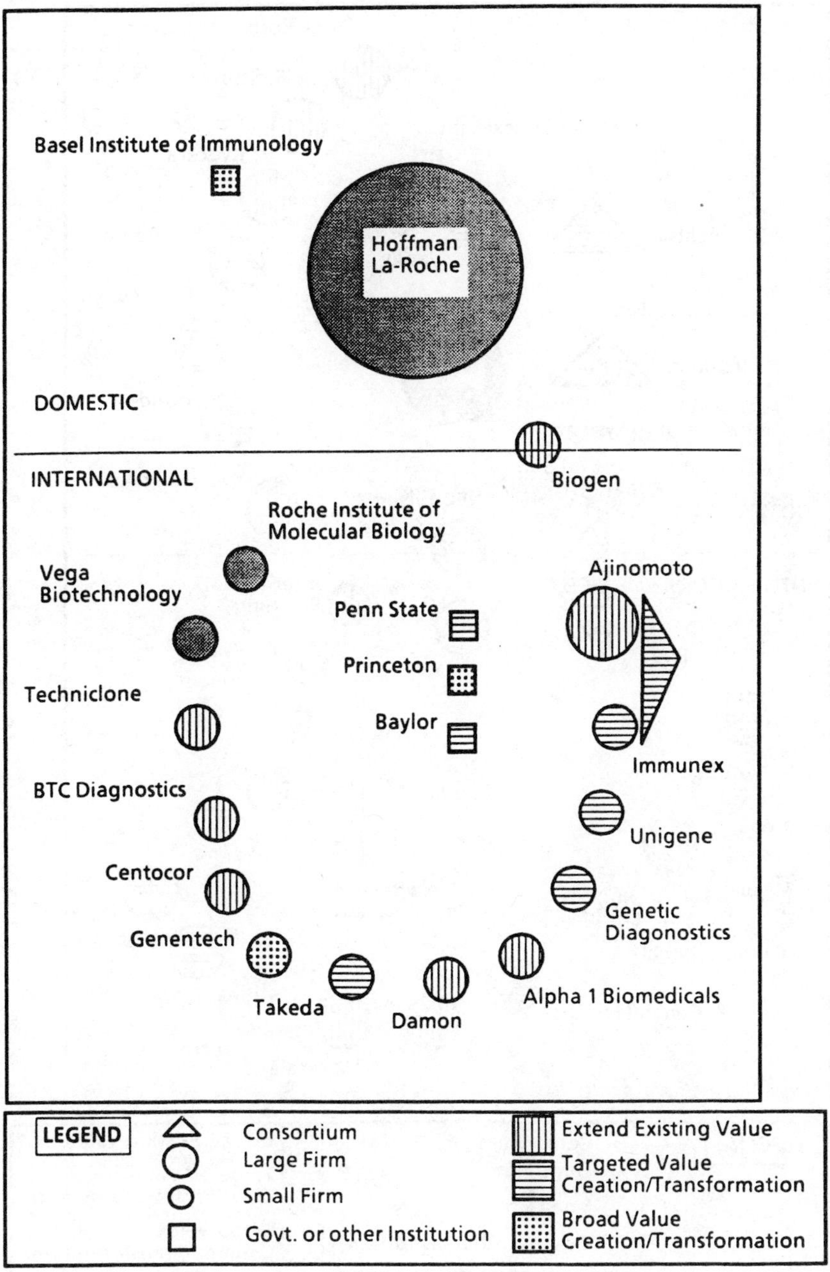

Figure 6. NEC-New Linkages: Selected Examples (1980–1985)

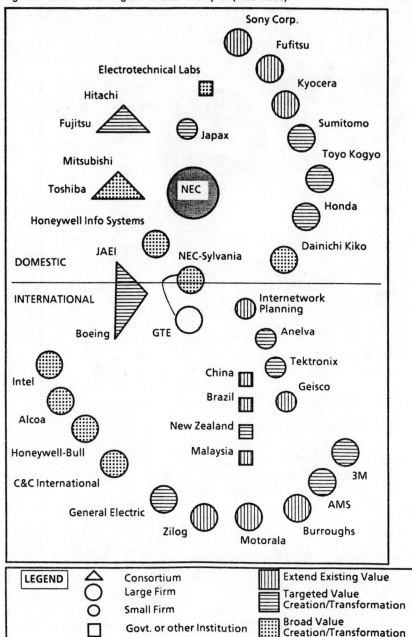

Figure 7. General Motors: Selected New Linkages with Technology Focus 1980–1985

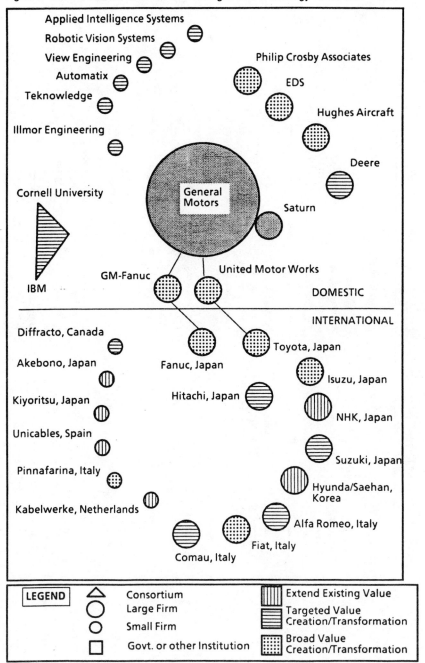

Table 10. Alternative External Collaborative Arrangements Possible for the Large Corporation

	Strategic Objective of Large Corporation		
Type of Partners/ Sponsor Chosen	Extension of Established Value	Creation or Transformation of Narrow or Targeted Value	Creation or Transformation of Broad Value
Another large corporation	Licensing Joint venture for manufacturing or marketing	Joint venture for new product development or new manufacturing methods	Joint venture for new sector development
Small firm	Distributor for limited market	Contracted research Joint venture for new product development	Portfolio of minority equity positions in selected small firms
Multiple firms			Multifirm consortia
Government programs		Governmental research program	Governmental research program
Others		University-industry association	University-industry association

ample, it is clear from Figure 7 that General Motors is exhibiting a clear strategy of using a portfolio of minority equity investments at least partially to keep abreast of technological developments in such fields as vision systems, artificial intelligence, and expert systems.

Finally, it is obvious that these interorganizational relationships often cross international boundaries and that some of these linkages are truly global in scope. Hoffman La-Roche has biotechnology-related agreements with three U.S. universities. NEC has ties with several U.S. firms and foreign governmental bodies. General Motors has foreign joint ventures with technology development objectives. GM's partners include Fanuc, Isuzu, Alfa Romeo, and Toyota.

These remarkably similar patterns of strategic-alliance structures used by such different corporations as Hoffman La-Roche, NEC, and General Motors are not simply due to coincidence. Instead, these patterns indicate a kind of convergence in the practice of strategic management by technology-intensive corporations in the advanced economies. Among many such firms, there is an intense search for effective higher-value strategies, which often involves considering technology as the critical strategic variable. Increasingly, firms are willing to "buy" such value-creating capability as well as investing in an internal capability to "make" high-value creation.

A GENERIC DISCUSSION OF VALUE-CREATING INTERORGANIZATIONAL STRATEGIC LINKAGES

The mid-1980s emergence of technology strategy has significant implications for modern strategic alliances. Companies increasingly are consciously designing concurrent, diverse, and even contradictory approaches for technology development and acquisitions. In particular, external linkages are an increasingly important component of technology strategy generally without regard often to the particular kind of firm, technology, industry, or home country under consideration. Firms appear relatively more active in employing the external approaches for technology development objectives. Firms also exhibit a general tendency in technology strategy toward more cooperation among competitors for technology development, using such methods as licensing, joint ventures, and acquisitions to share technology.

Going beyond technology-related issues, the rapid development of technology strategy was part of the general emergence of postmodern strategy. Technology strategy was the clearest indicator of simultaneity, of multiple organizational structures, and of the concurrent high priority of both effective disaggregation and complex reintegration. In this context, strategic alliances can be viewed as fundamentally value-creating moves, where the networks established in essence are pipelines to obtain resources from the outside that can enhance the value-creation capacity of an enterprise. Incorporating this concern for value in strategy, the various types of linkages are delineated in Table 10. The emphasis is shifting to the second and third columns of this chart where the creation or transformation of value occurs.

Using the formation of interorganizational networks for the purpose of creating value, often through technology development, the nature of the structure of the corporation is being altered. A large corporation might establish a variety of linkages for technology development. A vast number of different options are possible. A large firm might have alliances with other large domestic firms, small firms, other large foreign firms, and small foreign firms. It might also have strong associations with industry-wide consortia for technology development and a government-sponsored multi-firm R&D program. Moreover, the strength of these linkages is by no means uniform. Some of the relationships are quite strong—that is, they are relatively durable, difficult to break, and may be legally bound to last for a definite period or until some goal is achieved. Other relationships are quite easy to break—that is they can be quickly eliminated at almost any time, say, by selling stock or withdrawing funds arbitrarily. Many of these links are switchable in the sense that they can be turned off and possibly turned on again. Note also that this situation might be global; the linkages are not simply limited to the domestic setting.

These linkages may be controlled or monitored from different points within the formal internal organization of the large corporation, such as the chief executive officer's office, the internal venture unit, or one of the operating divisions. Any one of these places may have linkages with outside firms, although it is likely that high-level corporate or division managers control the linkages with the industry-wide consortium or the government-sponsored program. The formal internal organization itself is changing as a result of these linkages, and the corporation's boundaries can be stretched. The opposite can also happen. Small ventures that were once internal incubation efforts can be spun off with the large firm perhaps just keeping a piece of the resulting companies.

In reality, a flexible and malleable network of weak and strong relationships that may override the formal organizational boundaries of the firm has been created. The job of strategy has changed. Previously, the emphasis was on recognizing the opportunities and threats in the competitive environment and establishing within the firm the appropriate structure, systems, and processes. With the increasing importance of strategic networks, which have associations that pierce through the formal boundaries of a firm, the tasks of scanning, facilitating, and coordinating external entities assumes greater significance. In addition, the old make-versus-buy trade-off, found originally in purchasing and manufacturing, takes on greater general meaning. The creation of strategic networks can encourage a policy in which external entities play a high-value strategic role, and the notion of shrinking or "demassing" the internal structure gains enhanced legitimacy.

To repeat, value-creation strategic alliances are part of modern technology strategy, and technology strategy in turn is part of the broader transition toward postmodern strategy. Postmodern strategy is found in all the advanced economies. It requires a significant change of views concerning the basic elements of strategic management. Defining the domain of corporations is no longer simple. The inside structure has a more complex set of rules. The outside environment is no longer merely competitive. The distinction and boundaries between organization and environment are blurred. There are now a variety of ways to join forces with external actors. At least some of the linkages themselves can be changed or canceled. The growing diversity of enterprise certainly presents new difficulties for strategic management. But it also can mean enhanced strategic degrees of freedom and choice. New paths are now available for achieving meaningful strategic success.

NOTES

1. For a discussion of the general management heritage in strategic management, see Chester I. Barnard, *The Functions of the Executive* (Cambridge, Mass.: Harvard University Press, 1972); Philip Selznick, *Leadership in Administration* (Evanston, Ill.: Row, Peterson and Company, 1957); Kenneth R. Andrews, *The Concept of Corporate Strategy* (Homewood, Ill.: Richard D. Irwin).

2. For a discussion of strategic planning, see Arnoldo Hax and Nicolas Majluf, *Strategic Management: An Integrative Perspective* (Englewood Cliffs, N.J.: Prentice-Hall, 1984).

3. For an important critique of strategic planning, see Robert Hayes and William Abernathy, "Managing Our Way to Economic Decline," *Harvard Business Review* (July-August 1980). See also "The Future Catches Up With a Strategic Planner," *Business Week*, June 17, 1983, p. 62.

4. For a discussion on the role of strategic alliances for technology development, see Prafulla Joglekar and Morris Hamburg, "An Evolution of Federal Policies Concerning Joint Ventures for Applied Research and Development," *Management Science* 29, no. 9 (September 1983):1016-1026; "Suddenly U.S. Companies Are Teaming Up," *Business Week*, July 11, 1983, pp. 71-74; Januz A. Ordover and Robert Willig, "Antitrust for High-Technology Industries: Assessing Research Joint Ventures and Mergers," *Journal of Law and Economics* 28 (May 1985):311-333; Chauncy Starr, "Indus-

trial Cooperation in R&D," *Research Management* 28, no. 5 (September-October 1985):13-15; Hesh Wiener, "Beyond Partnership," *Datamation* (September 1, 1984):149-152; Norm Alster, "Power Partners," *Electronic Business* (May 15, 1986)50-64; William C. Norris, "Cooperative R&D: A Regional Strategy," *Issues in Science and Technology* (Winter 1985):92-102; "A New Weapon Against Japan," *Business Week* August 8, 1983, p. 42; William F. Baxter, "Antitrust Law and Technological Innovation," *Issues in Science and Technology* (Winter 1985):80-91; Philip Friedman, Stanford V. Berg, and Jerome Duncan, "External versus Internal Knowledge Acquisition: Joint Venture Activity and R&D Intensity," *Journal of Economics and Business* 30, no. 2 (Winter 1979):103-108. For the VLSI Project, see Kiyonori Sakakibara, *From Imitation to Innovation: Japan's Very Large-Scale Integrated (VLSI) Semiconductor Project*, MIT Sloan School Working Paper, #1490-83 (Cambridge, Mass.: MIT, October 1983); *Large Company/Small Company Alliances and Venture Capital* (Wellesley, Mass.: Venture Economics, February 8, 1985); Norm Alster, "Electronics Firms Find Strength in Numbers," *Electronic Business* (March 1, 1986):103; Carmela S. Haklisch, Herber I. Fusfeld, and Alan D. Levenson, *Trends in Collective Industrial Research* (New York: New York University, Center for Science and Technology Policy, August 1984); Herbert I. Fusfeld and Carmela S. Haklisch, "Cooperative R&D for Competitors," *Harvard Business Review* (November-December 1985):60-76; Carmela Haklisch, *Technical Alliances in the Semiconductor Industry* (New York: New York University, Center for Science and Technology Policy, February 1986); *Transnational Corporations in the Semiconductor Study* (New York: UN Center on Transnational Corporations, 1983); Kenichi Ohmae, *Triad Power* (New York: Free Press, 1985), pp. 125-148.

5. For a detailed discussion of technology strategy, see John Friar and Mel Horwitch, "The Emergence of Technology Strategy," in Mel Horwitch (ed.), *Technology in the Modern Corporation: A Strategic Perspective* (Elmsford, N.Y., Pergamom Press, 1986).

6. Mel Horwitch and C. K. Prahalad, "Managing Technological Innovation: Three Ideal Modes," *Sloan Management Review* (Winter 1976).

7. For a more extensive discussion of the previous two separate modes for technological innovation and the current blending and blurring of them, see Mel Horwitch, "The Blending of Two Paradigms for Private-Sector Technology Strategy," in Jerry Dermer (ed.), *Competitiveness Through Technology* (Lexington, Mass.: Lexington Books, 1986).

8. For a detailed discussion of the evolution of technology strategy in the personal computer manufacturing technology/robotics, medical equipment, and biotechnology industries, see John Friar and Mel Horwitch, "The Emergence of Technology Strategy."

9. Anne T. Fox, "Strategic Decisionmaking in a Global Technology-Intensive Environment: A Case Study of the Optoelectronics Industry" (Master's thesis, MIT, Alfred P. Sloan School of Management, June 1966). For AT&T in optoelectronics, see also *Wall Street Journal* July 18, 1986, p. 23; "Bell Labs Develops Optical Light Device, Draws Nearer to Light Beam Computer," *Byte* (October 1986):9; and "Where the U.S. Stands," *Fortune* (October 13, 1986):36-37.

10. Yano Research Institute, *Optoelectronic Industry in Japan* (Tokyo: Yano Research Institute, 1983), p. 2.

11. For an in-depth discussion of this study, see John Friar and Mel Horwitch, "The Emergence of Technology Strategy." For a similar, comparative study of U.S. and Japanese technology-intensive companies, see Toshiro Hirota, "Technology Development of American and Japanese Companies," *Kansai University Review of Economics and Business* 14, nos. 1-2 (March 1986):43-87.

12. John Friar and Mel Horwitch, "The Emergence of Technology Strategy."

DISCUSSION SUMMARY

As the U.S. high-tech surplus of $27 billion in 1980 decreases to a possible deficit in 1987, it might be more accurate to refer to a "clash of the titans" rather than patterns of cooperation, one discussant noted. Concern in recent publications about the United States giving away its technology and simply becoming a market for goods was pointed out. Despite this, there are increasing examples of the growing interdependence of Japan and the United States in joint licensing agreements and joint venture arrangements.

One reason for the need for cooperative efforts is the change in the consumer environment. Previously, corporations developed technology and products and created a demand for those products. Today almost everyone has the basics in durable goods. Companies must consider the diversification of requirements and needs of the consumer, but the cost of developing new products over a broader field of interests is prohibitively expensive, and no one company can satisfy the changing demands of the consumer. More coordination between the "seeds" of new technology and the needs of the consumer is needed.

New technology must reflect the needs of the consumer, not dictate them. In developing new technology, few people actually understood what that new technology was. For example, in the space industry, life sciences, telecommunications, marine resources, and other areas, the by-products of research were passed on to the consumers without understanding the cost of development or the technology involved. Currently, the United States and Japan are envisioning "megaprojects" such as the "Oriental Express" supersonic airplane that would fly to Tokyo from New York in two and one-half hours. Development of this plane will be costly and will be a high risk venture for one single company. The amount of research and funding necessary to bring a new product to market underlines the need for cooperative efforts: A new drug requires fifteen to twenty years of testing and $150-200 million in investment to bring the drug to market. Finally, only three out of one thousand products is even marketable.

Japan began cooperative efforts domestically following World War II when each discipline was devastated by war and Japan had to draw all its basic research from external sources. Government, industry, and academia banded together to survive. Today, Japan sees the need for international participation to strengthen its strategic alliances. Japan can offer human resources, a highly educated and highly disciplined work force, and a rich natural environment ideal for biotechnology research and development. Japan's role can also be to continue assimilating other technologies while adding value to that technology. Japan also stresses human values in developing its technology. A question from the floor indicated the need for an introduction of ethics to biotechnical research.

On the U.S. side, the government has changed its investment in research and development from one that fostered federal projects, such as the supersonic transport and breeder reactors. Now states have become the leaders and leverage economic growth at the state level. In 1982, forty states created centers of excellence with a total investment of $450 million. However, this trend is weighted toward the larger states with substantial access to larger technological power. The states are linking up with universities that already have ties to industry and federal support programs. The critical question is whether state legislatures will have the patience to wait for the gestation of technology when there are no immediate results apparent.

On the industrial side, multiple agreements among companies throughout the world may not always be to the best advantage of the company. One question pointed out the problems when corporations may not be fully aware of the various connections to other companies through separate project agreements, and this, in turn, can stifle a company's own technological development.

Implications for federal agencies of the new technological federalism may be the turning away by government agencies from in-house projects to more outside work. National laboratories may be rethinking their role as clients of federal agencies and may wish to work more closely with states and industry.

10

A New Era for U.S.-Japanese Technical Relations? A Cloudy Vision

Justin L. Bloom

The title of this chapter is ambiguous—and deliberately so. Those of us who are optimistic about the strength and importance of the political, economic, and scientific or technological relationships between the United States and Japan see mostly good for the future. In forty years, Japan has grown from a country devastated by war to the second largest economic entity in the Free World, and from an exporter of cheap toys to the world's supplier of sophisticated consumer and industrial products, thereby taking traditional markets away from the United States and the countries of Western Europe. Thus, Japan has achieved a position of economic equality and perhaps superiority in some instances and has demonstrated that its industrial technology is at the leading edge.

The more constructive observers say that now the time has come to recognize Japan's stature, to reorganize its relationships with the United States at the governmental, industrial, and academic levels to reflect this stature, and to enter into an enlightened era in which the two countries working together can achieve synergistic results beyond the capability of either. At least one well-known author, John Naisbitt, has suggested in a best-selling book that if harmony can be established and maintained between them for another ten years, the United States and Japan will be a dominant force internationally through a relationship he has called "U.S.-Japan, Inc."(1). Another positive and related approach, using technological cooperation as the salve for what is at times bitter friction between the two countries, has been suggested by Marvin Ott(2), who is now on the staff of the Senate Select Committee on Intelligence. Even those who number themselves as strong advocates of increased cooperation temper their views with cautionary statements to the effect that success in this regard could seriously damage relations with Europe and the Third World (2, 3).

It is clear that another set of forces is at play, stimulated by those whom I hesitate to describe as xenophobes or chauvinists but who believe that the United States must make every effort to retain or recapture its domination of Western trade, culture, and even science. This group is active in looking for ways to impose more restrictive conditions on the relationship in the hope of maximizing returns to the United States. I suspect that something of the same kind of dichotomy exists in Japan, but it is not as open, verbal, or focused.

As so often happens in complex interactions, the course of future events more than likely will lie along a path that is neither completely constructive nor completely destructive. However, the nature of the forces is such that no one—at least me—can safely predict whether this path will be biased more toward one side than the other.

My purpose here is to examine only one subset of the multidimensional matrix that forms the bilateral relationship, namely, scientific and technological cooperation. In doing so, it should be absolutely clear that this form of cooperative activity does not and cannot exist in a vacuum. Political, economic, and strategic considerations will come to bear as well and may in fact be the determinants. Thus, a new era in U.S.-Japanese scientific and technical cooperation, which is certain to occur, may be a time of greatly enhanced interaction or a time of increasing the distance between the two countries. It is no secret that I believe that the best course for both the United States and Japan is the former, as proposed by Ott, but that cannot be mandated.

THE BASELINE FOR MEASURING
TECHNICAL COOPERATION

I have analyzed the structure of the bilateral technical relationship between the United States and Japan in some depth and have concluded that the relationship is the most extensive and intensive of any that exists between two countries (4, 5). So far there has been no refutation of this claim, to my knowledge. All socioeconomic segments of the two societies are involved—government, industry, and universities.

The two governments maintain an elaborate network of agreements covering cooperation in essentially every aspect of science and technology. For the most part, these agreements have prospered technically, although they were entered into largely for political reasons. As Japan has reached maturity in science and engineering, the flow of useful information between the two countries has shifted from a condition where Japan was the principal beneficiary to one where equilibrium and parity obtain and both countries benefit equally in a qualitative if not absolutely quantitative sense. Another feature of the governmental relationship is the heavy investment that Japan has made in U.S. government research and development (R&D) programs, perhaps as much as $200 million. Counterinvestment by the U.S. government in Japanese government programs has been minimal.

A similar pattern has been followed by the industrial sector. Whereas in the early years of the postwar period technology flowed almost unilaterally from the United States and other countries to Japan, today a striking amount of Japanese technology is created indigenously and is transferred to the United States either in the form of products or as software through patents and other intellectual property media. As far as I can ascertain, there is no system in the United States that accurately accounts in quantitative fashion for the two-way flow. The Japanese periodically publish statistics on the financial value and nature of technology transfer agreements entered into by their industrial firms, but these are not particularly useful in gauging the total impact or the quality of the technology flow. Still, they provide a measure of the direction of technology flow and its monetary value. The latest statement I have found on technology trade indicates that Japan exported 241 billion yen worth of technology in the fiscal year ending March 31, 1983, which was up 30 percent from the previous year, and imported 279 billion yen worth of technology during the same period (down 1.2 percent from the previous year). Although a deficit in technology trade is still apparent, the value of technology exported under new contracts during that year exceeded that of all *new* contracts signed since 1972(6). Of these amounts, 2 percent of payments received from exports came from the United States and 68 percent of the payments made for imports went to the United States, so Japan's deficit in technology trade with the United States is still significant but mostly due to contracts still in force that were signed decades ago(7).

Although we have had to rely on Japanese data to measure technology flow, a growing number of investigators in the West are trying to analyze the situation through their own processes. These may not be comprehensive enough to make broad assertions or conclusions, but such analyses are certainly helping to clear the air of misunderstandings. The Office of Technology Assessment (OTA) of the U.S. Congress and the United States International Trade Commission seem to lead the way among government agencies in making studies of this sort that are directed toward specific industrial sectors and that are primarily concerned with competitiveness(8). An important exception is the objective and detailed analysis of technology transfer issues made by Dr. Martha Harris of OTA in a study performed for the Joint Economic Committee of the U.S. Congress. Dr. Harris identifies the following issues as impeding the flow of technology:

(1) Different approaches to protecting innovation; (2) an
imbalance in flows of technical information and personnel between the two countries; (3) difficulties in evaluating long-term costs and benefits of bilateral science and
technology cooperation; (4) sensitive issues surrounding
military technology cooperation; (5) competition between the United States and Japan for sales of technology and products in LDC [less-developed country]
markets; (6) structural barriers impeding foreign access
to Japanese technology; (7) differences in government
resources devoted to formulating and implementing
technology transfer policies.(9)

The National Science Foundation (NSF), both unilaterally and in conjunction with the Japan Society for the Promotion of Science, has analyzed
bilateral science and technology flow largely from the point of view of publications and interactions among technical personnel(10).

Among recent private investigators of technology flow to and from Japan
are Professor Leonard Lynn of Carnegie-Mellon University(11), Jon Choy
of the Japan Economic Institute(12), and Dr. Lois Peters, recently at New
York University but now at Renssalaer Polytechnic Institute(13). Dr.
Peters' work is particularly timely in that it analyzes in some depth the potential outcome of technical cooperation at the industrial level between the
United States and Japan. (By citing the work of these authors, I am not by
any means shunting aside the influential publications of major investigators
such as Ezra Vogel, Gary Saxonhouse, Daniel Okimoto, Richard Nelson,
and Hugh Patrick. My intent is to concentrate on cooperation rather than
competition.)

An interesting and potentially more important phenomenon has begun to
appear on the scene within the past few years and constitutes another form
of technology transfer. Japanese corporations have begun to let R&D contracts at U.S. universities and to establish R&D laboratories in the United
States that employ U.S. scientists and engineers. Although the extent of this
kind of entry is still relatively small and not well quantified, it is certainly
growing. The converse — United States entry into the Japanese R&D
scene — is also taking place, but as far as I know, Japanese universities have
not been involved. Rather, U.S. corporations are substantially increasing
their R&D investment in Japan, either through joint ventures with Japanese
companies or by the construction of wholly owned laboratories. Although
Japanese investment in U.S. R&D facilities has attracted some attention
here, mostly negative(14), U.S. corporate involvement in R&D in Japan has
passed largely unrecognized, although it is significant. A few examples will
suffice.

For more than a decade, IBM Japan has operated a large complex of research facilities adjacent to its manufacturing plant in Fujisawa. In July 1985, IBM opened a new building at the same site and consolidated the research operations. This building is said to have cost 15 billion yen (about $100 million), and it houses fifteen hundred research employees. Du Pont Japan is just completing a new research laboratory near Yokohama at a cost of 16 billion yen. It will employ an initial cadre of 180, which is expected to grow to 300(15). More recently, W. R. Grace has announced that it will build a research institute at the plant of its Japanese subsidiary located near Atsugi(16).

At the academic level, formal exchange agreements between U.S. and Japanese universities are rare, but substantial numbers of academic scientists and engineers move back and forth between the two countries. Much of this traffic is financed by the National Science Foundation and the National Institutes of Health for the United States and by the Japan Society for the Promotion of Science for Japan. In general, the number of scientists from Japanese universities studying or performing research in the United States far exceeds counterpart Americans in Japan. The reasons for these are primarily (1) that the Japanese have reasonable English language capability and the Americans ordinarily have no capability in Japanese; (2) U.S. university laboratories, taken as a whole, are better equipped and better supported than those at Japanese universities; (3) both the Japanese government and Japanese industry are willing to commit the large financial resources needed to support studies by promising scientists abroad. However, the number of Japanese university students who go on to graduate school or who perform postdoctoral research is small by U.S. standards(17).

RETHINKING THE BILATERAL S&T RELATIONSHIP

During the past five years or so, growing concern has been expressed by some influential members of Congress, prominent industrial leaders, U.S. government officials, and even a few academics about what is perceived as an imbalance in the flow of scientific and technical information and, more broadly, of intellectual property between the United States and Japan, all in favor of Japan. These analysts believe, among other things, that Japan has had a "free ride" at the expense of the United States; Japan has obtained advanced technology at little or no cost because of the U.S. propensity to publish technical results voluminously and to license technology at an abnormally low price. Some also believe that the presence of large numbers of Japanese graduate students and postdoctoral researchers at U.S. universities and government laboratories constitutes a channel for the unilateral flow of valuable information to Japan even before it is published. Still another view that has been propounded on occasion is that the U.S. national security is endangered by this flow because the Soviet bloc can more easily obtain illicit advanced technology from Japan than from other sources.

These arguments are invoked as one kind of explanation for Japan's economic successes, and proposals have been made to restrict or cut off the free flow of scientific and technical information to Japan as one device for restoring the U.S. position in international trade of high-technology products. What has to be a fundamental tenet of such positions is that the Japanese are merely copiers of U.S. technology or that they are incapable of performing basic research, so that restricting the flow of information would have a large, negative effect on Japanese innovative processes. I think that this myth—I use the word advisedly—has been largely dispelled in recent times, as is evidenced by even stronger proposals being made to increase U.S. knowledge of Japanese research results and to increase the presence of U.S. scientists and engineers in Japan.

In a hypothetical world free of trade friction among the advanced nations, there would seem to be little reason to question the validity of the existing bilateral technical relationship in its many ramifications, but the real world is facing strains that must be recognized and resolved.

In summary, the issues concerning science and technology that appear to be of most concern to the involved public in the United States appear to boil down to the following:

1. Better access to Japanese technical literature and to information on the status and accomplishments of Japanese research and development, thereby redressing a perceived historical imbalance.
2. Alleviation or elimination of technological aspects of tariff and nontariff trade barriers, including measures for the protection of intellectual property.
3. Increasing the number of U.S. scientists and engineers who study, perform research, or work in Japan (really a subset of [1] but involving different considerations).
4. Increasing the Japanese contribution and role in international "big science" projects.

I have avoided addressing a parallel and interrelated set of issues that are primarily domestic—namely, how the United States should employ science and technology to make itself more competitive with Japan. This subject has consumed the attention of innumerable government and industrial leaders and volumes have been published on it. It will continue to receive more thought than the narrower subject covered by this chapter.

Because of the clamor that has appeared in the press, in congressional hearings, in technical conferences and symposia, and in other forums about the aforementioned issues, the Japanese are well aware of them and have been seeking means to accommodate them. The Japanese also have their own concerns about the future of the S&T relationship, and these must be factored into the equation to the extent it is possible for an outsider to do so.

GOVERNMENT PROPOSALS AND ACTIONS

On the face of it, the U.S. government has been the most active in pursuing avenues, both positive and negative, that affect technical cooperation with Japan. This is not hard to explain since it is the government that presents positions to the Japanese government and because it is the function of the government to represent the views of its many constituencies to a large extent. The U.S. Department of State has overall policy responsibility for the agreements concerning science and technology that have been entered into by the United States and Japan. Between 1983 and 1986, the Department of State has sponsored a number of reviews of this relationship to determine if the many agreements in effect are useful, redundant, or prone to enhance an imbalance in the flow of technical information. The Office of Science and Technology Policy in the White House is usually the initiator of these reviews. The fact that there has been no major modification to or cancellation of the agreements indicates that there is general satisfaction with them, but this does not guarantee that the status quo will persist. Each year the Department of State is required by law to submit a report to the Congress that describes how science and technology are being used to support U.S. foreign relations objectives. Excerpts from the report for 1986 are pertinent to this chapter:

> Science and technology cooperation with Japan has for more than three decades served overriding U.S. foreign policy interests. Japan's access to Western science and technology has made a major contribution to its development into a stable and prosperous democracy closely allied with the United States and the West. Japan is now a recognized competitor in commercial technology, but it also presents opportunities for participation in new research and development through bilateral S&T cooperation. The State Department continues to review the science and technology relationship with Japan and most exchange programs are operating

well. Areas for strengthening the program have been
identified and are being discussed with Japanese government officials(18).

During 1985, discussions have also been held with the
Japanese concerning large-scale research facilities, particularly in the fields of breeder reactors, fusion reactors,
and high energy physics, for the purpose of trying to
identify next steps which might be jointly undertaken.
Success in these endeavors would be a significant step
forward in achieving the U.S. objective of sharing the
burden of supporting this advanced research and providing for timely access by U.S. researchers to the results of
Japanese research and development(19).

These official policy statements are constructive and will be the policy
backbone of U.S. government actions. However, I believe that ingrained attitudes of government officials, government-supported scientists, and the
members of Congress who ultimately appropriate funds for science and technology will have to undergo some change before technical cooperation at
the governmental level can be increased significantly. As I pointed out earlier, Japan already has invested more than any other country (and maybe
more than all other countries collectively) in U.S. government R&D
projects. Japan has done so for three reasons, in my opinion: to obtain access to the advanced technology involved, to compensate the United States
for technical assistance already received, and to purchase goodwill for the
future. As Japan's own domestic programs have grown in size and quality,
there is reason to doubt that Japan will be willing to continue in the role of
junior partner — always supporting U.S. programs with no reciprocity from
the United States. The fast breeder reactor program is a case in point. After
spending billions on fast breeder R&D, only to cancel the Clinch River
demonstration reactor project, the United States no longer has a focused
program. Japan does. Its Monju demonstration reactor is now under construction. It would be completely logical from a technical point of view for
the U.S. Department of Energy and its contractors to participate actively in
the Monju project, even to the extent of partially financing it, so that the
United States could obtain some future benefit from its "sunk" domestic investment. However, I am not sanguine that funds appropriated by Congress
could ever be obtained for this purpose. As far as I know, the United States
has been willing to accept foreign contributions to U.S. R&D programs but
has never been a major contributor to foreign programs, with the exception
of studies or projects carried out by multilateral or international agencies.

Perhaps an even better justification can be made for strong technical and financial collaboration with Japan in fusion research. Both countries are now at about the same level of sophistication in their mainline fusion projects (the Japanese JT-60 and the U.S. TFTR). The next generation of machine to be built will be designed as a prototype power reactor that produces more electrical energy than it consumes. It will be very expensive, but it will still be far from a commercially viable producer of electricity. Because proprietary concerns are still relatively minimal, this would be a good time to join forces. Again, I am not optimistic that this can be accomplished, particularly if Japan were to be placed in the role of leader and if the next-generation machine were to be built in that country.

The situation is turned around when one analyzes cooperation in the construction and operation of the National Aeronautics and Space Administration (NASA) space station. Here the United States has a lead of many years, and it is logical for Japan to invest in the U.S. project rather than attempting to duplicate it. Japan already has agreed to participate in the preliminary design (phase B) of the space station by development of a Japanese laboratory module, but problems remain to be resolved on how much technology concerning the rest of the station will be given to the Japanese and how much proprietary information generated by Japanese use of its module in the station will be transferred to the United States. If issues of this kind can be treated satisfactorily, Japan could ultimately invest more than $2 billion in its part of the space station[20] and also would reimburse NASA in excess of $1 billion for costs incurred by NASA to enable Japan to participate.

Without trying to be encyclopedic, I would like to mention some other governmental activities that are taking place within the context of increasing access to Japanese industrial R&D on a cooperative basis. In 1983, the National Bureau of Standards (NBS) signed an agreement with the (then) Nippon Telegraph and Telephone Public Corporation (NTT) to exchange basic technological information on telecommunications and allied fields[21]. Although the NBS role as a government agency in telecommunications R&D is quite small and NTT operates the second largest laboratory complex in this field, the two organizations have established a harmonious relationship in an important high-tech area. Beginning with the exchange of written information and of short-term visits by scientists, NBS and NTT are now arranging for the assignment of resident scientists at each other's facilities. Subsequent to the entry into force of the agreement, NTT was converted from a quasi-governmental agency to a private corporation (although all of its stock is still owned by the Japanese government). However, the agreement remains in effect and is being exploited actively.

Independent of its subordinate agency, NBS, the Department of Commerce also undertook to acquire a deeper understanding of Japanese industrial R&D capability and technology by awarding a contract to Science Applications International Corporation (SAIC) in 1983 for the purpose of assessing Japanese accomplishments in the fields of computer science, microelectronics, biotechnology, and robotics. Under this Japanese Technology Evaluation Program (JTECH), SAIC assembled panels of experts in these fields who visited Japanese laboratories, read translations of technical reports, and performed comparative evaluations. Subsequently, management of this program was transferred to the National Science Foundation and the Defense Research Projects Agency, and the program's scope was extended to cover telecommunications and advanced materials. Reports on the six subjects of study have been published(22).

Without going into the fine detail contained in these useful documents, a picture emerges that is most interesting. Many of the panel members appeared to have no previous in-depth involvement with the Japanese research scene, although they were acknowledged experts in their fields. The panelists were strongly impressed by the quality of Japanese research and were alarmed in some cases to find that the Japanese were abreast or ahead of U.S. counterparts in a significant number of subfields. The panelists also were surprised to find that Japanese laboratories opened their doors to them and gave them essentially as much information as they wished. For most of the panel members it was their first exposure to details of how the Japanese government and the private sector organize and fund their R&D programs.

I believe that the JTECH program has been extraordinarily valuable in demonstrating that Japanese industrial R&D is at the leading edge and that access to advanced technical information is possible if a reasonable attempt is made to find it. This may well be a significant step toward eliminating the ingrained not-invented-here (NIH) syndrome prevalent in the United States and accepting the fact that Japan is a technical equal in several fields as well as an economic competitor. At the same time, one has to question why it has taken the United States so long to engage in an activity of this sort. The Japanese have been doing it for decades.

Historically, the Department of Commerce has looked upon its subordinate agency, the National Technical Information Service (NTIS), to obtain technical information from Japan for the U.S. consumer. Sporadic attempts to increase the scope and magnitude of what NTIS does have been only modestly successful because NTIS does not usually receive congressional appropriations and must conduct its operations out of revenues received from the sale of its products and services. NTIS now holds agreements with a large number of private companies and government agencies in Japan to make their technical reports available in the United States. However, NTIS has had two strikes against it: It has been unable to provide large numbers of translations of documents originally written in Japanese, and its sales of Japanese technical documents have been disappointingly small(23). Within the past year or so, NTIS has concluded negotiations with the Japan Information Center of Science and Technology (JICST) whereby NTIS will operate a computer terminal giving access to an international data base of Japanese technical information that has been established by JICST. This data base is called the JICST Online Information System. Unfortunately, the data base will have only English titles and keywords, so it will still be necessary to arrange for translations of substantive material(24). An element of uncertainty about the future role of NTIS in collecting and disseminating Japanese technical information has been introduced recently by a directive from the Office of Management and Budget that requires a study to determine what functions of NTIS should be transferred to the private sector(25).

NSF also is undertaking two other programs that could form the basis of waves in the future. These derive, I think, from a marked change in policy at NSF under its current director, Dr. Erich Bloch, who has come to NSF from IBM. The foundation has begun a small program to dispatch a scientist to Japan for a year or so of postdoctoral research in semiconductor materials. The scientist will be selected from candidates who are junior faculty members at U.S. universities. A venture like this is expensive, so it is not surprising that only one scientist will be supported in the first year. Again, Japan has been using this approach to provide research opportunities for hundreds of its scientists. If the United States accepts the principle that it has something to learn in Japan, then the NSF program should be considered the harbinger for a much larger effort in the future.

To identify the extent to which private companies in Japan would be willing to accept U.S. scientists and engineers as temporary or permanent employees, the NSF Tokyo office conducted a poll of some three hundred companies and found that a surprisingly large proportion were willing to consider such employment(26). A catalog is now available to assist Americans to locate potential employment in Japan(27), but it is still too early to tell whether any significant number of Americans will grasp this potential opportunity. My guess is that additional incentives will be required from the government. Another field of potentially valuable cooperation that lies solely within the governmental policy province is military or defense R&D. Authority for the transfer of U.S. military technology and ordnance to Japan has existed for a long time, but interest in the reverse flow is a recent phenomenon. In 1983, a new bilateral agreement was signed providing for a two-way exchange. The arrangement is unique and derives, of course, from the military protection given to Japan by the United States since the end of World War II. Surveys of Japanese military and industrial technology made by the United States Department of Defense (DOD) have indicated that technology of potential benefit to U.S. defense systems is available in Japan, and mechanisms have been established for arranging transfers through industrial channels(28). However, few such transfers have occurred, mostly because of concerns by Japanese corporations that their technologies will be used for commercial purposes in the United States. Apparently, only so-called dual-use technology is of interest to the DOD; Japan's primary military technology does not appear to be involved, but the line of demarcation is a hazy one(29).

At this writing, an affirmative decision has been made by the Japanese government to authorize the participation by Japanese firms in the U.S. Strategic Defense Initiative (SDI)(30). This will mean that Japanese companies could become eligible for R&D contracts awarded by the DOD, bringing Japan into an arena now occupied by West Germany, the United Kingdom, and Israel. This arrangement could have implications that reach far beyond SDI, provided that Congress does not restrict or forbid the award of SDI R&D contracts to foreign companies(31).

In contrast to these efforts by the DOD to extract Japanese technology for use in U.S. weapons systems, the DOD also has been active in trying to limit the flow of U.S. scientific and technical information to Japan and other countries. Some of this activity is directed by law and is justified when classified information is involved. However, officials of the DOD have gone beyond this boundary in recent years when they tried to persuade universities to restrict participation of foreign students in unclassified, high-technology curricula and research programs. After meeting strong objections from university presidents and others, the DOD moderated its position drastically, and the issue is now moribund unless Congress or the administration chooses to open it again as a device for maintaining a U.S. lead in advanced technology. One of the best analyses that I have seen of the conflict between the desire for enhancing technology transfer and concerns for national security in the case of the United States and Japan is an exhaustive study performed by Anthony T. Green at Harvard University(32).

CONGRESSIONAL CONCERNS

Aside from continuing concerns about the transfer of advanced technology from the United States to the Soviet Union with consequent harm to the U.S. strategic position, the Congress probably has shown more interest in the flow of scientific and technical information to and from Japan than for any other democratic country. Several hearings have been held within the past few years that have related directly or indirectly to this subject. For example, the Committee on Science and Technology of the House of Representatives held hearings in 1983 on Japanese technological advances and possible U.S. responses using research joint ventures(33). Hearings before the House Committee on Foreign Affairs in 1982 addressed the gamut of U.S.-Japanese relations, with quite a bit of attention paid to the technological aspects of bilateral trade issues(34). However, in terms of a specific issue of a technical nature, the most attention has been paid to examining means for increasing access to the Japanese technical literature. At the initiative and through the persistence of Cecil H. Uyehara, the House Science and Technology Committee's Subcommittee on Science, Research, and Technology held hearings in 1984 and 1985 to assess the state of availability of Japanese technical information in the United States. The record of these hearings is a valuable statement on what was and was not being done at that time(35). Two efforts by the committee to enact legislation that would have increased government funding for acquisition and translation of Japanese documents were unsuccessful but were revived in 1985 by Senators Max Baucus and John D. Rockefeller. They were instrumental in introducing legislation in the Senate that ultimately passed both houses of Congress in 1986 and was signed into law by the president as the Japanese Technical Literature Act of 1986(36). Although the act as passed does not appropriate new funds, it authorizes the expenditure of $1 million by the Department of Commerce to analyze the status of Japanese science and technology, to catalog efforts by the public and private sectors in the United States to acquire Japanese technical information, to translate and disseminate such information when services are not already available, and to report periodically on the status of this program. Administration of the act has been delegated by the secretary of commerce to the National Bureau of Standards, not to NTIS.

PRIVATE-SECTOR PROPOSALS AND ACTIONS

Many individuals and organizations in the private sector have considered the technological aspects of the bilateral economic relationship between the United States and Japan (or more broadly, international competitiveness in high technology) but relatively few have looked upon scientific and technological *cooperation* as an important element in maintaining and increasing bilateral political, social, or economic stability. An even smaller number of the latter have proposed mechanisms for increasing cooperation.

In recent years, there have been a large number of studies and conferences that have addressed the competitiveness of the United States in international markets. Although this subject forms the backdrop for this symposium, it is not the focus, and I will not spend much time discussing it. Rather, I believe that the voluminous printed record can be read for the gamut of views that have been presented. Among the more important documents are some of those published by organs of the National Academies(37-39). However, the most widely read and quoted document on this subject is the report of the President's Commission on Industrial Competitiveness (the Young Commission)(40). Among other things, this report led to a conference on cooperation and competition in the global economy sponsored by the National Science Foundation, held in San Antonio in April 1986. With the exception of the keynote address by Professor Ezra Vogel of Harvard University, neither the theme of the conference nor the chapters presented were openly focused toward relations with Japan, but essentially every speaker couched his or her remarks in terms of Japanese competition. It was also a characteristic of the conference that there was essentially no "Japan-bashing" (41).

The Japan-America Society of Washington was among the first to recognize the need to examine technical cooperation with Japan and to do something about it. The society's 1981 symposium on technological exchanges with Japan constituted a watershed, and the papers presented at that symposium continue to be pertinent to any discussion of the issues entailed(42).

Although it is dangerous to quote selectively, two excerpts will suffice to frame the philosophies expressed. Dr. James Abegglen said the following in his keynote address:

> Japan's move to significant innovation in science and technology is a natural and logical extension of Japan's economic development to this time. For the United States and the world, in need of innovation and in need of capital, the emergence of Japan as a major source of technology and capital is an encouraging one.
>
> As U.S. businessmen, however, we need to address urgently the question of whether we are so organized, and whether our investment, personnel relations and national policy systems are so constituted as to allow us to take advantage of Japan as an important source of needed technology. Can we in fact assimilate substantial flows of technology and effectively apply that technology? What changes must we make as our relative technological advantage diminishes so that we can import more from abroad. It is not clear that we can compete with Japan in our ability to use imported technology, but clearly this is a topic whose time has come(43).

Dr. George Keyworth, then science adviser to the president, pointed out that concerns in the United States arising from the competitiveness of Japan in high-technology fields had to be recognized as part of the free enterprise system, but he welcomed such competition as long as it was "open and fair."

> When it comes to cooperation with Japan we are, of course, dealing not only with a very advanced nation but with a good friend and a very special partner. Ours is a partnership of countries that have risen to world leadership in a technologically mature world. We have benefited from each other's stability and growth. Our relationship has been as good as that of any two nations in the world. It is essential that such a partnership continue to flourish — and with scientific and technological cooperation as a key element. President Reagan considers this cooperation with Japan to be of paramount importance(44).

In 1984, the Conference Board and the Japan External Trade Organization jointly sponsored a conference in San Francisco with the title, "Japan and U.S.: Cooperating in High Tech." Most of the participants were from the private sectors of the two involved countries and were at the company chairman or president level. A few high-level government officials also spoke. Unfortunately, the Conference Board does not usually publish proceedings of its meetings, so a record of the discussions is not available to the general public. I was able to obtain a partial transcript of the remarks that were made, and it indicates that the meeting was of unusual value in explaining the R&D process in each country, defining issues related to technology transfer, and exploring opportunities for or constraints on cooperation. In my opinion, Dr. Frank Press, the president of the National Academy of Sciences, gave a seminal speech at that conference that should have been afforded a larger audience. Given that Dr. Press is the chief spokesman for the U.S. scientific community, his views are of the utmost importance. Let me quote his concluding remarks, taken from the unpublished transcript.

> This conference affirms that leaders in both countries believe in cooperation, in the absolute necessity of it. Our two countries are allied in their belief in free trade and in the centrality of advanced technologies to their national futures. Our two countries know that

competition is not a zero sum game, as many of the
speakers have said—that both can build major and
mutually profitable industries in the same field.

And governmental and scientific leaders in both
countries recognize that cooperation is not only important for what it produced, but also for what it symbolizes,
that in a miasma of tensions owing to economic competition, we can still cooperate on an intellectual enterprise,
because we believe it is worth doing and because we
believe that we both can gain.

Still, the forces driving us to cooperation have
changed. And acting on that recognition is the surest
road to future cooperation and to helping us to avoid the
destructive paths which lie before us.

Other evidence of Dr. Press' philosophy had appeared in print somewhat
earlier(45).

Another landmark event to take place was the convening of a quasi-offi-
cial body, the United States-Japan Advisory Commission, better known col-
loquially as "the Wise Men." This group (the second of its kind) of
distinguished representatives of the private sectors of the two countries met
several times during 1983 and 1984 to discuss the gamut of bilateral issues
lying before their nations. The commission was headed jointly by David
Packard for the United States and the late Nobuhiko Ushiba for Japan. Although previous like-minded committees and commissions had given lip service to scientific and technological cooperation and in fact had made some
explicit recommendations for increasing cooperation, this subject was addressed in far greater depth by the Wise Men than had been the case. There
should be no illusions, however, that cooperation was given high priority on
the list of issues facing them.

The report published by the commission has not yet been supplanted by
any other document endorsed at such a high level that could serve as a guide
for future relations in science and technology(46). Therefore, it is necessary
to quote liberally from it; the recommendations made are still valid to an extraordinary extent. As has happened before, the report seems to have attracted more attention and action in Japan than it has in the United States.

Under the rubric of science and technology, the commission made the following executive statement:

The scope of public and private scientific and technological cooperation between the United States and
Japan is unique. There is now an excellent qualitative
balance in the flow of technological ideas between the

two countries. To further capitalize on our individual strengths and develop expertise in additional areas, we recommend that:

* There should be a review of the thirteen government-to-government agreements to determine possible improvements and new directions.
* Japan should take a stronger role in the generation of basic knowledge, while the United States should devote greater attention to new-product innovation and production technology.
* Joint efforts between U.S. and Japanese high-technology firms should be encouraged, particularly where initial costs of product development are high.
* A variety of measures, including increased Japanese-language training for Americans, should be taken to enlarge opportunities for scientists from both countries to work together and have improved access to each other's research.
* A joint advisory body should examine technical-standards development in the two countries for purposes of harmonization(47).

Among its defense recommendations, the commission explicitly stated:

* Japan and the United States should pursue joint research and development of advanced defense systems.
* The United States and Japan should work bilaterally and through COCOM to stop detrimental transfers of technology(48).

Among its recommendations for energy cooperation, the commission held that:

* A long-term nuclear energy cooperation agreement should be concluded promptly. The United States should not ask more of Japan than it does of other close allies; Japan should be willing to set a world example for safeguards.
* Both countries should collaborate on nuclear-waste disposal and policies governing nuclear-technology exports to third countries.

        * Industry-to-industry cooperation should be pur-
    sued in the development of the next generation of
    nuclear technology(49).

These summary recommendations were backed up in the report of the
Wise Men by more explicit recommendations concerning science and technology and the technical aspects of energy and defense cooperation. Background material leading to the policy statements of the Commission was
prepared by individual experts in the United States and Japan and is available to the public(5, 50).

As is being shown throughout this chapter, some of the general and
specific recommendations are being implemented in either the public or
private sectors, but it is doubtful that this has occurred because of the Wise
Men's actions. At a minimum, the report serves as a useful yardstick against
which progress can be measured. At a maximum, it is a recipe for the future.

It is interesting to examine how other high-level groups and individuals in
the private sector have handled this broad issue of technological competition versus cooperation with Japan in the few years that have passed since
the Wise Men made their report. I find that polarization is the most striking characteristic—that is, most groups or individuals concerned with the
technological interface between the two countries look upon Japan as a competitor and not as a current or potential cooperator. These groups look for
ways by which the United States may regain or hold on to its competitive advantage (vis-à-vis Japan) in science and technology. Most often the
proposals made are constructive, although there are some who propose a
Fortress America approach. This is a subject all to itself, and I must limit
my comments to those who fall outside this category.

A noteworthy but not widely publicized example of the latter is a comprehensive paper that was presented originally at a meeting of the Japan-
Western U.S. Association in San Francisco in 1983 by two prominent
Americans who work in Tokyo. A revised version, in both Japanese and
English, was published in January 1985(51). This report examines the basis
for high-technology issues between the two countries and sets forth some
unusual suggestions for increasing cooperation. Not all of them will receive
hearty bilateral support, but they are worthy of consideration and debate.
The authors, Herbert L. Hayde of the Burroughs Co., and Jack L. Osborn
of TRW Overseas, propose that

        * Japanese firms seeking joint venture partners in the
    United States should go beyond marketing considera-
    tions and should actively stress joint production facilities

and R&D. These firms should encourage the licensing of fundamental technologies developed in Japan to U.S. firms.

* Japanese trading companies should provide some of the capitalization required to fund basic R&D in the United States.

* Major Japanese corporations should provide large U.S. universities with advice and financial support to enhance the development of technology relevant to commerce and should increase opportunities for U.S. graduate students and corporate employees to work in Japanese laboratories.

* The two countries should initiate a major exchange program similar to the Marshall or Rhodes scholarships.

* The United States at both the state and federal levels should provide incentives to secondary schools and universities to emphasize the teaching of Japanese and other Asian languages.

* U.S. industry should encourage, and perhaps require, U.S. graduate students, engineers, scientists, and business majors to go to Japan to study Japanese culture and business.

* The U.S. government should markedly increase its presence in Japan to a level matching that of Japan in the United States.

* The U.S. government should develop policies defining clear separation between commercial and military technologies that will encourage and not discriminate against Japanese investment in the United States.

The authors then go on to make recommendations to the Japanese:

* The government of Japan should give clear support to U.S. companies wishing to establish R&D centers in Japan by creating incentives for such companies to do so, by ensuring that U.S. firms have equal access to the joint R&D programs of the government, and by ensuring timely protection of industrial and intellectual property.

    * As the logical counterpart of free Japanese access to strong U.S. universities, U.S. firms should be given greater access to government industrial laboratories and to corporate research institutions.

    * The activities of industry associations, research associations, joint research centers, and working groups concerned with technological development should be opened to foreign participation. Foreign commentary on evolving legislation, standards, and national policies concerning high technology should be solicited.

As for ongoing efforts to maintain a continuing bilateral policy dialogue on issues concerning science and technology, I know of only one forum in the private sector that is doing so. It was created at the instigation of Dr. Frank Press, president of the National Academy of Sciences. As I have described earlier, Dr. Press has held the view for a number of years that scientific and technological cooperation between the United States and Japan is of great importance and that it is threatened by the trade friction that exists between the two countries. In 1985, the Academies of Science and Engineering joined forces to create a panel of senior executives from industry and distinguished professors from universities who were experts on Japan, and a counterpart panel was established in Japan, for the purpose of holding discussions on advanced technology and the international environment. The chair of the U.S. panel is Dr. Harold Brown, former secretary of defense and now chair of the Foreign Policy Institute at the Johns Hopkins School of Advanced International Studies. The chair of the Japanese panel is Professor Takashi Mukaibo, professor emeritus at the University of Tokyo and now deputy chair of the Japan Atomic Energy Commission. (Dr. Mukaibo acts in a private capacity on the panel because there is no formal governmental participation or involvement on either side.) The two sides met for the first time in August 1985 in Santa Barbara and concluded a second meeting in November 1986 in Kyoto. The panels have supported many studies on the innovative process in each country, looking for causes of friction and their amelioration. It is disappointing to observe how little attention this large-scale effort has drawn, perhaps because the deliberations were kept private in order to avoid publicity before a useful meeting of the minds could occur. There have been no documents published on behalf of the panels, and there was no press release or communiqué after the first meeting. However, members of the press were briefed in both countries, and a few articles on the work of the panels have appeared, primarily in Japan(52).

Because of the stature of the members of the panels and the degree of influence they are able to exert in government, industry, and academia, it is important to report on their common findings and their proposals for future action. It should come as no surprise that the findings are already relatively well known to those who keep a close watch on the U.S.-Japanese relationship or that the proposals duplicate at least in part those made in other forums.

The panels concluded in 1985 that they shared a common interest in science and technology and in the health of relationships between the two countries. The panels also shared a common concern about the tensions that exist and a common belief in the critical role of the innovation process in the two countries. More specifically, the two sides agreed on the following points:

> * The pool of basic research is a global, free commodity; hence contributions and access should be universal.
> * There are significant differences between the United States and Japanese basic science and research infrastructures that have important implications for exchanges.
> * Research results in pure science generally flow from the United States to Japan.
> * Japanese science and technology are more accessible than those in the United States realize or use to their advantage.
> * As a great technological power, Japan should increase its participation in world basic science.
> * Japan increasingly believes that to remain competitive, it must contribute to the world's scientific stock.
> * There is growing appreciation of the need for enhancement of basic research in Japan.
> * A patent treaty should be explored for reconciling differences between the two countries and for providing better protection of intellectual property.

The Japanese participants expressed the following views of the bilateral relationship:

> * The United States is leading in basic research on a global scale.
> * Basic research in the United States is not always well channeled into development and production.

* The United States expends insufficient effort to produce goods adapted to the Japanese market.
* Complex legal procedures in the United States are not constructive in enhancing cooperation between the two countries.

Therefore, the United States should:

* Deepen its understanding of the Japanese situation.
* Create incentives for U.S. scholars to take long-term assignments in Japan.
* Encourage U.S. scholars to accept Japanese living conditions.
* Encourage U.S. scholars to read and cite the Japanese literature.
* Recognize the need to adapt products to the Japanese market.

U.S. participants expressed the following points:

* Japan is the leading manufacturing power on a global scale, and its actions consequently have a global impact.
* Japan's patterns of behavior effectively block a fair return to foreign innovators (increasingly so in view of the shortened innovation cycle and its close linkage to basic science).
* Ways must be found to reduce the asymmetric treatment of intellectual property that leads to advantages for the Japanese side.
* Current trade problems have brought the United States dangerously close to the point of broad retaliatory actions that will damage the relationship between the two countries and the free interchange of science, technology, and innovation.
* The U.S. business community should have access to Japanese markets fully equal to Japanese access to U.S. markets.
* The U.S. industrial and scientific community wants symmetrical access to Japan's science and technology. Japan should make contributions to basic research commensurate with its standing as a global technological power.

> * The transfer of technology to Japan from the
> United States is not matched by the flow from Japan to
> the United States. The barriers to achieving greater
> equity in such transfers need to be addressed and
> reduced.

It is clear from these various statements that the two sides were extraordinarily frank and open in presenting their opinions, which was a result of the stature of the participants and the informal, private environment of the meeting. To the objective, outside observer, there can be little quarrel with the conclusions reached. However, these conclusions do not necessarily represent a broad consensus in either country or even the individual views of the participants. It is clear, however, that a heavy dose of position-taking on trade issues has dominated the discussions, rather than a search for mechanisms to increase technical cooperation.

Keeping in mind the science and technology issues that I postulated earlier, the private sector seems to be responding to a degree. For example, one entrepreneur after another has entered the market for supplying Japanese technical information. The largest endeavor in this regard is the Japanese Technical Information Service, a subsidiary of University Microfilms International(53). Approximately seven hundred Japanese journals are abstracted in English, thereby resulting in the distribution of five thousand abstracts per month to subscribers. George Mason University is offering a more limited service for abstracting and translating technical articles from the Japanese literature, and a Japanese data base will be added to other international data bases in late 1987 by STN International(54). What is not yet clear from all of this activity is whether the demand by scientists and engineers in the United States for the various services proffered matches the supply in a commercially viable sense.

There is also much ferment about increasing the opportunities for learning the Japanese language, particularly by scientists and engineers. Two conferences have been held that have addressed this subject in some depth(55, 56). Because of the difficulties entailed in achieving proficiency in Japanese, various shortcuts are being examined, such as the use of machine-assisted translation, abbreviated courses in learning limited numbers of Chinese characters without learning to speak Japanese, and total-immersion introductory summer courses. My own feeling is that the shortcuts may act to stimulate interest in the language among those who intend to spend much of their careers working with Japanese science and technology but will not replace the years of dedicated effort required to achieve real proficiency. The fact remains that only a relative handful of U.S. technical professionals are studying the Japanese language intensively.

There also is pressure in Japan to increase the volume of English-language technical publications, not only to defuse some of the criticism from abroad about the inaccessibility of Japanese technical information but also to increase international recognition of Japanese accomplishments.

Solution to or at least amelioration of the complex problem of equitable protection of intellectual property may be more difficult to achieve. Systems for issuance and enforcement of patents are quite different in the two countries, and neither the United States nor Japan has a well-developed, operational system for the protection of trade secrets (proprietary information not covered by patents). One important segment of this field, the protection afforded computer software — whether by patents or copyrights — is in an evolutionary stage and has been the cause of considerable friction all by itself. Another field, genetic engineering, may see the need for entirely different approaches to the protection of intellectual property. This general subject requires the attention of specialists on both sides, and a number of professional organizations are attempting to deal with it. Among them are the U.S. Chamber of Commerce and the American Chamber of Commerce in Japan, the Semiconductor Industry Association, the U.S. Electronics Association, and the Licensing Executives Society (an international organization).

What is needed most is a forum where these groups and corresponding groups in Japan could work together on a general solution to the protection problem, rather than addressing specific complaints. Such a consolidated approach might require action by the two governments. Perhaps the negotiation of a patent cooperation treaty as proposed by the Brown/Mukaibo panel could provide the vehicle for concerted attention. For those wishing to understand the issue in greater depth, publications of the Licensing Executives Society and similar organizations are particularly useful(57-59).

PERCEPTIONS OF JAPANESE ATTITUDES TOWARD COOPERATION

It is really up to representatives of corresponding sectors in Japan to present their views about the bilateral relationship in science and technology, and they are doing so increasingly. I will not attempt to usurp this role and therefore will mention only a few points that I trust are cogent.

The report of the Wise Men and the deliberations of the Brown/Mukaibo panel are cases in point. Beyond these, it is clear that expanding and consolidating international cooperation are policies of the Japanese government and are reflected in actions taken by almost every ministry and agency and extending into the private sector as well. Although these actions are in the self-interest of Japan (as they should be), they also reflect an improved attitude toward Japan's place in the world. Political and sociological changes occur slowly in Japan because of the consensus process required, and this leads to misunderstandings and frustrations in other countries. Thus, although policy and legislative actions have been taken to permit foreign scientists, engineers, and professors to work in Japan, the actual number of new hires is still small and has not exactly generated waves of enthusiasm. Likewise, efforts to increase the proportion of basic research in Japan are well codified, but budgetary constraints have limited actual increases in funding to relatively small amounts. Rather, the private sector has been called upon to increase its share of basic research, but this is self-defeating from the international point of view. It is not easy for private companies to disseminate the results of basic research when these results have implications for creating future commercial technology.

A related problem is the perception that changes of this sort occur in Japan only in reaction to foreign pressures, particularly from the United States. Japan can really help its image abroad and make a substantive contribution to international cooperation at the same time by taking initiatives that are generated internally rather than being forced by external demands. Genya Chiba of the Research Development Corporation of Japan has expressed this view eloquently in his analysis of the problems of internationalization in Japan(60), so, again, the Japanese are aware of the need for action.

The winds of change are blowing rather gently at this time, but there is hope for the future. One concept that has not yet fully materialized is the Human Frontiers Program that Prime Minister Yasuhiro Nakasone is propounding. This multibillion dollar international fundamental research effort, primarily in the life sciences field, is reputed to be one that Japan would fund heavily even in other countries — something like the way the SDI program has been structured but of course for peaceful rather than military purposes. However, it was revealed prematurely at the time of the Tokyo Economic Summit and more groundwork must be done both in Japan and abroad before the program becomes a reality. If Japan could take other initiatives of great magnitude that address the issues described earlier, international perceptions could change markedly.

A PROPOSAL FOR U.S. ACTION

I assume that there is a substantial body of goodwill toward Japan in the United States that can form the basis for carrying further the many suggestions that have been made for improving the bilateral scientific and technological relationship. What is missing is a structure or mechanism for converting positive attitudes into actions. It will always be true that the negative aspects of the relationship, particularly those concerning trade, will dominate the attention of the press and of the public generally. Those who wish to work toward improvements outside the immediate area of trade friction may well find themselves in the uncomfortable position of swimming upstream. Like salmon, however, they may also find that the rewards justify the effort. I do not think that it is necessary to establish a new professional society or other formal organization to take on the responsibility for this. Rather, something has to be done to alert existing organizations to the need and persuade them to tackle one aspect or another of the problem. If I can go back to the generic issues I have identified, I can generate the following scenario, involving both the public and private sectors in what could be a synergistic relationship.

1. Improve access to Japanese technical information.

Notwithstanding all the talk, there is no clear indication that there is a shortage of technical information from Japan. The problem may simply be that what is available is not read and absorbed. The JTECH studies seem to bear out this point. I note that the Japanese Technical Literature Act of 1986 calls on the Department of Commerce to "consult with businesses, professional societies, and libraries in the United States regarding their needs for information on Japanese developments in technology and engineering." (I do not know why science is not mentioned, but let us ignore that discrepancy.)

Consultation is hardly enough. What is needed is an in-depth survey of information needs and what has been done to satisfy them. I suggest that this could best be performed by highly qualified organizations already operating in the technical information field. I have in mind the U.S. Association for the Advancement of Science, the U.S. Federation of Information Processing Societies, or the National Federation of Abstracting and Information Services, but there are undoubtedly others. For sponsors, I think of the Department of Commerce, the National Science Foundation, the Japan Society, the United States-Japan Foundation, or a consortium of them.

Once it has been established that there is an unsatisfied need, then the private sector knows how to mate supply with demand. In this era of Gramm-Rudman, I do not think that the government can be called upon to provide any services. If no latent need emerges, we can cross this item off our list.

2. Investigate the technological aspects of trade barriers.

As far as I can tell, the two most important problem areas within this category worthy of examination are patents and copyrights and scientific and engineering standards. Concerning patents and copyrights, there is both a governmental and a private role. Negotiation of a patent cooperation treaty, as has been proposed, is clearly a governmental responsibility, and it is beyond my expertise to know whether such a treaty would be either useful or necessary. At least pressure could be brought on the Patent and Trademark Office by the private sector to explore the pros and cons.

However, the private sector has a more important role. If the sector can free itself from concentration on specific cases of delays in handling patent applications, alleged infringements, and complaints about discriminatory treatment, the private sector could address generic differences between the systems of the two countries and seek resolution or amelioration of these differences. Such an approach requires two other considerations: acceptance of the principle that this is not a short-term matter and that it will require many meetings, the use of working groups, and a sponsor or sponsors who can act on the results achieved; and the equal involvement of counterparts in Japan. A beginning has been made through the studies performed by members of the Licensing Executives Society; presumably associations of patent attorneys have similar interests. As for sponsors, I suggest government entities unless the U.S. Chamber of Commerce or the National Association of Manufacturers were willing to accept the responsibility for the U.S. side and perhaps Keidanren (the Federation of Economic Organizations) for the Japanese side. Let me repeat that I am not recommending this approach to solve existing, individual complaints, but as a more fundamental way of heading off friction in the future. This could be more cost-effective to the industrial sectors of both countries.

My argument for a better working relationship in setting standards employs a similar philosophy, but there is less of a legal input required. Typically, standards for products are set when the nature of the technology that will be brought to commercialization becomes clear. I have in mind the development of a bilateral process that starts much earlier — when scientific and engineering standards are being set. In the United States, product standards are set to a large extent by private organizations such as Underwriters Laboratories, the U.S. National Standards Institute, and the U.S. Society of Mechanical Engineers. However, the Food and Drug Administration, the U.S. Department of Agriculture, the Federal Aviation Agency, and other agencies also set standards in their respective areas of responsibility. The National Bureau of Standards has a clear responsibility for developing scientific and engineering standards outside of biology.

In Japan, the situation is different and is the cause of some friction. All industrial standards are set by a government organization, the Japan Industrial Standards Committee (JISC), which is part of MITI's Agency of Industrial Science and Technology. Biological and medical standards fall under a committee of the Ministry of Health and Welfare, and food standards are the responsibility of the Ministry of Agriculture, Forestry, and Fishery. Thus, there is a mismatch when any one of several private organizations concerned with industrial standards in the United States attempts to negotiate with JISC. I would like to see the National Bureau of Standards assume an oversight responsibility in a new relationship with AIST, bringing in representatives of industry organizations as needed and appropriate. Also, I would like to see a new cooperative agreement established between NBS and AIST wherein joint or coordinated development of scientific and engineering standards is carried out to a much greater extent than now. This would benefit both countries technically and politically, ultimately would save money for both industrial sectors, and would lead to a more harmonious sharing of markets.

3. Increase the number of U.S. scientists and engineers in Japan.

My suggestion here is simple. I propose that the National Academies of Science and Engineering sponsor a promotion wherein each of the five hundred largest manufacturing corporations in the United States that do not have technical personnel working in Japan at the present time would agree to sponsor a year of research or study in Japan by one of their scientists or engineers, or alternatively, would sponsor a year of residence by a scientist or engineer drawn from U.S. university. The unit cost would be modest (but not small), and the overall impact would be enormous by U.S. standards. By this technique the United States would begin to match what Japan has been able to do in this country. There is an equally good argument for seconding technical personnel from government agencies to Japan, but again Gramm-Rudman rears its ugly head.

4. Increase the Japanese contribution and role in "big science."

Here my feelings are ambivalent. The Japanese acknowledge that they should do more to increase the world's storehouse of basic scientific knowledge. If there are ways that the U.S. scientific community can employ to assist Japan along this path, all well and good. However, I am not necessarily in favor of another reading of the proposition—that Japan should increase its financial contributions to U.S. scientific projects. As I have pointed out, there are places where increased investment in the United States makes sense and other places where it does not. The same might be said for increasing U.S. expenditures for basic research conducted in Japan, where the United States would be starting from an almost zero base. If the United States were to find it feasible and indeed attractive to invest in the proposed Japanese Human Frontiers Program, then a logical quid pro quo could be sought from Japan. Funding for "big science" projects comes essentially from governments, so the responsibility for pursuing this issue should rest with the respective governments. It would be helpful to form a bilateral working group that could examine the several proposals on the table calling for large-scale investments in projects that are beyond the capacity of any single country to finance. Perhaps the U.S. government would be willing to delegate its responsibility to the National Academy of Sciences. The name of this game ought to be "trade-offs."

SOMEWHAT AMBIGUOUS CONCLUSIONS

Probably the greatest barrier to a new era of greatly enhanced technical cooperation between the United States and Japan is the abysmal lack of knowledge that exists about the extent and depth of current relations. I honestly believe that there would be much less talk about protectionist legislation if the Congress were better informed about the positive aspects of technological trade and scientific and cultural exchanges between the two countries, but those who are satisfied with the relationship simply do not register their views with the same vehemence as those who are trying to redress grievances. The timing of this present conference may coincide with the consideration of trade legislation in Congress that could undo forty years of effort to build better relations in all sectors, so we are at a turning point. If the trade atmosphere can be cleared — giving both sides some time and breathing space to take up new initiatives for cooperation — we just might find ourselves embarked on the new era that I have postulated.

Dr. Daniel Koshland, the editor of the journal *Science*, has written an editorial for the special issue of the journal devoted to science in Japan and from which I have drawn some of the material for this chapter. Dr. Koshland's remarks could well provide the framework for how the United States treats Japan in the future. The concluding paragraph of his remarks also forms a fitting, optimistic conclusion for this chapter:

> It is a noteworthy and rare human being who is highly disciplined and yet readily adaptable to change. It is astonishing when a nation is capable of being introspective, rational, and decisive. If Japan were perfect for this instant in time, we would admire it as a rare, artistic creation of beautiful glass sculpture whose fragility would be vulnerable to future shock. That it is less than perfect, yet constantly willing to examine its imperfections and act on them, means that it is made of a metal that will last for ages. No one magazine issue — in fact, no book — can analyze comprehensively the phenomenon of modern Japan, but readers of this issue will be able to infer on reasons for its past accomplishments and will be able to recognize some of the seeds of future greatness(61).

SPECIAL NOTE

One week before the second symposium, the second joint United States-Japan meeting of senior executives from industry and distinguished professors was held in Kyoto, Japan, on November 9-11, 1986, to discuss advanced technology and the international environment. Justin Bloom, who was the consultant to the U.S. delegation, gave the following account to the second symposium on the results of this special high-level meeting:

As you know, the meeting in Kyoto was sponsored by the U.S. Academy of Sciences and Academy of Engineering and their counterpart in Japan. It is with pleasure that I provide you with an account of what transpired at this meeting with the prospect that greater publicity will be given to the findings of these distinguished representatives of the two countries and that these findings will influence decisionmakers in a positive fashion during the tumultuous period which is almost certain to be upon us starting early in 1987.

The U.S. panel was headed by Dr. Harold Brown, the former secretary of defense. Ex-officio members included Dr. Frank Press, the president of the National Academy of Sciences, and Dr. Robert White, the president of the National Academy of Engineering. Other Americans on the panel well known to you who were present in Kyoto included Professor Ezra Vogel of Harvard University; William Norris, the retired chairman of Control Data Corporation; Fred Bucy, the former chairman of Texas Instruments; and former ambassador to Japan Robert Ingersoll. The Japanese panel was chaired by Dr. Takashi Mukaibo, former president of the University of Tokyo. Other well-known Japanese participants included Professor Hiroshi Inose, dean of the School of Engineering at Tokyo University; Dr. Michiyuki Uenohara, executive vice president of NEC Corporation, who is with us this morning; Dr. Keichi Oshima, professor emeritus of Tokyo University; Mr. Shoichi Saba, chairman and chief executive officer of Toshiba Corp.; and Dr. Dogo Okamura, former president of the Japan Society for the Promotion of Science. All together, there were twelve U.S. panel members and twenty-nine Japanese present, not to mention various consultants and administrative staff members on both sides.

After two days of intensive discussion on their perceptions of the innovation cycle and the causes of trade friction resulting from innovation, the two sides found that they were in good agreement on most issues. This contrasted with the first meeting, where there was more of an air of confrontation, as described in my chapter. In Kyoto, a joint statement was prepared that made the following major points:

1. The delegates supported economic coordination, symmetrical access to scientific, technological, and economic resources, and the formulation of agreed-upon practices of commerce, as steps to avoid unwise, unilateral actions that may occur.

2. They applauded the intent of the recent bilateral agreements by the United States and Japan to coordinate macroeconomic policies affecting exchange rates, interest rates, rates of economic stimulation, and other steps to reduce the extent and mitigate the effects of severe trade imbalances.

3. They agreed that poor performance at the level of the firm or industrial sector should be addressed at the level of management or structural changes rather than through protective measures.

4. The delegates noted that defining "fair" or "unfair" practices that affect trade or technology transfer is a most difficult endeavor, in view of the differing cultures and attitudes of the two countries. To mitigate the consequences of perceived or real unfair practices, they recommended that a series of programs be undertaken to achieve symmetrical access to the elements of innovation: knowledge, technology, finance, and markets.

You will note the use of the word *symmetrical* a number of times. This proved to be the theme of conclusions, replacing the use of *fair* or *equal* in previous debates. The difference in meaning is far from trite. In its recommendations for future action, the joint statement employs the heading, "Symmetrical Access — An Approach to Avoiding Conflict."

Concerning access to new knowledge, Japan is called upon to exert more effort in all fields of science, not just in fields with presumed applications. Both countries are asked to participate in arrangements to improve access to Japanese institutions engaged in basic research, considering that the nature of these institutions in Japan is different than in the United States.

On access to new technology, mutual accessibility to institutions engaged in precommercial development is called for, while noting that negative political reactions may occur from excessive corporate acquisitions that tend to dominate an industrial sector. Copyright and patent policies in the two countries are found to differ for historical and cultural reasons, generating a perception on both sides that these policies put the other side at a disadvantage. International consensus should be sought on the protection of intellectual property rights, since innovations appropriated without proper compensation to the creator result in denying the creator the fruits of his [or her] work.

Addressing the issue of symmetrical access to capital, the group found that it would be desirable to have more equitable access to the financial markets of each country to allow market forces to determine the cost of capital.

With respect to foreign subsidiaries, the two governments are asked to provide the same treatment to them as is received by domestic firms. Foreign subsidiaries should support the welfare of the communities where they are located, including undertaking high-value-added operations when possible.

Reduction of trade barriers that restrict access to markets in each country should be sought, so that competition is based on quality and price. American companies in particular are asked to pay more attention to consumer requirements in international markets.

In addition to making these rather general recommendations, the joint statement also proposes that a series of conferences, workshops, and studies be employed to follow up the recommendations with more specific plans for action. However, further consultations will be required to determine which of the several proposals will receive priority. Time does not permit me to go into further detail, but the text of the statement should be available now to any interested party from the executive office of the National Academy of Sciences, and a full report of the conference will be prepared and published within the next two months or so.

As you can tell, no really novel ideas emerged from this meeting, and probably none should have been expected. What is important, however, is that a spirit of reconciliation and mutual determination to work together seems to have emerged — encouraged no doubt by the imminent threat of a trade war. Both sides were united in strongly rejecting these prospects. One striking event did take place in Kyoto that is worthy of note. The Japanese panelists announced that they had decided to create a Japanese Academy of Engineering, completely within the private sector, to act as a counterpart to the U.S. organization, and there also was some talk of forming a Japanese Academy of Sciences. Such moves had been long sought by senior American scientists and engineers. Dr. Dinneen speculated on this possibility yesterday. Dr. Koji Kobayashi, chairman of NEC Corporation, is destined to be the president of the new academy, and Professor Mukaibo will become the vice president.

REFERENCES

1. Naisbitt, John, *Megatrends* (New York: Warner Books, 1984), p. xxx.

2. Ott, Marvin, "Which Way for U.S. and Japan?" *Los Angeles Times*, January 2, 1985, p. II:5.

3. For example, see remarks by Prosser Gifford, cited in *The Wilson Center Reports* (November 1984).

4. Bloom, Justin L., "The U.S.-Japan Bilateral Science and Technology Relationship: A Personal Evaluation," *Scientific and Technological Cooperation Among Industrialized Countries: The Role of the United States*, Mitchell B. Wallerstein, ed. (Washington, D.C.: National Academy Press, 1984), pp. 84-110.

5. Bloom, Justin L., and Yakushiji, Taizo, *Stabilization and Expansion of Long-Term Scientific and Technological Cooperation Between the United States and Japan* (Washington, D.C.: United States-Japan Advisory Commission, September 1984).

6. Science and Technology Agency, *White Paper on Science and Technology 1985* (Tokyo: Foreign Press Center, December 1985), p. 20.

7. Science and Technology Agency, *Indicators of Science and Technology (1984)* (Tokyo: STA, March 30, 1985), pp. 138-140 (in Japanese and English).

8. See, for example, Office of Technology Assessment, *International Competitiveness in Electronics*, Report OTA-ISC-200 (November 1983); Office of Technology Assessment, *Commercial Biotechnology: An International Assessment*, Report OTA-BA-218 (January 1984); and U.S. International Trade Commission, *International Developments in Biotechnology and Their Possible Impact on Certain Sectors of the U.S. Chemical Industry*, Publication 1589 (October 1984).

9. Harris, Martha Caldwell, "Japan's International Technology Transfers," *Japan's Economy and Trade with the United States* (Washington, D.C.: Joint Economic Committee, Congress of the United States, December 9, 1985), pp. 114-142.

10. See, for example, Gerstenfeld, Arthur, ed., *Science Policy Perspectives: USA-Japan* (New York: Academic Press, 1982); and Bartocha, Bodo, and Okamura, Sogo, eds., *Transforming Scientific Ideas into Innovations: Science Policies in the United States and Japan* (Tokyo: Japan Society of the Promotion of Science, 1985).

11. Lynn, Leonard H., "Technology Transfer to Japan: What We Know, What We Need to Know, and What We Know that May Not Be So," *International Technology Transfer: Concepts, Measures, and Comparisons*, Rosenberg, Nathan, and Frischtak, Claudio, eds. (New York: Praeger, 1984): "Japanese Technology at a Turning Point," *Current History* (December 1985).

12. Choy, Jon, *U.S.-Japan Technology Flows: A Two-way Street?* Japan Economic Institute Report no. 48A (Washington, D.C.: Japan Economic Institute, December 20, 1985).

13. Peters, Lois S., "Technical Cooperation: U.S.-Japan, A Case History" (Paper presented at International Conference on Technical Cooperation and International Competitiveness, Lucca, Italy, April 2-4, 1986). This is to be published in a book edited by Dr. Richard Nelson of Yale University.

14. *Science* 233 (July 18, 1986):270-272.

15. *Japan Economic Journal* (November 30, 1985):11.

16. *Japan Economic Journal* (August 16, 1986):20.

17. *Science* 233 (July 18, 1986):267-270.

18. *Science, Technology, and U.S. Diplomacy, 1986*, Seventh annual report submitted to the Congress by the president pursuant to Section 503(b) of Title V of Public Law 95-426 (Washington, D.C.: U.S. Government Printing Office, May 1986), p. 37.

19. Ibid., p. 38.

20. *Japan Times Weekly*, August 23, 1986, p. 5.

21. "Framework of Cooperation Between the National Bureau of Standards and the Nippon Telegraph and Telephone Public Corporation," signed August 9, 1983.

22. JTECH panel reports are published by Science Applications International Corp.: *Computer Science in Japan*, JTECH-TAR-8401 (December 1984); *Mechatronics in Japan*, JTECH-TAR-8402 (March 1985); *Opto- & Microelectronics*, JTECH-TAR-8403 (May 1985); *Biotechnology in Japan*, JTECH-TAR-8404 (June 1985); *Telecommunications Technology in Japan*, JTECH-TAR-8501 (May 1986); *Advanced Materials in Japan*, JTECH-TAR-8502 (May 1986).

23. See, for example, testimony before Congress by David B. Shonyo of NTIS: "The Collection and Dissemination of Japanese Technical Report Literature at the National Technical Information Service," reproduced in *The Availability of Japanese Scientific and Technical Information in the United States*, Hearings before the Committee on Science and Technology, House of Representatives, March 6-7, 1984, Committee Print no. 85, pp. 167-178.

24. Kanda, Toshihiko, "The Japan Information Center of Science and Technology." Morse, Ronald A., and Samuels, Richard J., eds., *Getting America Ready for Japanese Science and Technology*, Proceedings of a conference at the Woodrow Wilson International Center for Scholars (Lanham, Md.: University Press of America, 1986), pp. 101-104.

25. "Sale of Federal Agency Debated," *Washington Post*, August 24, 1986, p. H2.

26. *More Foreigners for Japanese Research Laboratories? Response of Japanese Industry*, NSF Tokyo Report Memorandum no. 86 (Washington, D.C.: National Science Foundation, November 8, 1985).

27. *Directory of Japanese Company Laboratories Willing to Receive U.S. Researchers*, NSF Tokyo Report Memorandum no. 92 (Washington, D.C.: National Science Foundation, January 31, 1986).

28. *Science, Technology, and American Diplomacy, 1986*, p. 155. For complete details, see Office of the Under Secretary of Defense for Research and Engineering, *Japanese Military Technology. Procedures for Transfers to the United States* (February 1986).

29. Defense Science Board Task Force, *Industry-to-Industry International Armaments Cooperation* (June 1984), p. 42 in particular.

30. *Washington Post*, September 8, 1986, p. A24. For an analysis of reaction in Japan, see *New Scientist* (September 11, 1986):16.

31. "U.S. Senate Puts a Shield Around SDI Contracts," *New Scientist* (August 14, 1986):11.

32. Green, Anthony T., *U.S.-Japan Technology Transfer: Accommodating Different Interests* (Cambridge, Mass.: Program on Information Resources Policy, Center for Information Policy Research, Harvard University, February 1986).

33. *Japanese Technological Advances and Possible United States Responses Using Research Joint Ventures*, Hearings before the Committee on Science and Technology, U.S. House of Representatives, June 29-30, 1983, Committee Print no. 45.

34. *United States-Japan Relations*, Hearings before the Committee on Foreign Affairs, House of Representatives, March, April, June, and August 1982.

35. *The Availability of Japanese Scientific and Technical Information in the United States*, Hearings before the Committee on Science and Technology, House of Representatives, March 6-7, 1984, Committee Print no. 95.

36. For a description of the Senate bill and an analysis of it, see Report 99-618 accompanying S. 1073, House of Representatives, *Japanese Technical Literature Act of 1986*, June 4, 1986. As passed, the bill became Public Law 99-382, 100 STAT. 811, August 14, 1986.

37. *International Competition in Advanced Technology: Decisions for America* (Washington, D.C.: National Academy Press, 1983).

38. Keatley, Anne G., ed., *Technological Frontiers and Foreign Relations* (Washington, D.C.: National Academy Press, 1985).

39. A series of articles on "High Tech Trade: United States Versus Japan," *Issues in Science and Technology* (Spring 1986).

40. *Global Competition: The New Reality*, The report of the President's Commission on Industrial Competitiveness, January 1985.

41. *Cooperation and Competition in the Global Economy*, Proceedings of a National Science Foundation conference on industrial scientific and technological innovation, San Antonio, Texas, April 27-29, 1986 (to be published).

42. Uyehara, Cecil H., ed., *U.S.-Japan Technological Exchange Symposium, Sponsored By the Japan-America Society of Washington, 1981* (Washington, D.C.: University Press of America, 1982).

43. Abegglen, James C., "U.S.-Japan Technological Exchange in Retrospect, 1946-1981," ibid., p. 11.

44. Keyworth, George A., II, "International Scientific and Technological Exchange and the Future of U.S.-Japan Relations," ibid., pp. 35-36.

45. Press, Frank, "The U.S. and Japan: Renaissance and Cooperation," *Journal of Japanese Trade & Industry* 3 (1983):25-27.

46. *Challenges and Opportunities in United States-Japan Relations*, A report submitted to the president of the United States and the prime minister of Japan by the United States-Japan Advisory Commission, September 1984 available from Office of Public Communications, Department of State, or Japan Center for International Exchange, Tokyo.

47. Ibid., pp. xvii-xviii.

48. Ibid., p. xvi.

49. Ibid., p. xiii.

50. Frost, Ellen L., *U.S.-Japan Security Relations in the 1980s and Beyond* (Washington, D.C.: United States-Japan Advisory Commission, September 1984). Available from Office of Public Communication, Department of State.

51. Hayde, Herbert F., and Osborn, Jack L., *The United States and Japan: High Technology—From Competition to Cooperation* (Tokyo: American Chamber of Commerce, January 1985).

52. "A Meeting of Minds," *Look Japan* (November 10, 1985):19.

53. Baron, Herman, and Satoh, Tomoyuki, "Establishing a Japanese High Technology Information Company in the United States," Morse and Samuels, *Getting America Ready*, pp. 91-92.

54. Advertisement in *Science* (July 18, 1986):264.

55. See Morse and Samuels, *Getting America Ready*.

56. Brady, Edward L., ed., *U.S. Access to Japanese Technical Literature: Electronics and Electrical Engineering*, Proceedings of a seminar held at the National Bureau of Standards, Gaithersburg, Maryland, June 24-25, 1985. NBS Special Publication 710 (Washington, D.C.: National Bureau of Standards, January 1986).

57. See, for example, Pegan, John R., and Armstrong, James E., III, "Protection, Use and Transfer of Intellectual Property Rights in Japan" (Paper presented at the Eleventh Annual Symposium on International Licensing, Technology Transfer and Distribution, New York, November 4, 1985).

58. "Probing for the Source of Japan's Intellectual Property Trade Frictions," *Patents & Licensing* (June 1984):18-23.

59. Guttman, David S., "Effects of Japanese Intellectual Property Laws on Trade with and Investment in Japan," *Patents & Licensing* (December 1982):7-12.

60. Chiba, Genya, *The Trend in Science and Technology and Problems of Internationalization in Japan* (Tokyo: Research Development Corporation of Japan, January 29, 1985).

61. Koshland, Daniel E., Jr., *Science* (July 18, 1986):261.

DISCUSSION SUMMARY

U.S.-Japanese interdependence in science and technology comes as a result of the very nature of science and technology, which have crossed international barriers from the time of the philosopher-scientist. The difference today is that governments have taken science and added it to the web of relations with other governments. In postwar Japan, the United States supported a number of intergovernmental agreements, some dating from 1958, in science, medicine, nuclear energy, radiation, environment, and space.

It was recognized that U.S. policy had been fairly open to the rest of the world and that reciprocity on the part of Japan was important, that more research by foreigners should be done in Japan. In Japan, technology meant development for economic *and* social reasons. It has taken Japan many years to clearly recognize the role it has to help protect the shared values of its Western allies through the exchanging and extending of military technology. In the area of the Strategic Defense Initiative, discussions have been ongoing to structure a framework within which the two private sectors can cooperate in R&D.

In the United States, there is a recognition of the need for a more competitive atmosphere in all trade areas including high technology, but there was agreement among discussants that the Congress should avoid any severe protectionist legislation. U.S. industry has failed to take advantage of technical information from thousands of technical publications and still suffers from the NIH syndrome to some extent. It was noted that government actually plays a rather small role in the technology exchange process, but government can help by identifying the needs of industry. Recent legislation for access to Japanese technical literature was pointed out as an example, but it was noted that companies still fail to take advantage of what is already available.

On the U.S. side, expansion in the standards area from the National Bureau of Standards was welcomed, as was a suggestion of an exchange of five hundred U.S. corporate personnel in a program similar to the Fulbright program.

Several areas were singled out where governments must become involved in order to avoid duplication of effort, to save money, and to complete projects: aerospace, nuclear fusion, high-energy physics. It was noted that Japan and the United States are currently updating a 1980 agreement in those areas. Japan, the United States, and Europe are cooperating in building a space station, with each side making major contributions in the form of habitable experimental models of space stations and participation of crew for the operation of those stations. All partners will derive more good from the project than they would if each developed separate programs.

Despite examples of cooperative efforts and public policy dating back to the late 1940s, little is publicly known of successful cooperative efforts in science and technology exchange. The United States has a psychological problem — the country is adversarial in its approach to ongoing issues, it was noted, because the private sector does little to advertise its successes in Japan. In fact, thousands of U.S. scientists and engineers have gone to Japan and established numerous constructive working relationships.

The need to inform the public as to these successes is crucial in keeping an open door policy in the area of science and technology while still protecting technology that is transferred. Expanded cooperation in both the public and private sector is needed, with Japan increasing its side of the two-way flow of technology.

11

Concluding Remarks

Cecil H. Uyehara

During the past decade, there has been a swing from ignoring Japanese science and technological potential and holding it in contempt for its alleged "copycat" characteristics, to fear of the threat and the challenge it presents and the obvious slowness, reluctance, and inability to organize a systematic response and mobilization of resources. As the consciousness in the United States about the real and potential challenge from Japanese scientific and technological prowess—more technological than scientific at this time—rose, there have been more and more meetings, papers, conferences, and symposia to assess this challenge and debate the appropriate response. In 1986, a modest bill about Japanese technical literature was even signed into law. The increased tempo of activity seems almost frenetic.

Academic studies, such as "Technology," by Merton J. Peck of Yale University, in *Asia's New Giant* (1975), assessing Japanese technology, research and development (R&D) organization, and factors contributing to technological success appeared more than a decade ago. Generally, science and technology were treated as part of a broader analysis. Only in more recent years have there been studies devoted exclusively to this subject, such as *Japan's High Technology Industries* (1986), edited by Hugh Patrick. There have been an increasing number of academicians participating in the dialogue about and specializing in the analysis of Japanese science and technology.

The depth and breadth of the U.S. private sector's interest in Japanese science and technology, meaning principally that of the larger industrial corporations and nonprofit research institutions, are understandably more difficult to fathom, appreciate, and understand for proprietary and commercial reasons. For example, one of the more recent studies known to this writer, *Japanese Science and Technology Literature: A Subject Guide*, by GM's Research Laboratories Library (1979) listed more than nine thousand Japanese technical journals and suggested a number of actions to ensure a greater degree of utilization of Japanese scientific and technical results by Western researchers: U.S. government support of surveys of published Japanese literature, cooperative programs between Western indexing and abstracting services and the Japan Information Center of Science and Technology and improved holdings of Japanese technical literature by Western academic and corporate libraries.

In 1981-1982, a group of like-minded academicians from a number of universities, private consultants, U.S. government officials, and a modest representation from private industry met under the auspices of MIT and then under the National Science Foundation in Washington to discuss what might be done to stimulate the effective utilization of Japanese science and technological results. A fair amount was learned about what U.S. federal agencies were doing to collect information on Japanese science and technology (JSTI) and what private firms had been created to disseminate that information on a commercial basis.

In 1981, the Japan-America Society of Washington, D.C., sponsored the first known symposium devoted exclusively to an assessment of U.S.-Japanese science and technology exchange. Most of the papers presented at this symposium described a basically one-way street of technology transfer from the United States to Japan. Because one of the major objectives of this symposium was consciousness raising among Americans, no recommendations were expected to result from this meeting. It was obvious, however, from the papers, the questions, and corridor conversations that the Japanese technological challenge to the United States was at the door and could not be ignored.

The U.S. Department of State and the National Technical Information Service (Department of Commerce) sponsored a meeting at MIT in January 1983 to evaluate the availabilities of Japanese science and technology in the United States. The speakers were from public agencies, libraries, and a few corporations (IBM, GTE Microcircuits, and Corning Glass Works). The workshop called for additional studies in JSTI availability, library holdings, language training, access to JSTI, etc.

For the first time, the U.S. Congress held hearings in March 1984 to assess the availability of scientific and technical information in the United States. Again, many federal agencies reported on their efforts to gather JSTI, and several private libraries and extracting services informed the House Subcommittee on Science, Research, and Technology on their continuing efforts to collect and disseminate JSTI. As in the past, U.S. industry's participation in this kind of exchange was slight (this is understandable but unfortunate). Numerous actions were urged upon the subcommittee to study the collection and utilization of JSTI in the United States, take legislative action to encourage the study of the Japanese language in order to foster a more effective dialogue between the engineers and scientists of the two countries, foster the translation services of JSTI, stimulate the systematic collection of JSTI journals by U.S. libraries, increase responsibilities and funding of federal agencies to collect and disseminate JSTI, and urge the establishment of a U.S. national information policy. In September 1984, Congress directed that $500,000 out of a larger appropriation for part of the Department of Commerce be spent on JSTI. This bill was vetoed by the president, and unfortunately this tiny sum was not included in final fiscal year 1985 appropriations. Thus, despite the apparent need and urgency, JSTI was not sufficiently important even to appropriate the paltry sum of $500,000. The subcommittee held a second set of hearings in June 1985, which probably contributed to the passage of a JSTI bill in 1986.

Two other events of note concerning JSTI also took place in 1984. The Defense Science Board Task Force issued a report in June on industry-to-industry international armaments cooperation with Japan. The task force admitted even in 1984 that it had become "clear how relatively little we [presumably the U.S. Department of Defense] know of Japanese scientific and technical work." Of course, the task force recommended a number of actions, which have been oft-repeated in other forums. The second Japanese and U.S. "Wise Men's Report" was issued in September. For the first time, it contained a chapter on Japanese science and technology and included a number of recommendations for actions by both the United States and Japan.

A significant meeting on "Getting America Ready for Japanese Science and Technology" was sponsored by the Woodrow Wilson Center (Smithsonian Institution) and the MIT-Japan Science and Technology Program in May 1985 to assess the preparedness of the critical tools to effectively internalize and utilize JSTI: language training in technical Japanese, translators, the availability and survival potential of JSTI service companies, machine translation, language technologies. The findings were not encouraging.

The dialogue between the United States and Japan was significantly escalated in summer 1985 when the U.S. National Academy of Science and the Japan Society for the Promotion of Science convened a meeting of company chief executive officers, professors, university presidents, and other senior officials to discuss the international environment and science and technology exchange. After this distinguished panel's second meeting in Kyoto, Japan, in November 1986, the combined groups called for "symmetrical access" to science and technology information and institutions in each country, accelerating scientific communication via satellite link ups, the study of common problems facing Pacific Rim countries in science and technology transfer, discussion of advanced technology issues at summit and General Agreement on Trade and Tariffs meetings, and creation of bilateral workshops on these issues.

In addition, mention should be made of the 1984 Report of the President's Council on Competitiveness (The Young Report), the series of hearings by the Science and Technology Committee in the U.S. House of Representatives on cooperative research among U.S. corporations and competition with Japan, and the February 1987 Report on Defense Semiconductor Dependency by the Defense Science Board Task Force. They are mentioned because of their focus on what needs to be done to make the United States "more competitive" and not on the issue of U.S.-Japanese science and technology exchange.

It could be said that the 1984 and 1985 subcommittee hearings mentioned previously although seemingly unsuccessful at that time, laid the groundwork for the successful introduction of the Japanese technical literature bill by Senators Max Baucus of Montana and John D. Rockefeller of West Virginia; the bill was signed into law by the president on August 14, 1986. Yet even this act did not include any new funds for JSTI, which everyone declared to be of utmost concern and even impinging in some aspects on U.S. national security; the law only stipulated that the Commerce Department would set aside $1 million from its existing appropriations for this purpose! Under this act, the Commerce Department will monitor JSTI, consult with various organizations on JSTI needs, translate selected documents, and coordinate with other federal agencies to avoid duplication and gaps in JSTI efforts in the government. The department shall also prepare an annual report on Japanese scientific discoveries and technical innovations and compile an annual directory on commercial services on JSTI and translations of Japanese materials in the federal government.

It was against this rather monotonous litany of what should be done that the Japan-America Society of Washington and its other co-sponsors optimistically decided to convene the Second Symposium on U.S.-Japan Science and Technology Exchange in fall 1986 to mark the fifth anniversary of the first symposium. The 1986 symposium's subtitle, "Patterns of Interdependence," symbolized a distinct philosophical difference from its 1981 predecessor and emphasized the reality of growing interdependence and the need for further broadening, deepening, and strengthening of this bilateral relationship. It was also in sharp contrast to the characterization of the U.S.-Japanese competition in science and technology as a "decisive battle" or "science and technology war" between the two countries. All the papers presented and the Japanese and U.S. discussants emphasized a positive approach rather than the potentially destructive martial cry voiced by some.

The following observations can be distilled from the papers and discussion during the symposium:

1. In many areas there has been a radical shift from the one-way street to a more balanced exchange, even to a Japan-to-United States transfer of technology in some instances.

2. We now have a better appreciation from a strategic point of view that there is a need for the United States and Japan to strengthen, broaden, increase, and deepen their scientific and technological relations. Societal requirements are apparently driving both countries in this direction, and there is a concomitant need to take actions that facilitate these trends.

3. We have a better understanding of the relative standings of the United States and Japan in selected technical areas.

4. One of the major achievements of this symposium was its ability to conduct a constructive dialogue between U.S. and Japanese colleagues. For once, there was less discussion about what the Japanese should do and more about what Americans should call upon themselves to do in order to make a much greater, systematic, and continuing effort to maintain the U.S. leadership position.

5. Both the United States and Japan are faced with a situation in the science and technology areas that neither side has experience. The situation appears uncomfortable for both, and both are struggling to formulate a national response appropriate to this challenge. Both have been flexible in the past; both have responded. Some have raised the question, "Will Japan change?" The more appropriate question is, "Will the United States *and* Japan change?": This change is going to be very difficult, but in light of the determination and commitments expressed by those present, a reasonable solution will be devised and executed.

6. The solutions and the obstacles to them are rooted in both cultures and in the interaction of culture and technology, not in the so-called "objectivity" of science and technology. Although mentioned last, this point should perhaps have been placed at the top of these observations; it needs to be stated over and over again. Although each country can obviously learn from the other, what might be learned should first be internalized and digested and then recreated in each cultural context.

> This cultural factor kept recurring in the dialogues at the
> symposium. Although the U.S. participants persistently
> reiterated – almost to the point of boredom – the
> dangers of the not-invented-here syndrome, the latter
> cannot be overemphasized.

This symposium was intended to strike a positive note in order to understand a dynamic and fluid situation and to be helpful to R&D managers in industry and to government officials in their assessments of U.S.-Japanese relations. It was not intended that a set of recommendations for action by both governments or by private industry would be adopted, but a number of suggested actions have been offered. The principal ones are summarized as follows and are focused mainly on the United States.

- 1. Retain safeguards on intellectual property (a point mentioned several times in the past).
- 2. U.S. businesses need to take more systematic and continuing action to position themselves for commercial and technical exchange with Japanese organizations.
- 3. Greater, more systematic, and more sustained study of Japanese technical research by U.S. business and science needs to occur as well as an in-depth study of what the United States needs from Japanese technological findings.
- 4. Greater effort should be made to study the Japanese language. (Although this is a worthy objective, realistically this will be extremely difficult to achieve in light of the obvious lack of funds from either private industry, Congress, or the federal government. Even symbolic encouragement is hard to find.)
- 5. Increase the number of U.S. scientists and engineers in Japanese laboratories. It is reported that there are more slots in Japanese laboratories for foreigners with a working knowledge of the Japanese language than there are available candidates.
- 6. Increase Japanese contributions and role in "big science." (This is an excellent idea, but are the U.S. government and industry really willing to make such potential projects truly bilateral; in funding and utilization of findings?)
- 7. Extend and expand cooperative research in the United States.
- 8. Continue the Engineering Research Centers Programs in the United States.
- 9. Engage in joint ventures and research in the precompetitive stage.
- 10. Recognize the need for international agreement on engineering standards.

- 11. Improve the U.S. educational systems, particularly in the K-12 grades.
- 12. Create a Japanese Academy of Engineering, similar to that in the United States. Subsequently, it was announced that the Japanese had created such an academy.

As the participants returned to their home offices, they were asked to contribute to creating a critical mass to have some of these proposed actions put into reality.

Appendix A:
Symposium Program
November 17-18, 1986

NOVEMBER 17

OPENING REMARKS
Ambassador Marshall Green, President, Japan-America
Society of Washington, D.C.

COMPARATIVE ASSESSMENT OF U.S.-JAPANESE
SCIENCE AND TECHNOLOGY

Speaker: *Gerald P. Dinneen*, Corporate Vice President, Science
and Technology, Honeywell, Inc.

Moderator: *Raymond G. Kammer*, Deputy Director, National Bureau
of Standards, U.S. Department of Commerce

Discussants: *Shojiro Aoki*, General Manager, Technical Development
Center, Mitsui & Co., (USA)
George Gamota, President, Research and
Development/New Business Center,
Thermo-Electron Corporation

TECHNOLOGICAL PROGRESS AND R&D
SYSTEMS IN JAPAN AND THE UNITED STATES

Speaker: *Gary Saxonhouse*, Professor, Department of Economics,
University of Michigan

Moderator: Carl Kaysen, Director, Program in Science, Technology
and Society, Massachusetts Institute of Technology

Discussants: *Hisashi Kobayashi*, Dean, School of Engineering and
Applied Science, Princeton University
Sheldon Weinig, Chairman, Materials Research
Corporation

THE JAPANESE TECHNICAL
LITERATURE ACT OF 1986

Speaker: *Mark R. Policinski*, Associate Deputy Secretary, U.S.
Department of Commerce

CASE STUDIES OF INTERDEPENDENCE

NEW MATERIALS

Speaker: *George B. Kenney*, Assistant Director, Materials Processing Center, Massachusetts Institute of Technology

Moderator: *A.R.C. Westwood*, Corporate Director, R&D, Martin Marietta Corporation.

Discussants: *Kiyoshi Sugita*, Executive Counsellor, Nippon Steel Corporation
Leon Starr, President, Celanese Research Company

MECHATRONICS

Speaker: *James L. Nevins*, Division Leader, Robotics & Assembly Systems Division, Charles Stark Draper Laboratory

Moderator: *M. Eugene Merchant*, Director, Advanced Manufacturing Research, Metcut Research Associates, Inc.

Discussants: *Hajimu Inaba*, Executive Vice President, GM Fanuc
Mike Kutcher, Automation Consultant, IBM

COMPUTERS AND COMMUNICATIONS

Speaker: *Morimi Iwama*, Executive Director, Switching Systems Engineering Division, AT&T Bell Laboratories

Moderator: *Lee W. Hoevel*, Director, Advanced Systems Architecture Program, NCR

Discussants: *Michiyuki Uenohara*, Executive Vice President, NEC Corporation
George L. Turin, Professor, Department of Electrical Engineering and Computer Science, University of California, Berkeley

BIOTECHNOLOGY

Speaker: *Arthur E. Humphrey*, Director, Biotechnology Research Center, Lehigh University

Moderator: *Kevin Ulmer*, Director, Center for Advanced Research & Biotechnology, University of Maryland

Discussants: *Yasuo Iriye*, Director, Basic Research, Maryland Research Laboratories, Otsuka Pharmaceutical Company
David V. Goeddel, Director, Molecular Biology Department, Genentech, Inc.

PLENARY SESSION ON CASE STUDIES

SCIENCE AND TECHNOLOGY
POLICY IN JAPAN

Speaker: *Yoshimitsu Takeyasu*, Council of Science and Technology
                of Japan

NOVEMBER 18

THE EMERGENCE OF VALUE-CREATION
NETWORKS IN CORPORATE STRATEGY

Speaker: *Mel Horwitch*, Professor, Alfred P. Sloan School of
                Management, Massachusetts Institute of Technology
Moderator: *Shinzo Kobori*, Senior Vice President, C. Itoh & Com-
                pany
Discussants: *Jiro Kamimura*, General Manager, Mitsubishi
                International Corporation, Washington Office
                David L. Bodde, Executive Director, Commission on
                Engineering and Technical Systems, National Research
                Council

A NEW ERA FOR U.S.-JAPANESE TECHNICAL
RELATIONS? PROBLEMS AND PROSPECTS

Speaker: *Justin L. Bloom*, President, Technology International,
                Inc.
Moderator: *Max Baucus*, U.S. Senator
Discussants: *Peter Y. Sato*, Minister, Embassy of Japan
                Robert G. Morris, Deputy Assistant Secretary for Science
                and Technology Affairs, Bureau of Oceans, Internation-
                al, Environmental, and Scientific Affairs, U.S. Depart-
                ment of State

CONCLUSIONS AND SUGGESTIONS

Speaker: *Cecil H. Uyehara*, President, Uyehara International
                Associates

CLOSING REMARKS

Speaker: *Ambassador Marshall Green*

Appendix B:
About the Symposium Participants

SHOJIRO AOKI has been general manager of the Technical Development Center, Mitsui & Co. (U.S.A.), in New York City since 1982. Born in Shizuoka City in 1936, he graduated from Shizuoka University, School of Industrial Chemistry in 1961, majoring in polymer chemistry. He began his career in the Mitsui Company's Technical Development Division and was assigned to the Technical Development Center in New York from 1964 to 1967. He then returned to Tokyo where he worked in the Technical Development Division until 1969, when he was assigned to a sales division in the Chemical Plant and Machinery Division. In 1972, he returned again to the Technical Development Division for promotion of pollution control and new energy technology development.

MAX BAUCUS has been a U.S. Senator (Democrat) from Montana since 1978. He serves on the Senate Finance, Environment, and Small Business Committees. Previously, he served in the U.S. House of Representatives, 1974-1978, and the Montana House of Representatives, 1973-1974. He was a staff attorney with the Civil Aeronautics Board (1967-1969), and the Securities and Exchange Commission (1969-1971), and had his own law business, George and Baucus, in Missoula, Montana (1971-1974). In the U.S. Senate, he has worked to strengthen the competitiveness of U.S. industry as a member of the International Trade Subcommittee. He was in the forefront of the movement to tighten subsidy laws against Canadian timber imports in order to protect the U.S. timber industry from unfair competition. He coauthored (with Senator Rockefeller of West Virginia) the 1986 Japanese Technical Literature Translation Act signed into law by the president.

JUSTIN L. BLOOM is president of Technology International, Inc., of Potomac, Maryland, a consulting organization specializing in foreign scientific and technical information and international technology transfer. His career has spanned thirty-eight years, following his graduation from the California Institute of Technology. He has worked as an engineer and manager in petrochemicals development, nuclear materials production, nuclear weapons development, and radioisotope applications. During twenty-four years of service with the U.S. government, he was technical assistant to the chairman of the Atomic Energy Commission and counselor for Scientific and Technological Affairs at the U.S. Embassies in Tokyo and London. He retired from the Foreign Service in March 1983 with the rank of minister-counselor and with a Presidential Meritorious Service Award.

DAVID L. BODDE is executive director of the Commission on Engineering and Technical Systems of the National Research Council where he supervises the engineering and policy studies of the National Academy of Sciences. Prior to this, he was assistant director of the Congressional Budget Office and a deputy assistant secretary in the Department of Energy. His business experience includes managing an energy engineering group at TRW. Dr. Bodde is a 1965 graduate of the U.S. Military Academy. After army service in Vietnam, his graduate education included nuclear engineering at MIT and business and economics at the Harvard Business School.

H. KENT BOWEN has been Ford Professor of Engineering at the Massachusetts Institute of Technology since 1981. He completed a B.S. degree in ceramic engineering in 1967 at the University of Utah and received a Ph.D. degree from MIT in 1971. He joined the MIT faculty in 1970 in the Department of Materials Science and Engineering, later receiving a joint appointment in electrical engineering and computer science, and became a full professor in 1976. He has served as director of the Materials Processing Center and currently serves as director of MIT's Ceramics Processing Research Laboratory. He has served on numerous professional, societal, government, and corporate advisory committees related to developments in advanced materials and high technology engineering systems. Professor Bowen's research has focused on ceramic materials and materials processing, which has lead to more than one hundred published papers. He is the co-author of a key textbook in the field. Among other honors, Dr. Bowen was named the 1986 Scientist of the Year by the *Research and Development Magazine* and is a member of the National Academy of Engineering.

GERALD P. DINNEEN is corporate vice president for science and technology at Honeywell Corporation. He received his B.S. (mathematics) from Queens College, New York, in 1947; and his Ph.D. and M.S. in mathematics from the University of Wisconsin, Madison, in 1952 and 1948, respectively. He was director from 1970 to 1977 at MIT Lincoln Laboratory and concurrently MIT professor of electrical engineering, 1971-1981. Under President Jimmy Carter he was assistant secretary of defense for communications, command and control and intelligence, and principal deputy under secretary of defense research and engineering. In 1981, he received the Distinguished Public Service Award, Department of Defense. He is a board director of

Votan, Microelectronics and Computer Technology Corporation (MCC), Science Museum of Minnesota, Honeywell Foundation, and the Council of National Academy of Engineering.

GEORGE GAMOTA was appointed president of Thermo Electron Corporation's Research and Development/New Business Center in March 1986. The New Business Center is involved in research, development, and new business creation in high-technology areas such as new materials, terrestrial and space power sources, instrumentation, lithography, and infrared sensors and lasers. From 1981 to 1986, Dr. Gamota was director of the University of Michigan's Institute of Science and Technology and professor of physics, and from 1976 to 1981, he was director for research in the U.S. Department of Defense, Office of the Secretary of Defense. Before 1976, Dr. Gamota was with Bell Laboratories where he performed research in solid state physics. He has published extensively on research and development and science and technology policy, including international R&D. Dr. Gamota is currently involved in the Japanese Technology Program (JTECH) supported by the National Science Foundation, Department of Commerce, and the Defense Advanced Research Projects Agency.

DAVID V. GOEDDEL received his B.A. in chemistry from the University of California at San Diego in 1972 and his Ph.D. in biochemistry from the University of Colorado, Boulder, in 1977. He did postdoctoral research at SRI International for one year before joining Genentech in 1978. Goeddel's research at Genentech has focused on the cloning and expression of genes for medically important proteins. This work has included the successful production via recombinant DNA technology of human insulin, growth hormone, interferon-a, -B, and -Y, tissue-type plasminogen activator, and tumor necrosis factor. Three of these products have been approved by the Food and Drug Administration as therapeutic agents, and the others are in various stages of clinical testing.

MARSHALL GREEN is president of the Japan-America Society of Washington, one of the several sponsors of the Second Symposium on U.S.-Japan Science and Technology Exchange. He began his long career in foreign affairs after graduating from Yale University in 1939, as the private secretary to Joseph Grew, U.S. ambassador to Japan, until the outbreak of the Pacific War. During the war he was a Japanese interpreter and translator for the U.S. Navy. His career in the U.S. Foreign Service from 1945 to 1979 involved eight assignments overseas and four in Washington, including regional planning advisor for Asia, minister in Korea, consul-general in Hong Kong, deputy assistant secretary for the Far East, ambassador to Indonesia and Australia, assistant secretary of state for East Asia and the

Pacific, delegate to the Paris Peace Talks on Vietnam, chief of Delegation to the U.N. Population Commission, and chairman of the NSC Task Force on World Population. Since 1979, Ambassador Green has been active in organizations concerned with U.S.-East Asia relations and with world population and refugee issues.

LEE W. HOEVEL is the director of the Advanced Systems Architecture Program, a management position which reports to the vice president of the Research and Development Division at NCR Corporation. The objective of this program is to formulate and identify an advanced systems architecture framework and elements of platforms to meet NCR's needs in the early 1990s. Dr. Hoevel previously was with IBM Corporation in Yorktown Heights, New York, where he was the manager of environment architecture at the T. J. Watson Research Center. Dr. Hoevel holds degrees in economics and mathematics from Rice, has done postgraduate studies in computer science at Stanford, and received a Ph.D. in electrical engineering from Johns Hopkins in 1978.

MEL HORWITCH is a member of the strategic management group at the Alfred P. Sloan School of Management at MIT. He has taught courses on technological innovation, technological strategy, strategic management, managing large-scale enterprises, production operations, and energy economics. He has written extensively on management, technology, and energy affairs. He is the editor of *Technology in the Modern Corporation: A Strategic Perspective* (Pergamon Press, 1986). He is the author of *Clipped Wings: The American SST Conflict* (MIT Press, 1982) and a contributor to *Energy Future: Report of the Energy Project at the Harvard Business School* (Random House, 1979). His articles have been published in *Policy Science*, *Sloan Management Review*, *Technology in Society*, and *Management Science* (forthcoming). He received his A.B. from Princeton University and an M.B.A. and Ph.D. from the Harvard Business School. He served as a Peace Corps volunteer in Thailand and consults for several corporations and government agencies in the United States and abroad.

ARTHUR E. HUMPHREY is T. L. Diamond Professor of Biochemical Engineering and director of the Biotechnology Research Center at Lehigh University. He received his B.S. (chemical engineering) in 1948 and M.S. (chemical engineering) in 1950 from the University of Idaho. He received a Ph.D. (chemical engineering) in 1953 from Columbia University and majored in biochemical engineering. Later he went to MIT and received an M.S. (food tech.) degree in 1960. Beginning in the fall of 1953 and for the next twenty-seven years, he taught biochemical engineering at the University of Pennsylvania. While there, he served as chairman of the Department of Chemical Engineering for ten years and as dean of engineering and applied science for eight years before going to Lehigh University in 1980, where he served as provost and academic vice president for six years. In 1986, he returned to full-time teaching and research as the T. L. Diamond Professor of Biochemical Engineering. Professor Humphrey has authored three books, written more than two hundred fifty research papers, and has been granted four patents. Dr. Humphrey is a fellow in AIChE and a member of the National Academy of Engineering. He has been a director of fermentation design and biochem technology. In 1984, Dr. Humphrey chaired the Research Briefing Panel for the Office of Science and Technology Policy on "Chemical and Process Engineering for Biotechnology." Dr. Humphrey has been a Fulbright lecturer on biotechnology to several countries, including Japan, China, India, and Australia.

HAJIMU INABA has been executive vice president of GMF Robotics Corporation and a member of the Board of Directors since 1982. He joined Fujitsu, Ltd., in 1968 as an engineer on numerical control systems. In 1972, he transferred to FANUC Ltd., continuing his work in factory automation, direct numerical control systems, and automatic programming; in 1976 he began work in the Automation System Laboratory. He received his B.S. (1966) and M.S. (1968) degrees for applied mathematics and physics from Kyoto University.

YASUO IRIYE is director of basic research at the Maryland Research Laboratories of the Otsuka Pharmaceutical Company. After graduating with a B.A. degree (1973) in pharmaceutical sciences from Kyoto University, he joined the Tokushima Research Institute of the Otsuka Pharmaceutical Company. Subsequently, he became assistant manager, Division of Research Administration, (1979-1980); manager (1980-1981) of the Division of Cellular Technology of the Tokushima Research Institute (1981-1983); and director of the Otsuka Pharmaceutical Company's Maryland Liaison Office (1983-1985). He has been a member of the Japan Association of Biological Chemistry and the Japan Association of Pharmacy and has published numerous articles in Japanese and European technical journals.

MORIMI IWAMA is executive director, Switching Systems Engineering Division at AT&T Bell Laboratories. Following a brief teaching career at the University of California at Berkeley, he joined Bell Labs as a member of the technical staff in 1961. His initial assignment was Project TELSTAR. During the ensuing ten years, he worked on numerous defense projects. In these assignments, his contributions were primarily in system engineering, encompassing concept formulation, system synthesis, analysis and evaluation. His responsibilities from 1974 to 1979 included private network and new telecommunications services planning for Bell System customers. Between 1979 and 1982, he was responsible for systems engineering and development of computer-based systems for mechanizing, provisioning, and maintaining the Bell System network. He returned briefly to defense systems work in 1982. In November 1983, he was appointed executive Director, Operations and Network Planning Division at AT&T Bell Laboratories. Dr. Iwama received B.S., M.S. and Ph.D. degrees in electrical engineering from the University of California at Berkeley in 1954, 1955, and 1960, respectively. He is a senior member of the IEEE.

JIRO KAMIMURA is general manager of Mitsubishi International Corporation's Washington, D.C. office. After graduating from Georgetown University, School of Foreign Service in 1957, he joined Mitsubishi Corporation, Tokyo, Chemicals Department. From 1968 to 1976, he served at Mitsubishi International Corporation, New York office, establishing extensive relationships with U.S. chemical firms through technical licensing and joint venture arrangements. Returning to Tokyo he engaged in planning and development of fine chemicals related to biochemistry, electronics, alternative energy, and other high-technology industry. After a two and a half years assignment in Saudi Arabia to complete the petrochemical project sponsored jointly by the Saudi Arabian and Japanese governments, he assumed his Washington position in July 1986.

RAYMOND G. KAMMER became deputy director of the National Bureau of Standards in 1980. He joined NBS in 1969 as a management intern and subsequently served as senior budget analyst; associate director for programs, budget, and finance; and director of administration and information systems. In 1981, Mr. Kammer chaired an eight-month technical review of the EPA study of Love Canal to evaluate the measurement procedures used by EPA in arriving at its determinations as to the habitability of the Love Canal area. From April 1983 until September 1983, Mr. Kammer served as chairman of the Source Evaluation Board for Civil Space Remote Sensing. He served as chairman of the Advisory Committee for NEXRAD System Requirements Evaluation and recently led a review of the OMNI-STAR proposal to fly the LANDSAT sensors on a space platform.

CARL KAYSEN is director, Program in Science, Technology, and Society at the Massachusetts Institute of Technology. He received his B.A. degree from the University of Pennsylvania in 1940 and his Ph.D. from Harvard University in 1954. He became Lucius N. Littauer Professor of Political Economy at Harvard University (1964-1966), was director of the Institute of Advanced Studies at Princeton University (1966-1976), and has been David W. Skinner Professor of Political Economy at MIT since 1977. He was deputy special assistant on national security affairs to President Kennedy from 1961-1963. Dr. Kaysen has been a director of the Polaroid Corporation, United Parcel Service; member of the editorial board of *Foreign Affairs*; life trustee of the University of Pennsylvania; and trustee of the German Marshall Fund and the Russell Sage Foundation.

GEORGE B. KENNEY, co-author of the chapter on new materials with D. Kent Bowen (Ford Professor of Engineering, MIT) is assistant director of the Materials Processing Center at MIT. After receiving his B.S. and M.S. in metallurgy and materials science and his Ph.D. in materials systems analysis, all from MIT, he joined his alma mater's staff in 1978 as a research associate. In 1980, when the Materials Processing Center was first established within MIT's School of Engineering, Dr. Kenney was appointed its assistant director. The next year he was made director of the Materials Processing Center/Industrial Collegium, which currently has sixty-five worldwide corporate members. Dr. Kenney consults internationally in materials engineering, economics, and systems analysis, and in 1981 he founded a company engaged in metals processing analysis and control.

HISASHI KOBAYASHI has been dean of the School of Engineering and Applied Science, Princeton University since July 1986. He also holds the Sherman Fairchild University professorship and is a professor of computer science and electrical engineering. Prior to joining Princeton University, he had been with the IBM Research Division for nineteen years. From 1982 to 1986, he was the founding director of IBM Japan Science Institute in Tokyo. Dr. Kobayashi received his B.S. and M.S. degrees from the University of Tokyo and his M.A. and Ph.D. degrees from Princeton University in electrical engineering. The areas of his research contributions include radar signal design, data transmission theory, magnetic recording, computer performance modeling, computer network, and queuing theory. While with IBM, he held visiting professorships at UCLA (1969-1970), University of Hawaii (1975), Stanford University (1976), Technical University of Damstadt, West Germany (1979-1980), and University of Brussels, Belgium (1980). He holds seven U.S. patents, authored more than sixty research articles, and published a graduate textbook *Modeling and Analysis* (Addison-Wesley, 1978). He was the past editor in chief of an international journal, *Performance Evaluation*. Among the various honors and awards that he has received are the 1979 Humboldt Award (Senior U.S. Scientist Award) from West Germany, IFIP Silver Core Award (1980), and IBM Outstanding Contribution Award (1975, 1984). He is a fellow of IEEE since 1977.

SHINZO KOBORI presently is senior vice president of C. Itoh & Co. (America), Inc., and general manager of its Washington office. He obtained his B.A. degree (economics) from Tokyo University and spent one year (1980-1981) at the Brookings Institution in Washington, D.C. as a guest scholar before he was posted to Washington (1981-1987). His previous overseas assignments were in New York and Toronto with C. Itoh. He is a trustee, secretary, and vice president of the Japan-America Society of Washington and a member of the National Press Club.

MICHAEL KUTCHER is presently automation consultant with IBM. From 1979 to 1985, he organized and chaired IBM's Corporate Automation Council. He has been a consultant to various government agencies including the U.S. Air Force's ICAM Program and Commerce's Mechatronics Panel. He is a member of IEEE and a recipient of the IBM President's Award for process control systems. He also holds patents on robots and manufacturing and testing systems.

FRANCIS R. MAGEE, JR., co-author of the chapter on computers and communications with Morimi Iwama, is a technical supervisor at AT&T Bell Laboratories, where he started working in 1972. From 1972 to 1978, Dr. Magee worked on applied research data transmission over voiceband telephone lines, which resulted in many publications in technical journals and conferences. In 1979-1982 he worked on specification of basic data network services and algorithmic development for the internal protocol of these products. His current group is responsible for technical planning of foreign data networks for AT&T. In 1982-1985, he worked on systems engineering of data networks for enhanced services and initial planning of a large-scale corporate network for AT&T Information Systems. Dr. Magee earned his B.S. (with highest honors), M.S. and Ph.D. degrees at Northeastern University. He received a NSF graduate fellowship to support his graduate training. He is a member of Sigma XI, Tau Beta Pi, Eta Kappa Nu, and Phi Kappa Phi honor societies, is a senior member of the IEEE, and has recently completed a two-year period as the chairperson of the Computer Communications Technical Committee. He also received an IEEE Computer Society Certificate of Appreciation for his work as the chairperson of IEEE INFOCOM '83.

M. EUGENE MERCHANT has been director, Advanced Manufacturing Research, Metcut Research Associates, Inc., since June 1983 after retiring from Cincinnati Milacron, Inc., where he engaged in the performance and direction of manufacturing research for forty-six years. He holds a B.S. degree (mechanical engineering) from the University of Vermont in 1936 and a Ph.D. from the University of Cincinnati in 1941. He also holds honorary Doctor of Science degrees from the University of Vermont (1973) and the University of Salford, England (1980). His research activities have included basic and applied research on manufacturing processes, equipment and systems, and the future of manufacturing technology. He is a member of the National Academy of Engineering and has been the recipient of a variety of awards and honors, worldwide.

ROBERT G. MORRIS is deputy assistant secretary for science and technology affairs in the Department of State's Bureau of Oceans and International Environmental and Scientific Affairs. He received his Ph.D. in physics from the Iowa State University. After postdoctoral study in Zurich, he was professor of physics and performed research in solid state physics at the South Dakota School of Mines and Technology from 1958 to 1968, with a second year in Zurich during that time. He was a research administrator at the Office of Naval Research in Washington (1968-1974). He entered the Foreign Service in 1974 and has served in Washington, Paris, and Bonn.

JAMES LAWRENCE NEVINS is division leader, Robotics and Assembly Systems Division in the Charles Stark Draper Laboratory, Cambridge, Massachusetts, which conducts automation projects sponsored by industry, the National Science Foundation, and the Office of Naval Research. His past responsibilities included co-principal investigator of the NSF-sponsored Product System Productivity Research Study, the direction of an ARPA-DOD project on computer-controlled manipulators, the Space Nuclear Systems Office (SNSO) project in support of the development of the NERVA Engine Instrumentation and Control System, the SNSO project to develop a multimoded remote manipulator system, and the man-machine design and implementation for the Apollo and Lunar Module guidance, navigation and control systems. He is a former consultant to NSF. He was the chairman of the U.S. Department of Commerce Japanese Technology Evaluation Committee Mechatronics Panel. After receiving his B.S. degree (electrical engineering) in 1952 from Northeastern University, he joined the Draper Lab (formerly the MIT Instrumentation Lab) as a test engineer in the Inertial Gyro Group. In 1956, he received his M.S. degree from MIT in the Department of Aeronautics.

MARK R. POLICINSKI has been associate deputy secretary of commerce since September 14, 1983. As the principal executive to the deputy secretary of commerce, he oversees the development and implementation of departmental policies and programs. Prior to his present position, he was senior economist for the Joint Economic Committee, U.S. Congress, 1976-1983. From 1973 to 1976, Mr. Policinski was director of student activities for Western Kentucky University in Bowling Green, Kentucky.

PETER Y. SATO is economic minister with the Embassy of Japan. Since joining the Japanese Foreign Service in 1958, he has served in London, Jakarta, Washington, D.C. (on three occasions), and Hong Kong. In 1980, Mr. Sato was assigned to the Economic Affairs Bureau in charge of both bilateral and multilateral economic affairs, including U.S.-Japanese trade issues. During 1978-1980, Mr. Sato was executive assistant to the late prime minister M. Ohira in charge of foreign policy. His latest post in Tokyo was as deputy director-general of the Economics Affairs Bureau.

GARY SAXONHOUSE is professor of economics at the University of Michigan. In addition to holding his present position, Professor Saxonhouse has taught at Harvard, Yale, and Brown universities. While at Brown, Professor Saxonhouse was Henry Luce Professor of Comparative Development. He has written widely on the structure and operation of the Japanese economy, on U.S.-Japanese trade relations, on technology transfer, and on econometrics. His co-authored book, *Technique, Spirit and Form in the Making of the Modern Economies* was published in 1984, and this year Macmillan will bring out another co-authored book, *Comparative Technology Choice*. The Association for Asian Studies awarded Professor Saxonhouse its distinguished lectureship for 1979-1980. During the academic year 1984-1985, Professor Saxonhouse was a fellow at the Center for Advanced Study in the Behavioral Sciences in Stanford, California.

LEON STARR has served as President, Celanese Research Company, since January 1983 and as vice president, technology, Celanese Corporation, since August 1986. Dr. Starr joined Celanese Plastics Company research facility in Clark, New Jersey. He has held both management and technical management positions in the corporation and in operating companies. He is a member of various industry organizations and is a member of the Board of Directors of Codenoll Technology Corporation and the Materials Properties Council. He holds a B.S. degree (organic chemistry) from the Polytechnic Institute of New York and a Ph.D. (organic chemistry) from the University of Missouri.

KIYOSHI SUGITA is executive counselor of Nippon Steel Corporation, responsible mainly for ceramics-related technical activities in the Central R&D Bureau of the corporation. After receiving his B.S. degree (applied chemistry) from Osaka University in 1954, he joined Nippon Steel Refractories Laboratory. He received a Ph.D. in 1965 from Osaka University. He had been general manager of the Heat Technology Division until 1985 and chair of the Heat Technology and Economy Committee of the Iron and Steel Institute of Japan. He is now chairing the International Relations Committee of the Technical Association of Refractories, Japan.

YOSHIMITSU TAKEYASU has been a member of the Japanese Council for Science and Technology since 1984. He has also served on many policy-making advisory bodies to the Japanese Government, such as the Patent Right Council, the Council for Aeronautics, Electronics, and Other Advanced Technologies, and the Industrial Technology Council. After receiving a B.S. (electrical engineering), he worked for the Japanese government in various capacities. In 1955, he became director, Research Division of the Agency for Industrial Science and Technology in the Ministry of International Trade and Industry. In 1956, he joined the newly established Science and Technology Agency (STA); in 1964 became director, Personnel Division; in 1965, the deputy-director general, Atomic Energy Bureau; and in 1967, the director-general of the Planning Bureau. He joined the Power Reactor and Nuclear Fuel Development Corporation established under STA in 1967 and served as a member of its Board of Directors (1968-1972). He later returned to the STA as vice minister, 1973-1975. Mr. Takeyasu became president of the Research Development Corporation of Japan, 1975-1983, which assists the private sector to utilize the results of R&D conducted by academic, government, and public institutions as well as by individuals under the supervision of the STA.

GEORGE L. TURIN is a professor in the Department of Engineering and Computer Science, University of California, Berkeley, and was chairman of the Department of Electrical Engineering and Computer Science at the University of California at Los Angeles. He was recently chairman of the Panel on Telecommunications of the NSF- and DARPA-sponsored Japanese Technology Evaluation Program, which evaluated and compared the status of telecommunications R&D in the United States and Japan and attempted to predict the future of trade between the two nations in this area. He is a member of the National Academy of Engineering and a fellow of the Institute of Electrical and Electronics Engineers.

MICHIYUKI UENOHARA has been executive vice president and director of the NEC Corporation, Tokyo, since 1982. He is responsible for NEC's R&D Group and Production Engineering Development Group. He received his B.S. degree (electrical engineering) from Nihon University in Tokyo in 1949, Ph.D.s from Ohio State University in 1956 and from Tohoku University in 1958. He worked at the Bell Telephone Laboratories, 1957-1967, and since that time has been with NEC in various capacities. He has written on semiconductors and optoelectronics. He has served on many government committees, most recently on the Council for Science and Technology chaired by the Japanese prime minister. He is a foreign associate member of the U.S. National Academy of Engineering and a Fellow of IEEE.

KEVIN M. ULMER is director of the Center for Advanced Research in Biotechnology, a joint endeavor of the University of Maryland and the National Bureau of Standards to develop protein engineering technology. After receiving his Ph.D. in molecular biology from MIT in 1978, Dr. Ulmer spent a year as Chaim Weizmann Postdoctoral Fellow in the Department of Applied Biological Sciences at MIT. He joined Genex Corporation as one of its first research scientists in 1979 and later became vice president for advanced technology. While at Genex, he helped establish the Applied Molecular Biology Program at the University of Maryland, Baltimore County (UMBC), the nation's first undergraduate academic program for training genetic engineers; he is presently adjunct professor, Department of Biology, UMBC. Genex's protein engineering project was an outgrowth of this activity, and Dr. Ulmer served as research director of the Protein Engineering Division. On April 1, 1985, Dr. Ulmer joined the University of Maryland as the first director of the Center for Advanced Research in Biotechnology (CARB). CARB is a joint activity of the University of Maryland and the National Bureau of Standards and will focus on developing protein engineering technology.

CECIL H. UYEHARA is president of Uyehara International Associates, Bethesda, Maryland. He organized the First (1981) and Second (1986) Symposium on U.S.-Japan Science and Technology Exchange and played a major role in holding the first congressional hearings in 1984 on Japanese science and technology information. He served for twenty-four years in the U.S. government: Agency for International Development, the Office of Management and Budget, and the U.S. Air Force in Dayton, Ohio, in long-range weapon systems planning, programming, budgeting and planning and policy analysis in military assistance and economic development. He received his B.A. from Keio University (1948) and his M.A. from the University of Minnesota (1951). He also studied at the Kennedy School of Government, Harvard University (1963-1964), where he produced The Nuclear Test Ban Treaty and Scientific Advice in *Knowledge and Power* (1966). He co-authored *Socialist Parties in Postwar Japan* (1966), and compiled *Leftwing Social Movements in Japan: An Annotated Bibliography* (1959). He attended the Federal Executive Institute in 1978 for senior management training and was given the Career Education Award for Civil Service Employees in 1963, which allowed him to study at Harvard University.

SHELDON WEINIG is chairman and founder of Materials Research Corporation, a multinational company supplying sophisticated materials and equipment to the electronics and computer industries. He received a Ph.D. in metallurgy from Columbia University and an honorary Doctor of Laws degree from Saint Thomas Aquinas College. He received the 1980

SEMMY Award of the Semiconductor Equipment and Materials Institute for developing the critical materials necessary for the growth of the semiconductor industry. Dr. Weinig is a member of President Reagan's Board of Advisors on Private Sector Initiatives. He is a member of the National Academy of Engineering, a member of the Columbia University East Asian Institute Visiting Committee, a fellow of the Polytechnic Institute of New York, a fellow of the American Society for Metals, and a member of the New York Academy of Sciences.

A.R.C. WESTWOOD is corporate director, R&D, for the Martin Marietta Corporation. He received his B.Sc., Ph.D., and D.Sc. degrees from the University of Birmingham, England. He joined Martin Marietta Laboratories (then RIAS) in 1958, becoming its director in 1974 and assuming his present position in January 1984. He has published more than one hundred technical papers, mostly concerned with environment-sensitive mechanical behavior and, lately, R&D management, and has presented numerous keynote and invited lectures around the world. His scientific contributions have been recognized by a variety of awards and fellowships, including the Beilby Gold Medal (1970) and election to the National Academy of Engineering (1980). Current professional responsibilities include the Commission on Engineering and Technical Studies of the National Research Council, the Board of Directors of the Metallurgical Society, the Advisory Council to the Oakridge National Laboratory, the School of Arts and Sciences at the Johns Hopkins University and the School of Engineering at Maryland, and to the foreign secretary of the National Academy of Engineering.